D1321043

Holy and Noble Beasts

Encounters with Animals in Medieval Literature

Holy and Noble Beasts

Encounters with Animals in Medieval Literature

DAVID SALTER

D. S. BREWER

First published 2001
D. S. Brewer, Cambridge

Transferred to digital printing

ISBN 978–0–85991–624–0

D. S. Brewer is an imprint of Boydell & Brewer Ltd
PO Box 9, Woodbridge, Suffolk IP12 3DF, UK
and of Boydell & Brewer Inc.
668 Mount Hope Ave, Rochester, NY 14604, USA
website: www.boydellandbrewer.com

A CIP catalogue record for this book is available
from the British Library

Library of Congress Catalog Card Number 2001025980

This publication is printed on acid-free paper

Typeset by Joshua Associates Ltd, Oxford

Contents

List of Illustrations   vi

Acknowledgements   vii

Abbreviations   viii

Introduction   1

I. Return to Paradise: Animals in the Lives of the Saints

  1   St Jerome and the Lion   11
  2   The Patron Saint of Ecologists: St Francis and the Wolf
      of Gubbio   25
  3   Dominion over Animals: The Taming of 'Brother Ass'   33
  4   Reading the Book of Nature: St Francis, the Bible, and
      the Natural World   39

II. Knights and the Brute Creation:
Nobility and Sanctity in Four Middle English Romances

  5   Romance and Hagiography: *The Vision of St Eustace*
      and *Sir Isumbras*   55
  6   *Sir Gowther*   71
  7   *Octavian*   82
  8   *Sir Orfeo*   96

III. Nature and Supernature:
The Middle English Romances of Alexander the Great

  9   Alexander: Romance and History   111
 10   Alexander's Miraculous Conception and Birth   123
 11   The Wonders of the East   134

Conclusion: Representing Nature in Medieval Literature   147

Bibliography   150

Index   163

List of Illustrations

Plate 1. Niccolò Colantonio, *St Jerome and the Lion*. National
Museum of Capodimonte, Naples   15

Plate 2. Pisanello, *The Vision of St Eustace*. National Gallery,
London   54

Acknowledgements

The origins of this book lie in a doctoral thesis undertaken in the Department of English at the University of Leicester. I am greatly indebted to the University for the award of a three-year scholarship which enabled me to carry out most of the research towards the thesis, and to Professor Vincent Newey, the then head of Department, for his support and guidance throughout. In addition, I am grateful to the *Soprintendenza per i beni artistici e storici di Napoli* for permission to reproduce Colantonio's *St Jerome and the Lion*, and to the Board of Trustees of the National Gallery, London, for permission to reproduce *The Vision of St Eustace* by Pisanello.

I should also like to thank the friends and colleagues who have helped me in so many ways while I was writing the book; in particular, Michael Davies, Carina Vitti, Michael and Andrew Hagiioannu, Lucy Faire, Peter Smith, and Sara Schivappa. I am especially grateful to Steve Glosecki and Julie Coleman, for the very useful comments they made after reading a draft of the manuscript. The anonymous reader's report commissioned by Boydell & Brewer highlighted a number of weaknesses in an earlier version of the book, and I should like to express my gratitude to that reader for offering such careful and incisive criticisms. Marina Spunta read and commented upon the final draft of the manuscript, for which I am enormously grateful. Special thanks must also go to my parents, and to my brother and sister, Martin and Ann, for their encouragement. Finally, I should like to express my very deep gratitude to Greg Walker and Elaine Treharne, who supervised the doctoral thesis on which the book is based, and who have been such good friends over the years.

Abbreviations

AAS	*Acta Apostolicae Sedis*
ANTS	Anglo-Norman Text Society
AUMLA	*Journal of the Australasian Universities Language and Literature Association*
EETS OS	Early English Text Society, Original Series
EETS ES	Early English Text Society, Extra Series
EETS SS	Early English Text Society, Supplementary Series
MS	Manuscript
OED	*The Oxford English Dictionary*
FS	*Franziskannische Studien*
JEGP	*Journal of English and Germanic Philology*
JHS	*Journal of Hellenic Studies*
PL	Jacques Paul Migne, ed. *Patrologia Latina Cursus Completus*, 221 Vols (Paris, 1844–1864)
PMLA	*Publications of the Modern Language Association of America*
STS	Scottish Text Society

All biblical quotations are taken from the Authorised King James Version of the Bible

Introduction

Who peyntede the leon, tel me who?
Geoffrey Chaucer,
The Wife of Bath's Prologue and Tale

Near the end of the Prologue to her Tale, the Wife of Bath – perhaps the most vividly drawn and fully realised of Chaucer's Canterbury pilgrims – makes a brief but significant allusion to the Aesopian Fable, 'The Lion and the Man'. Describing her marriage to Jankyn, her fifth husband, the wife tells of his habit of reading aloud from his 'book of wikked wyves', a collection of anti-feminist writings from the likes of Tertullian and St Jerome, compiled to encourage men to adopt the celibate life. Feeling herself under attack from Jankyn's relentless reading of these tracts, the Wife encapsulates her criticism both of the book itself, and of the misogynistic tradition from which it derives, by quoting a line from the fable. The Wife fails to explain her allusion, a fact that suggests that 'The Lion and the Man' was sufficiently well known to Chaucer's contemporaries to require no further elaboration. Of course, for modern readers of *The Canterbury Tales*, unfamiliar with the fable, this lack of exposition may have the effect of investing the Wife's words with a cryptic, almost esoteric quality that they did not originally possess. The ingeniousness with which the Wife appropriates the fable for her own highly polemical ends is a fascinating subject, and one that is worthy of study in its own right.[1] But I have chosen to discuss it here because both 'The Lion and the Man', and the Wife's idiosyncratic use of it, raise a number of fundamental questions about how animals were represented in the literature of the period – questions that highlight some of the difficulties involved in using literary sources as a guide to uncovering the beliefs and attitudes of the people of the time.

The fable of the lion and the man, which has traditionally been attributed to Aesop, tells of an argument between a man and a lion about which of the two is the stronger. In order to prove that humans are more powerful than lions, the man shows the creature a painting (in the earliest versions of the fable, a sculpture), of a man killing a lion with an axe. But, rather than accepting the picture as evidence of the relative strength of their two species, the lion responds to this artistic assertion of human supremacy by asking, in the words of the Wife of Bath: 'Who

---

[1] For an analysis of the Wife's allusion to the fable, see Marjorie M. Malvern, ' "Who peyntede the leon, tel me who?": Rhetorical and Didactic Roles Played by an Aesopic Fable in *The Wife of Bath's Prologue*', in *Studies in Philology* 80 (1983), 238–52.

1

peyntede the leon, tel me who?'[2] Having thus drawn attention to the anthropocentric bias of the human artist, the animal goes on to claim that – had a similar conflict been depicted by a lion – a very different outcome would have been shown.[3]

The tale is in many ways a typical example of an Aesopian fable, in that lying beneath its clear and concise narrative – with its simple ideas and concrete images – it is possible to discern a fundamental truth about human existence. But my reason for discussing the fable here is that in addition to its wit, charm, and unpretentious wisdom, it shares with this book an interest in the representation of animals in art, and by extension, literature. For what the fable seems to imply is that human depictions of animals tell us more about the beliefs and attitudes of the artists who portray them, than about the actual creatures themselves. The lion in the fable can thus be said to resemble a modern critic, who looks beyond or behind the surface texture of a work of art in order to reveal the assumptions, preoccupations, and prejudices either of the individual artist, or of the broader social and cultural milieu in which that artist worked. Adopting the approach suggested by the lion, I shall examine the representation of animals in a number of key literary texts of the thirteenth and fourteenth centuries, with a view to uncovering the range of attitudes towards the animal kingdom that were current at the time.

As well as illustrating in narrative form the basic critical assumption underlying this study, the fable of the lion and the man also introduces one of the central ideas to which we shall repeatedly return in the chapters that follow; that of anthropocentricism – the inevitable tendency of men and women both to see and make sense of the world around them from an exclusively human point of view. It is this anthropocentric

---

[2] Geoffrey Chaucer, *The Wife of Bath's Prologue and Tale* (692), in Larry D. Benson *et al.*, ed. *The Riverside Chaucer* (Oxford, 1988).

[3] While its origins are classical, 'The Lion and the Man' enjoyed great popularity in the Middle Ages, and exists in many different versions, and in numerous languages. Perhaps the best known – and certainly the oldest surviving – translation of the fable into the vernacular is that of Marie de France, which dates from the second half of the twelfth century. See Marie de France, *Fables*, ed. and trans. Harriet Spiegel (Toronto, 1987), pp. 122–5. Marie's source was a Latin prose collection dating from the eleventh century known as the *Romulus Nilantii*, which was ultimately derived from the verse fables of the classical poet, Phaedrus (first century AD). An alternative Latin version of the fable which enjoyed an extremely wide circulation was written by Avianus (fourth / fifth century AD) in elegiac couplets, and was used as a school text throughout the Middle Ages. For an introduction to the medieval tradition of the Aesopian fable, and an overview of its complex textual history, see Jill Mann, 'Beast Epic and Fable', in *Medieval Latin: An Introduction and Bibliographical Guide*, ed. F. A. C. Mantello and A. G. Rigg (Washington D.C., 1996), pp. 556–61, and Ben Edwin Perry, ed. and trans. *Babrius and Phaedrus* Loeb Classical Library (Cambridge Massachusetts, 1965), pp. xi–cii. The fable was translated into English in 1483 by William Caxton. See R. T. Lenaghan, ed. *Caxton's Aesop* (Cambridge Massachusetts, 1967), pp. 132–3.

attitude towards the animal kingdom that the lion in the fable exposes through its rhetorical question, showing that the painting of the man killing the lion is nothing more than an expression of narcissistic, human wish-fulfilment. And yet, on a deeper level, the fable exhibits – and so is complicit in – the very anthropocentrism that it apparently seeks to condemn. The historian Keith Thomas has noted that because animals are neither wholly similar to, nor entirely different from, human beings, they have provided men and women with an endlessly fruitful point of departure from which to explore what it means to be human.[4] When viewed with Thomas's insight in mind, it becomes apparent that the fable is neither about, nor especially interested in, lions themselves, but is rather a rumination upon the nature of human society, which comments in particular on the ways in which rival groups of people misrepresent and misunderstand one another. Significantly, the lion in the fable possesses no recognisably leonine characteristics, and the story pointedly invites us to view the creature in human terms, presenting it not as a 'real' animal, but as a representative of an unjustly maligned social group. It is just such an interpretation that Chaucer's Wife of Bath places on the tale, when she appropriates the painting of the lion as an emblem of misrepresented womanhood. For, in the same way that the picture of the lion is distorted by the bias of the human artist, so, according to the Wife, women have habitually been slandered in the misogynistic writings of men.

Curiously, then, the fable of the lion and the man presents us with something of a paradox. The lion's witty and intelligent critique of the painting would seem to hint at an emotional and intellectual engagement with, as well as an aesthetic pleasure in, animals, on the part of the fable's audience. And yet, as we have seen, it is possible to draw the opposite conclusion, and view the fable simply as an allegorical tale about division and conflict within human society. My discussion of 'The Lion and the Man' therefore highlights one of the central questions that I shall explore in this book. Were medieval authors actually interested in the 'animalness' of the animals they depicted, or did they see the animal kingdom principally as a vehicle through which they could reflect upon their own humanity? In other words, were animals viewed as creatures in their own right, independent of any human claims over them? Or, conversely, were they regarded in utilitarian terms, and so seen simply as a means to a human end?

Of course, before embarking on such a study it must first be noted that animals abound in medieval literature, and are represented in every conceivable genre where they assume a huge variety of forms and guises. The treatment of the animal kingdom varies enormously depending on

[4] See Keith Thomas, *Man and the Natural World: Changing Attitudes in England 1500–1800* (Harmondsworth, 1984), pp. 40–1.

the type of literature concerned. For instance, detailed (if fanciful) pseudo-scientific descriptions of animal behaviour can be found in didactic and pedagogical works such as bestiaries and encyclopaedia, while fabulous accounts of creatures possessing magical or supernatural powers recur with great frequency in romance, saints' lives, and beast fable and epic. The types of animal that populate the pages of medieval literature are also astonishingly diverse, ranging from the familiar cat and mouse of everyday experience, through more exotic creatures such as lions and elephants, to such mythical beasts as griffins and dragons. In addition, the narrative function of animals and the range of meanings attributed to them – whether symbolic, allegorical, or metaphorical – vary dramatically from text to text and frequently from page to page. The task of charting a course through the myriad of different animal types and forms inevitably raises a number of methodological questions, the most pressing of which being: what principle of selection should underlie the choice of source material, and to what use should this material be put? Joyce Salisbury's well-received and frequently cited study, *The Beast Within: Animals in the Middle Ages*, examines similar issues to those that are explored in the present book.[5] By considering Salisbury's use of texts and the conclusions that she draws from them, it will be possible to highlight some of the inherent difficulties – as well as the intellectual possibilities – associated with this type of scholarship. Moreover, through a discussion of both the aims and the limitations of Salisbury's work, I hope better to explain the argument and rationale of my own study.

Although Salisbury brings to bear a wealth of literary and historical material to argue her thesis, her thesis itself is comparatively simple, and she states it at the very beginning of her book. She illustrates her argument at the outset by comparing two quotations; the first taken from St Augustine's *City of God* (written during the second and third decades of the fifth century), and the second from the work of Gerald of Wales, who was writing approximately eight hundred years later in the early thirteenth century. Both quotations are concerned with the phenomenon of humans supposedly mutating into animals. But whereas Augustine maintains that no such transformations occur in nature, Gerald asserts the contrary view, telling the story of a man who was driven mad when a woman whom he had been kissing was suddenly transformed into a hairy monster. Salisbury argues that these radically different views of the relationship between humanity and the animal kingdom reflect a broader shift in cultural attitudes that occurred over the course of the Middle Ages. According to Salisbury, Augustine's belief in the fundamental and unbridgeable difference between humanity and

---

[5] See Joyce Salisbury, *The Beast Within: Animals in the Middle Ages* (New York and London, 1994).

the animal kingdom – which she claims was typical of the time – was itself a reaction to the classical view of animals, which held that they were very similar to human beings. But Salisbury goes on to contend that from the twelfth century onwards, the early medieval position articulated by figures such as Augustine became increasingly untenable. As philosophers began to develop a much more detached and objective interest in the natural world, they increasingly came to observe many striking affinities between humanity and the animal kingdom. So by the end of the Middle Ages, Salisbury argues, there was a widespread belief that the boundary separating humans and animals was considerably narrower and less clearly defined than was previously thought to be the case.

As Salisbury notes in her introduction, *The Beast Within* is not a conventional work of literary or historical scholarship, but is rather an attempt to use literary and historical sources to chart the changing place of animals in human culture over a period of approximately a thousand years. Thus, when discussing attitudes towards animals in the later Middle Ages, Salisbury analyses a number of contemporary works of literature which either feature human–animal hybrids, or which attribute human characteristics to animals or animal characteristics to humans. From this, she concludes that the people of late-medieval Europe tended to believe that not only were the similarities between humans and animals more significant than the differences, but that under certain circumstances it was possible for the one to be transformed into the other.

While Salisbury argues her case very persuasively, her thesis nonetheless raises a number of questions about the use of literary sources as a means of uncovering the thoughts and feelings of the people of the time. For instance, can works of literature (as Salisbury seems to imply) be said to reflect in a simple and unproblematic way the kind of underlying attitudes and convictions of those who produced and consumed them? Or, is it not rather the case that all storytelling (at least to a certain extent), requires – in the famous phrase of Coleridge – the willing suspension of our disbelief? Surely, like their modern counterparts, the writers and readers of the late Middle Ages intuitively recognised (in however ill-defined a way), that narratives are governed by their own rules and conventions which are profoundly different from those that operate in the so-called 'real world'? If this argument is to be accepted, the presence in literary texts either of human–animal hybrids or of creatures (such as werewolves) that mutate from one species into another should not necessarily be taken as proof of widespread contemporary belief in such phenomena.

One further cautionary note should perhaps be added when considering Salisbury's use of literary sources. Salisbury claims that the animal stories to which she attaches such significance became increasingly popular from the twelfth century onwards, and she cites what she considers to be this new found popularity as evidence of a growing interest in animals – and a corresponding belief in their close affinity with humans – on the part of the contemporary population. However, there is an alternative explanation that might account for this increase in the production of animal-related literary texts. During the twelfth century there was a dramatic expansion both in literacy and in the demand for books. As a result, there was a very large increase in the number of books of all sorts that were actually produced.[6] It is quite possible, then, that the appearance in the twelfth century of the works to which Salisbury attributes such importance may have had very little to do with attitudes towards animals. Rather, it might simply reflect the great expansion in literacy and book production that occurred at the time. Because we possess such scanty information about how medieval literary texts were actually produced, disseminated, and then received by their audience, it is perilous to draw too many conclusions about the ways in which they either mirrored – or helped to condition – contemporary opinion.

Having argued that literary sources do not provide a straightforward and infallible guide to the underlying beliefs and attitudes of those who produced and consumed them, where then does this leave the present study? What can a book-length exploration of the representation of animals in medieval literature hope to tell us about the ways in which the animal kingdom was viewed during the Middle Ages? My discussion of 'The Lion and the Man' – which reveals such a profoundly anthropo-centric view of animals – perhaps provides us with a clue. It has become something of a commonplace amongst anthropologists to note that one of the crucial ways in which human beings define their own humanity is in opposition to the animal kingdom. So, rather than examining the ways in which literary depictions of animals reflect attitudes towards the animal kingdom itself, it is perhaps more useful to think of what they reveal about our perceptions of ourselves as human beings. What I shall concentrate on in the pages that follow are the ways in which human identity and notions of humanness are not only inextricably bound up with, but are actually defined and constructed in relation to, animals. This is particularly evident in late-medieval hagiography and romance, where we frequently find that both the holiness of saints and the heroism of knights are revealed through their miraculous encounters with wild beasts. I shall therefore examine the ways in which encounters between humans and animals are portrayed in a number of key texts dating from the thirteenth and fourteenth centuries, which are to be found in these two genres. In the process, I shall examine how ideas and models drawn from the animal kingdom were used by contemporary authors either to express, or to explore, different aspects of their own lives. We shall find that through their depictions of animals, medieval writers were able to

[6] See M. T. Clanchy, *From Memory to Written Record*, 2nd edn (Oxford, 1993), *passim*.

reflect upon their own humanity, as well as clarifying for themselves and for their readers the meaning of more abstract values and ideas – such as civility, sanctity, and nobility – that were central to the culture of the time.

Of course, discovering how far such texts give access to contemporary attitudes towards 'real' animals will also be a central issue in what follows, as will the extent to which the real and the imaginary interact. Did authors respond to the animals they wrote about in experiential terms, bringing their knowledge of the dogs, cats, and horses that they saw around them to bear upon their portraits of the animals' imaginary counterparts, or did the conventional and symbolic associations of such beasts take precedence over quotidian experience? And what about those authors who turned to animals of which they had no direct knowledge, not only exotic beasts like lions and crocodiles, but also mythical creatures such as griffins and dragons? What principles would seem to underlie their representation? Finally, what can one tell about attitudes towards nature and the 'natural' more generally from those texts popular in the thirteenth and fourteenth centuries? And how was the natural world represented in relation to human nature itself?

The book is divided into three parts. Part One takes as its subject the representation of animals in hagiography, concentrating in particular on the early lives of St Francis of Assisi. However, by way of an introduction to the subject, I shall examine the painting of St Jerome and the lion by the fifteenth-century Neapolitan artist, Colantonio, which I shall relate to a number of other hagiographical narratives, each involving saints and lions. The tale of Jerome's miraculous encounter with the lion was one of the most popular stories of the later Middle Ages, and my discussion of the incident is meant to act as a case study, demonstrating some of the insights into the subject that an analysis of narrative can yield. Moreover, through my reflections on the painting, I shall introduce a number of important themes and issues that I shall explore in greater detail in the chapters that follow.

Turning to the lives of St Francis of Assisi, I shall show how despite the seemingly novel and idiosyncratic nature of Francis's relationship with the animal kingdom, his medieval biographers exhibited little interest in, and attributed no intrinsic value to, the creatures themselves. Rather, the saint's 'love' of animals, and their affinity for him, was seen as a sign that he had returned to the state of innocence and holiness enjoyed by Adam and Eve before the Fall. As well as exploring the complex nature of Francis's emotional responses to animals, I shall also investigate the moral status that Francis and his biographers accorded to beasts, and shall question whether they considered members of the animal kingdom to be entitled to compassionate and sympathetic treatment from human beings.

Part Two shifts the focus from hagiography to romance, and explores

– through a discussion of both *The Vision of St Eustace* by the fifteenth-century Italian painter, Pisanello, and the Middle English romance *Sir Isumbras* – the strong affinities between the two genres, and in particular the close kinship of knights and saints. After this preliminary discussion of the subject, I shall go on to examine in detail the three Middle English romances *Sir Gowther*, *Octavian*, and *Sir Orfeo*, showing how motifs and story-elements drawn from hagiography exerted a major influence on both the treatment of animals in romance, and the romance ideal of the courtly, aristocratic hero. Part Two also investigates some of the ways in which the animal kingdom was thought to reflect the structure of feudal society, with 'noble' beasts such as lions, falcons, horses, and hounds sharing not only an instinctive empathy with their counterparts in the human world, but also a common aristocratic disdain for creatures of low birth.

Part Three investigates the Middle English romances of Alexander the Great, and examines how Alexander's decidedly pagan identity – which in the romance tradition he manifests in great part by asserting his god-like dominion over the natural world – elicited both from writers and their audiences strongly ambivalent feelings. Alexander was admired for the heroism and ambition that drove him to conquer his human adversaries, and which in the romances gave him power over animals and the world of nature, and yet it was his very refusal to accept the limitations of his own humanity that led to his condemnation as an irreligious overreacher. To a very great extent, then, it is through his relationship not simply to the animal kingdom but to the wider natural world, that Alexander's heroic identity – which encompasses both human and divine attributes – is revealed.

I hope that my discussion of the above saints' lives and romances will demonstrate both how and why – in an attempt to make sense of their own lives, and better to understand the place of human beings in the wider scheme of things – the authors of the later Middle Ages repeatedly turned to, and made use of, the animal kingdom.

Part I

Return to Paradise:
Animals in the Lives of the Saints

1

St Jerome and the Lion

OF all the animal stories that were circulating in Western Europe during the late Middle Ages, the one that appears to have exerted the strongest hold over the imagination of contemporary writers and artists was the tale of St Jerome and the lion. Its hero, Jerome, was born during the middle of the fourth century at Stridon in Dalmatia, and although the exact date of his birth is unknown, modern scholars estimate that it was some time between 331 and 347. Jerome's greatest contribution to history, and the achievement for which he was most revered during the ensuing Christian centuries, was his production of a Latin translation of the Bible (which became known as the *editio vulgata*, the Vulgate or popular edition), a text that for almost a thousand years, and throughout the Latin-speaking West, was regarded as the standard version of the Scriptures.[1] But, in addition to his skills as a linguist, scholar, and translator, Jerome was also famed for his advocacy of the monastic life (a life that he himself practised, first in solitude in the Syrian desert, and then as the leader of a community of monks at Bethlehem in Palestine), and it is while he was residing in Bethlehem during the second phase of his monastic career that his miraculous encounter with the lion is supposed to have taken place.[2]

Jerome's extensive writings, and in particular the many letters that he wrote to his friends (and enemies), are full of personal information about his life and work, and these scattered autobiographical references, along with testimonials to his character from such eminent figures as St Augustine, Sulpicius Severus, Gregory the Great, and Isidore of Seville, were the sources from which two ninth-century Latin Lives of the saint

---

[1] For an excellent modern biography of Jerome, see J. N. D. Kelly, *Jerome: His Life, Writings, and Controversies* (London, 1975). Useful essays on Jerome, his biblical scholarship, and the medieval history of his translation of the Bible can be found in the first two volumes of the *Cambridge History of the Bible*. See H. F. D. Sparks, 'Jerome as Biblical Scholar', in P. R. Ackroyd and C. F. Evans, ed. *The Cambridge History of the Bible*, Vol. 1 (Cambridge, 1970), pp. 510–41: Fr. E. F. Sutcliffe, 'Jerome', in G. W. H. Lampe, ed. *The Cambridge History of the Bible*, Vol. 2 (Cambridge, 1969), pp. 80–101; and Raphael Loewe, 'The Medieval History of the Latin Vulgate', in Lampe, ed. *The Cambridge History of the Bible*, Vol. 2, pp. 102–54.

[2] For an account of Jerome's monasticism, see Kelly, *Jerome: His Life, Writings, and Controversies*, pp. 46–55, and pp. 129–40.

were compiled. These Lives, written independently of one another by anonymous authors, are known as *Hieronymus noster* and *Plerosque nimirum*, and were used in turn as the primary sources for all of the subsequent medieval biographies of Jerome.[3] However, as well as recording the known facts of Jerome's life, the author of *Plerosque nimirum* also related the legendary story of the saint's miraculous encounter with the lion. The source for this story is an almost identical tale that had been told in relation to the Palestinian abbot, St Gerasimus – a near-contemporary of Jerome – by Joannes Moschus in his seventh-century collection of the lives of the desert fathers, the *Pratum Spirituale*.[4]

According to the author of *Plerosque nimirum*, the encounter between Jerome and the lion took place one evening while the saint was listening to the sacred lessons with his fellow monks in the monastery that he had established at Bethlehem. A lion suddenly came limping into the building, whereupon everyone fled except for Jerome, who confidently approached the animal as though he were welcoming an honoured guest. The lion showed Jerome his paw, and seeing that the creature was badly injured the saint summoned his brothers and instructed them to wash and bind the wound with care. As the monks were performing this task they observed that the lion's paw had been scratched and torn by thorns, but they washed and dressed the wound so carefully that they were able to restore the animal to full health. From then onwards the lion lost all traces of his former wildness, and lived tamely alongside the monks, helping them with their labours.

The story of Jerome and the lion was widely disseminated in the late Middle Ages thanks to its inclusion in two of the most popular and influential books of the thirteenth century; Vincent of Beauvais's *Speculum Historiale*, an account – completed in 1244 – of the history of humanity from the Fall to Vincent's own lifetime, and the *Legenda Aurea*,

---

[3] See *Hieronymus noster*, in *PL*, 22: 175–84, ed. Jacques Paul Migne (hereafter referred to as *PL*), and *Plerosque nimirum*, in *PL* 22: 201–14. For a discussion of the sources of these two works, and their influence on the subsequent biographies of St Jerome, see Eugene F. Rice, *Saint Jerome in the Renaissance* (Baltimore, 1985), pp. 23–48.

[4] For the story of St Jerome and the lion, see *Plerosque nimirum*, 209 ff. See also Joannes Moschus, *Vita Abbatis Gerasimi*, in *Pratum Spirituale*, in *PL* 74: 172–4. Eugene Rice has suggested that in all probability the story of Gerasimus's lion became attached to the figure of Jerome some time during the seventh century, after the military invasions of the Arabs had forced many Greek monks who were living in the deserts of the Middle East to seek refuge in Rome. Rice conjectures (*Saint Jerome in the Renaissance*, pp. 44–5), that because of the similarity between the names Gerasimus and Geronimus – the late Latin form of Jerome's name – 'a Latin-speaking cleric . . . made St Geronimus the hero of a story he had heard about St Gerasimus; and that the author of *Plerosque nimirum*, attracted by a story at once so picturesque, so apparently appropriate, and so resonant in suggestion and meaning, and under the impression that its source was pilgrims who had been told it in Bethlehem, included it in his life of a favourite saint otherwise bereft of miracles.'

a collection of saints lives written by Jacobus of Voragine, the Archbishop of Genoa, which dates from about 1260.[5] But the popularity of the story was not confined simply to the medium of literature; it is also reflected in the field of the visual arts. According to the art historian Grete Ring, Jerome was perhaps 'the most frequently represented saint in art from the fourteenth to the sixteenth century, with the exception of the members of the Holy Family and St John.'[6] Although a number of different episodes from the legend of St Jerome not involving the lion formed the subject of some of these fourteenth-, fifteenth-, and sixteenth-century representations, the saint was most commonly shown dressed as a cardinal and seated on a chair in his study (or on a rock in the wilderness), either removing the thorn from the lion's paw, or reading a book with the animal lying quietly at his feet.[7]

The eminent Italian canonist Giovanni d'Andrea, who taught law at the University of Bologna from 1301 until his death in 1348, and who commissioned a number of paintings of Jerome, is usually credited with introducing the motif of the lion into the visual arts, and combining it with images of the saint as a scholar and theologian.[8] In his book *Hieronymianus* – a work written in praise of St Jerome – Giovanni claimed:

> I have also established the way he should be painted, namely, sitting in a chair, beside him the hat that cardinals wear nowadays (that is, the red hat or *galerus ruber*) and at his feet the tame lion; and I have caused many pictures of this sort to be set up in divers places.[9]

[5] See Vincent of Beauvais, 'De Vita et Actibus Sancti Hieronymi Presbiteri', in *Bibliotheca Mundi. Vincentii Bellovacensis Speculum Quadruplex: Naturale, Doctrinale, Morale, Historiale*, ed. Benedictini Collegii Vedastini, 4 Vols (Douai, 1624), Vol. 4, Liber XVI, Cap. 18, p. 623, and Jacobus of Voragine, *The Golden Legend of Jacobus de Voragine*, trans. Granger Ryan and Helmut Ripperger (New York, 1941), pp. 587–92. The popularity of the two books is reflected in the large number of manuscripts that has survived from the period. Gregory G. Guzman has compiled a list of two hundred manuscripts of the *Speculum Historiale*, while according to Eugene Rice, there are over five hundred extant manuscripts of the *Legenda Aurea*. See Gregory G. Guzman, 'A Growing Tabulation of Vincent of Beauvais' *Speculum Historiale* Manuscripts', *Scriptorium: International Review of Manuscript Studies*, 122–5, and Rice, *Saint Jerome in the Renaissance*, p. 23.

[6] Grete Ring, 'St Jerome Removing the Thorn from the Lion's Paw', *Art Bulletin* 27 (1945), p. 190.

[7] See Herbert Friedmann, *A Bestiary for Saint Jerome: Animal Symbolism in European Religious Art* (Washington D.C.), p. 229.

[8] For a discussion of Giovanni's role in establishing the iconography of Jerome, see Rice, *Saint Jerome in the Renaissance*, pp. 64–68, and Ring, 'St Jerome Removing the Thorn from the Lion's Paw', p. 190.

[9] Quoted in Rice, *Saint Jerome in the Renaissance*, p. 65. According to Rice, p. 33, before Giovanni had identified the lion and the cardinal's hat as Jerome's two attributes or emblems, the saint 'was typically shown seated on a chair or throne,

The painting of St Jerome and the lion by the Neapolitan artist, Niccolò Colantonio (Plate 1), perfectly accords with Giovanni's prescriptions, and is one of the best known, and most interesting, artistic treatments of the subject.[10] The painting is dominated by the figures of Jerome and the lion, both of whom are situated in the centre of the composition, and perhaps what is most immediately striking (at least to the modern viewer), is not only the sense of the benevolence of the saint and the pathos of the injured animal, but also a strong feeling of trust and companionship between the two. However, the picture is also remarkable for the extraordinary detail with which it represents the interior of Jerome's cell.[11] The shelves are strewn with books, pens, and papers, along with all of the other equipment that one would expect to find in a scholar's study, while the book that is lying open on Jerome's desk, and the general atmosphere of disorderly clutter, gives the impression that the saint had been busy at work when the lion entered his room, seeking his help. Jerome himself is seated on an ornately carved chair. He is dressed in a brown habit and cloak, and is wearing a tightly fitting grey hat, while his tasselled, red cardinal's hat, the *galerus ruber*, is prominently displayed to the left of the lion, on a table in front of his desk. Finally, in the bottom right hand corner of the painting, behind Jerome's chair, a mouse can be seen eating a scrap of paper.

Amidst all the finely observed detail of Jerome's study, the lion remains a somewhat incongruous, almost enigmatic figure. Despite the animal's large size and enormously powerful frame, he is stripped of the conventional leonine attributes of wildness and courage, and is pictured instead with a slightly mournful and subdued expression, looking rather

---

made more comfortable by a cushion, his feet on a stool, reading from a book propped on a lectern, writing, dictating to a scribe or *notarius*, handing out copies of his translation of the Bible, or instructing one or two small figures, monks or clerics, who sit below him.'

[10] Very little is known about Colantonio. His artistic education is thought to have taken place under the patronage of René D'Anjou, who reigned in Naples from 1438 to 1442, while his last work was commissioned in 1460 by Queen Isabella Chiaromonte. The painting of *St Jerome in His Study* (which formed the lower section of an altarpiece, the upper panel of which was a depiction of *St Francis Giving the Rule to the First and Second Franciscan Orders*), was completed at the beginning of Colantonio's career, and although the circumstances of its composition are obscure, it is believed to have been commissioned by Alfonso of Aragon for the Franciscan church of San Lorenzo, Naples. For a discussion of Colantonio's life and work, see Giovanna Cassese, 'Niccolò Colantonio', in Jane Turner, ed. *The Dictionary of Art*, Vol. 7 (London, 1996), pp. 542–4. See also Penny Howell Jolly, 'Jan Van Eyck and St Jerome: A Study of Eyckian Influence on Colantonio and Antonello da Messina in Quattrocento Naples' (University of Pennsylvania, Ph.D. thesis, 1976), pp. 80–151.

[11] Penny Howell Jolly ('Van Eyck and St Jerome', p. 103), has suggested that Colantonio's painting 'is the first Italian representation of St Jerome in his study to make the setting of such great importance'.

Plate 1. Colantonio, *St Jerome and the Lion*. National Museum of Capodimonte, Naples.

ill at ease in the domestic setting of Jerome's book-lined chamber. The lion's former wildness stands in stark contrast to his present domesticity, and the encroachment of the animal into the indoor, human space of Jerome's study seems to blur the traditional opposition between the notions of nature and culture, wilderness and civilisation, and wild and tame. Moreover, Jerome's evident sympathy for the predicament of the lion, and the proximity and intimacy of the two, threatens to dissolve still further the conventional boundaries separating the human and animal worlds.

The story of Jerome and the lion, then, and in particular Colantonio's representation of it, would appear to suggest that the men and women of the late-medieval period were far from indifferent to the predicament of wild creatures, and that the plight of a suffering animal – at least when it was presented in the context of the life of a saint – was able to engage the interest of contemporary viewers and readers, and to elicit from them a compassionate and sympathetic response. The painting therefore poses interesting and important questions about how animals were perceived in Western Europe at the end of the Middle Ages, and how they were thought to relate to human beings; two of the questions with which this book is most concerned.

Of course, it is possible to criticise this reading of Colantonio's painting as subjective and impressionistic. It could be argued that in seeing the picture simply as an expression of human sympathy and affection for animals, there is the danger of both isolating the painting from the culture in which it was produced, and imposing upon it the humane, secular values of a modern, liberal sensibility. In order to arrive at a better understanding of what the painting can actually tell us about late-medieval attitudes towards animals and the natural world, it is first necessary to root the work much more firmly within not only the religious and cultural context of its time, but also the long-established tradition of hagiographical writing that takes as its subject the relationship between beasts and saints.

In contrast to the literary version of the story found in *Plerosque nimirum*, it is significant that Colantonio chose to locate the action not in one of the monastery's public, communal areas, but in the private space of Jerome's study, a setting that enabled him to depict an impressive array of books and papers in the background of the painting. Furthermore, rather than following literary versions of the story and portraying a scene in which Jerome at first examined the lion's wound, and then delegated the task of washing and dressing it to his monks, Colantonio showed the saint actually removing the thorn from the animal's paw. (According to *Plerosque nimirum*, the lion did not have a thorn stuck in his paw, but merely a wound that he had received when his paw had been pierced with thorns.) The effect of these two changes was to simplify the narrative while simultaneously amplifying the role that Jerome played in it. By removing the other monks from the scene, and so making Jerome solely responsible for healing the lion, Colantonio eliminated all the superfluous elements of the story that could divert attention from the saint, and reduce not just the dramatic impact of the miracle that he performed, but also the strength of the bond connecting him to the lion. With great narrative economy, then, Colantonio was able in the one painting to convey two quite distinct images or impressions of Jerome. On the one hand, he depicted a popular animal story in which (one can argue), a genuine sense of intimacy and companionship between the human and animal protagonists is conveyed. At the same time, he projected an image of the saint as a great scholar and theologian – reminding his audience of Jerome's reputation for erudition through the expedient of locating the action in his study.

Of course, in addition to these two aspects of Jerome's life and character, Colantonio – following the artistic convention established by Giovanni d'Andrea – also represented the saint as a cardinal, displaying his red cardinal's hat on the table situated in front of his desk. In the same way that the books and papers lining the shelves of Jerome's study lend intellectual weight to the portrait, so the presence of the *galerus ruber* invests the figure of the saint with considerable ecclesiastical authority, denoting as it does the important position that he was thought to have occupied in the governing hierarchy of the Church. However, it is important to note that this aspect of Jerome's biography is anachronistic. The College of Cardinals was not actually established until the eleventh century, over six hundred years after Jerome's death, and it was not until the Council of Lyons in 1245 that Pope Innocent IV declared that the red hat should be worn by members of the Sacred College.[12]

The anachronism of granting Jerome the title of cardinal reflects the way in which the writers and artists of the late Middle Ages tended both to visualise and understand historical figures in terms of the customs, fashions, and institutions of their own time. Interestingly, Colantonio's painting contains a number of such historical anomalies. For instance, the magnifying glass that is hanging from the shelf above Jerome's desk is clearly a late-medieval detail, as such devices did not come into use until the end of the thirteenth century,[13] while the folded document situated on the bench immediately above the mouse has a papal bull attached to it, which can be identified as late-medieval in origin from the heads of saints

---

[12] For a discussion of the origins of the Cardinalate, see Rice, *Saint Jerome in the Renaissance*, p. 37, and I. S. Robinson, *The Papacy 1073–1198: Continuity and Innovation* (Cambridge, 1990), pp. 33–120.

[13] As has been noted by George Sarton in his discussion of the technological developments that occurred in the field of optics during the late Middle Ages. See George Sarton, *Introduction to the History of Science*, Vol. 2 (Baltimore, 1931), p. 24.

Peter and Paul that are visible on its seal.[14] But, even more important than the anachronistic presence of these physical objects (at least from the point of view of the present discussion), is the fact that Jerome's relationship with the lion is also represented in an anachronistic manner, and an examination of this aspect of the painting will highlight discrepancies between the kind of attitudes towards animals and the natural world that were held by Jerome and his monastic contemporaries, and those that prevailed a thousand years later during Colantonio's lifetime.

Alison Goddard Elliott has observed that miraculous encounters with wild beasts are one of the characteristic features of the Lives of the early Christian anchorites, and that lions appear much more frequently in these stories than any other animal.[15] Significantly, Jerome himself was the author of three biographies of desert saints, two of whom – Paul the hermit and Malchus the monk – themselves had dramatic encounters with lions in the wilderness. Thus, it is possible to compare Colantonio's late-medieval treatment of the story of Jerome and the lion with two narratives, both involving saints and lions, written by Jerome himself.[16]

It is thought that Jerome wrote his *Life of St Paul the First Hermit* some time around 376, while he was living the life of a solitary hermit in the Syrian desert.[17] In this work, Jerome argued that contrary to received opinion – which regarded St Anthony as the instigator of the monastic movement – Anthony had merely followed the example of his master, Paul of Thebes, who was in fact the first Christian monk to withdraw into the desert.[18] After relating how, for almost a century, Paul had endured a solitary life of extreme hardship in the wilderness, Jerome concluded the hermit's biography with an account both of his death, and of the miraculous events that followed it. According to Jerome, Paul died alone in his cave in the desert, leaving his body to be discovered by Anthony, who grieved that he did not have any tools with which to dig a grave. However, two lions miraculously appeared from out of the

---

[14] According to Penny Howell Jolly ('Van Eyck and St Jerome', p. 102), 'the heads of Sts. Peter and Paul . . . [were] a commonly used form for the reverse of papal seals in the 14th and 15th centuries.'

[15] See Alison Goddard Elliott, *Roads to Paradise: Reading the Lives of the Early Saints* (Hanover, 1987), pp. 144–67.

[16] See St Jerome, *Life of St Paul the First Hermit*, trans. Sister Marie Liguori Ewald, in Roy J. Deferrari, ed. *Early Christian Biographies*, The Fathers of the Church, Vol. 15 (Washington D.C., 1952), pp. 217–38, and St Jerome, *Life of Malchus*, trans. Sister Marie Liguori Ewald, in Deferrari, ed. *Early Christian Biographies*, pp. 281–97.

[17] See the comments of Sister Marie Liguori Ewald (p. 221), in her introduction to Jerome's *Life of Paul the First Hermit*. J. N. D. Kelly suggests a slightly later date, arguing that Jerome wrote the work in Antioch, after he had returned from the first sojourn in the wilderness. See Kelly, *Jerome: His Life, Writings, and Controversies*, pp. 60–1.

[18] See Jerome, *Life of St Paul the First Hermit*, 1, p. 225.

wilderness and prostrated themselves before the dead body, wagging their tails and roaring loudly with grief. After communicating their feelings of sorrow in this way, the animals began to dig a hole in the ground not far from Paul's corpse, and when they had made a space large enough to contain the body, they respectfully approached Anthony, who sent them away with a blessing.[19]

The holy monk, Malchus, the subject of Jerome's second sacred biography, also had a miraculous encounter with a lion in the wilderness. After living in a monastery in the desert for a number of years, Malchus returned home to visit his widowed mother for one last time. On his way he was captured by Ishmaelites and sold into slavery. He eventually managed to escape with a fellow Christian slave, but they were pursued across the desert by their former master and his servant. Malchus and his Christian companion finally took refuge in a cave, convinced that they were about to be murdered, yet they were miraculously rescued from this fate by a lioness who attacked and killed their assailants, but left them completely unharmed.[20]

Alison Goddard Elliott has observed that the lions that feature in the Lives of the desert saints typically perform a similar function to the 'helpful beasts' of folklore, in that they willingly override or renounce their naturally bestial inclinations in order to grant their assistance to those holy figures whose innocence and sanctity they instinctively recognise.[21] But, as well as using this common folkloric motif as a way of highlighting the holiness of Paul and Malchus, it is also significant that the two stories share a similar location – a cave in the desert, beyond the boundaries of the civilised, human world. This wilderness setting, far from being incidental to the two narratives, actually reflects the theological concerns and convictions of the desert fathers themselves, for both Paul and Malchus chose to forsake the world and lead a solitary existence in the wilderness because they believed that the civic, humanistic values of late-classical society were incompatible with the ascetic ideals proclaimed by Christ in the Gospels.

The inherent sinfulness of human society, and the redemptive, purifying power of the wilderness, is a theme that is given particular prominence in the *Life of Malchus*. According to Jerome, Malchus first went into the desert in order to escape from those members of his family, who – ignoring his vow of chastity – were trying to force him to marry. Then, having lived as a monk in the wilderness for many years, Malchus decided to visit his widowed mother one last time before she died, only to be told by his abbot that this seemingly innocuous wish was in fact a temptation from the Devil, and that in succumbing to it he would be

---

[19] See Jerome, *Life of St Paul the First Hermit*, 16, p. 236.
[20] See Jerome, *Life of Malchus*, 9, pp. 296–7.
[21] See Elliott, *Roads to Paradise*, p. 159.

placing his soul in great jeopardy. The abbot's forebodings proved to be well founded, for as has already been noted Malchus was captured by Ishmaelites on his journey home, and sold by them into slavery. In this captive state his virginity was again imperilled, this time by his new master, who tried to force him to marry a fellow slave, and it was in order to escape this threat to his sexual purity that he once again sought refuge in the desert. Paradoxically, then, for Malchus, it was the harshness of the desert climate, and its general physical inhospitality, that made it a place of such spiritual safety, a religious haven where on two separate occasions he sought sanctuary from the moral corruption of human society.

Jerome's attitude towards the wilderness was identical to the view that he attributed to Malchus. In a famous letter that he wrote in 384 to Eustochium, the daughter of his friend, Paula, he reflected upon his own experiences of the austerities of the desert – with its potential for spiritual salvation – and compared it to the morally corrupt and decadent nature of life in the city:

> Oh, how often, when I was living in the desert, in that lonely waste, scorched by the burning sun, which affords to hermits a savage dwelling place, how often did I fancy myself surrounded by the pleasures of Rome . . . Filled with stiff anger against myself, I would make my way alone into the desert; and when I came upon some hollow valley or rough mountain or precipitous cliff, there I would set up my oratory, and make that spot a place of torture for my unhappy flesh. There sometimes also – the Lord Himself is my witness – after many a tear and straining of my eyes to heaven, I felt myself in the presence of the angelic hosts, and in joy and gladness would sing: 'Because of the savour of thy good ointments we shall run after thee [Song of Solomon 1: 3].'[22]

Like Malchus, Jerome would seem to have regarded human society as beset with moral dangers, dangers that could best be countered by withdrawing from civic life and retreating into the desert. Of course, as Charles Segal has noted, such a complete and absolute rejection of the values and institutions of human society represented a profound political and philosophical break with the traditions of classical antiquity:

> In classical thought the forms of civic life and social organisation differentiate man from the beasts and constitute the essence of his true estate. Only by being a 'political animal,' in Aristotle's celebrated formulation, does man fulfil his humanity. For the desert saints, on the other hand, man's real goal is the heavenly kingdom, and civic life constitutes a state of alienation from his true condition. Hence to

[22] St Jerome, 'Letter XXII: To Eustochium', in *Select Letters of St Jerome*, ed. and trans. F. A. Wright (London, 1933), pp. 67–9.

negate civilised life, to replace culture by nature, is also to bypass the fallen condition of humankind. To draw closer to the beasts is, paradoxically, to regain a lost proximity to the divine.[23]

Thus, the extreme asceticism of the desert fathers developed in part as a reaction to the civic values of classical society. The fathers' rejection of pagan religion led to their abandonment of pagan society's social and philosophical underpinnings, which in turn resulted in their withdrawal from urban life.[24] More than any other creature, the lion was thought of as the archetypal representative of the wilderness – the natural, non-human world that Paul, Malchus, and Jerome had so fervently embraced. It is perhaps for this reason, as Alison Goddard Elliott has argued, that the animal was viewed as the ally, as well as the emblem, of the early Christian hermits.[25]

Although Paul and Malchus's lions symbolise the willingness of the two saints to renounce human society and accept the rigours of the desert, the lion that features in Colantonio's painting carries a very different meaning. Whereas both Paul and Malchus encountered their respective lions in a cave in the wilderness – the animal's natural habitat – the story of Jerome and the lion is, as we have seen, located within the walls of the monastery itself, with Colantonio setting the scene in the highly rarefied atmosphere of the saint's book-lined cell. Rather than abandoning human civilisation and retreating into the natural world in the manner of Paul and Malchus, Colantonio depicted Jerome accommodating the lion, and, by implication, the world of nature, within his private study. Significantly, there is nothing in Colantonio's painting to suggest a desert location. On the contrary, even though the historical Jerome shared the same hostile and distrustful view of the city that he attributed to Paul and Malchus, Colantonio chose to portray the saint surrounded by the kind of cultural artefacts that one would normally associate with a highly sophisticated, urban civilisation. While both Jerome and Colantonio interpreted power over animals as a sign of sanctity, one could argue that the distinctive way in which they represented their respective lions points to a notably different understanding of

---

[23] See Charles Segal, 'Foreword', to Elliott, *Roads to Paradise*, p. x.

[24] Eugene Rice (*Saint Jerome in the Renaissance*, pp. 8–9) also places considerable emphasis on Jerome's militant opposition to civic life, and the radical break with traditional values that this constituted: 'His abandonment of the earthly city for a *civitas nova*, the citizens of which meditate night and day on Scripture and God's law, was . . . explicit. The wilderness and solitude, he thought, are lovelier than any city. Indeed, he believed the *civitas* incompatible with Christianity: "*quicumque in civitate sunt, Christiani non sunt*" [those who live in the city are not Christians]. From the remotest antiquity, urban living had distinguished the civilised from everything savage, rustic, and barbarous. Jerome's reversal of traditional values could hardly have been sharper.'

[25] See Elliott, *Roads to Paradise*, pp. 166–7.

the nature of holiness. Whereas for Jerome and the desert fathers the lion was an emblem of their complete rejection of the world, for Colantonio it was a much more optimistic symbol, speaking both of and to the capacity of individuals to lead a virtuous life within human society.

This brief examination of the role and significance of the different lions that feature in Jerome's Lives of Paul and Malchus, and Colantonio's painting of Jerome and the lion, demonstrates the kind of contribution that a study of narrative can make to our understanding of late-medieval attitudes towards animals and nature. Of course, because the story of Jerome and the lion describes a world that is extremely remote from ordinary experience, it tells us nothing directly about the kind of treatment that was daily meted out to wild and domestic animals by the people of the time. Rather, the value of such material lies in what it can tell us about the workings of the human imagination; suggesting some of the different ways in which medieval writers and artists thought about themselves, their society, and their religious convictions in relation both to the animal kingdom, and to the wider world of nature.[26]

But as well as acting as a case study, my discussion of Colantonio's painting is particularly apposite here because of the revealing light it casts on the relationship between animals and Franciscan spirituality – the subject of the following three chapters. As mentioned above, Colantonio's *St Jerome and the Lion* has a strong Franciscan connection. Although the circumstances of the picture's composition are obscure, it is known that the altarpiece of which it originally formed a part was

---

[26] Clearly, my brief reading of Colantonio's *St Jerome and the Lion* comes nowhere near to exhausting the painting's possible meanings. The taming of the lion can be seen as a metaphor for the subjugation of the bestial side of human nature, what Plato in the *Republic* referred to as 'the wild beast in us'. [*The Republic of Plato*, trans. Francis MacDonald Cornford (Oxford, 1941) IX: 571, p. 296.] Hence it is possible to see Jerome's mastery of the lion as representing the victory of human reason over animal passion, and civilisation over savagery. On a more overtly religious level, the thorn that Jerome removed from the lion's paw inevitably calls to mind Christ's crown of thorns, and Eugene Rice (*Saint Jerome in the Renaissance*, pp. 39–40), has suggested that whether it is protruding from the lion or piercing the head of Christ, the thorn symbolises sin, while Jerome – by removing the thorn from the lion's paw – is acting as a type of Christ, overcoming evil and redeeming human beings from their sins. The extent to which this kind of animal symbolism pervaded both Colantonio's thought and artistic method can perhaps best be demonstrated by considering the significance of one of the painting's more minor details – the mouse that can be seen in the bottom right hand corner of the composition. Herbert Friedmann (*A Bestiary for Saint Jerome*, p. 271), has pointed out that in Western art mice have traditionally symbolised the destructive power of time because of their habit of gnawing away at objects with relentless determination, eventually annihilating everything in their wake. It is therefore possible that Colantonio intended the mouse – like the hourglass on Jerome's desk – to be understood as an emblem of the transience of human existence, which was to stand as a warning against the vanity and futility of worldly pride and ambition.

initially housed in the Franciscan church of San Lorenzo, Naples. Moreover, this Franciscan association is further suggested by the subject of the altarpiece's upper panel: *St Francis Distributing the Rule to the First and Second Franciscan Orders.*

In her discussion of the overall iconographic design of the San Lorenzo altarpiece, Penny Howell Jolly argues that by juxtaposing the figures of Francis and Jerome, Colantonio was highlighting what were – amongst Franciscans – well-established connections between the two saints.[27] Jolly points out that Jerome was held in especially high esteem by Franciscan writers, who regarded him as a figure whose life in many ways anticipated that of their founder. Thus, like Francis, Jerome was thought to have turned his back on the allurements of worldly honours and preferment by adopting the *vita apostolica*, the apostolic life. As a result, he was believed to have attained such a state of grace and holiness that – once again anticipating St Francis – he was able to tame and befriend even the wildest of animals.

But while the altarpiece may have been designed both to emphasise and celebrate the similarities between the two saints, what my discussion of Colantonio's lion highlights is the extent to which Jerome and Francis actually differ from one another. The emergence of the Franciscan Order in the early years of the thirteenth century under the charismatic leadership of St Francis constituted a profound break with the traditions of monasticism. Whereas from the time of Jerome onwards, monks had withdrawn into their monasteries in open flight from the world, the Franciscans – along with their fellow Mendicants the Dominicans, Carmelites, and Augustinians – rejected the contemplative life in favour of an active, evangelical ministry, that necessitated their full participation in the life of the towns.[28] There are a number of stories both from the Life of Francis himself and from the Lives of his followers that reflect the urban orientation of the Franciscan Order.[29] Arguably, it is this major shift in religious and cultural sensibility away from the wilderness and towards the city that lies behind what can be thought of as Colantonio's anachronistic 'misreading' of Jerome's lion.

[27] See Jolly, 'Jan Van Eyck and St Jerome', pp. 150–1.

[28] For an account of the Mendicant Orders' 'mission' to the cities, see C. H. Lawrence, *The Friars: The Impact of the Early Mendicant Movement on Western Society* (London, 1994), pp. 102–26.

[29] Although powerfully drawn to the life of the desert fathers, Francis came to recognise that his true vocation lay not in withdrawing from human society, but in ministering directly to its needs. (See below, p. 39.) One Franciscan who famously felt particularly at home in an urban milieu was St Bernard of Siena (1380–1444). Like Francis, Bernard initially believed himself called to a solitary life in the wilderness, but – unable to survive on a diet of herbs and thistles – he returned to Siena and joined the Franciscan Order. See Cynthia L. Polecritti, *Preaching Peace in Renaissance Italy: Bernadino of Siena and His Audience* (Washington D.C., 2000), p. 11.

Unlike St Jerome, who had just the one miraculous encounter with a wild animal, the Life of St Francis abounds in such narratives. In the following three chapters, I shall examine in detail the most interesting and significant of these animal stories, exploring what they reveal about the beliefs, assumptions, and preoccupation both of Francis himself, and of his followers.

2

The Patron Saint of Ecologists:
St Francis and the Wolf of Gubbio

ON 26 December 1966, at a meeting of the American Association for the Advancement of Science, the historian Lynn White Jr delivered a lecture entitled: 'The Historical Roots of Our Ecological Crisis', in which he argued that St Francis of Assisi's attitude towards animals and nature was profoundly at odds with the official view that was disseminated by the medieval Church.[1] Characterising Christianity, particularly in its medieval, Latin form, as 'the most anthropocentric religion the world has ever seen',[2] White claimed that modern Western society has directly inherited from the Middle Ages an extremely destructive attitude towards the natural world; an attitude that not only regarded human beings as entirely separate from – and in a state of opposition to – nature, but one that also failed to place any moral impediment on the exploitation of natural objects, whether animal, mineral, or vegetable, for human advantage. However, White argued that in contrast to the harmful, oppositional view of nature typical of medieval Christianity, a radically different set of beliefs and assumptions about the natural world, and humanity's place within it, was held by St Francis of Assisi, a figure who according to White 'tried to substitute the idea of the equality of all creatures, including man, for the idea of man's limitless rule of creation'.[3] The tenor of White's argument is that it is only by rejecting the disastrous legacy of orthodox Christianity, and embracing instead Francis's democratic and respectful way of relating to animals and nature, that modern society can hope to avert the environmental crisis into which it appears to be falling, and he concluded his lecture by proposing that Francis should be declared 'the patron saint of ecologists' as a mark of his profound sympathy for the whole of creation.[4]

---

[1] For the text of the lecture, see Lynn White Jr, 'The Historical Roots of Our Ecological Crisis', *Science* 155 (1967), 1203–7. According to Keith Thomas, such has been the influence of White's article that it has come to be seen as 'almost a sacred text for modern ecologists'. See Keith Thomas, *Man and the Natural World: Changing Attitudes in England 1500–1800* (Harmondsworth, 1984), p. 23.

[2] White, 'The Historical Roots of Ecological Crisis', p. 1205.

[3] White, 'The Historical Roots of Ecological Crisis', p. 1205.

[4] White, 'The Historical Roots of Ecological Crisis', p. 1205.

Despite White's fiercely critical view of what he considered to be the harmful effects on the environment caused by the teaching of the Catholic Church, Pope John Paul II did indeed proclaim Francis 'the heavenly Patron of those who promote ecology' (in November 1979), a declaration that he reiterated on 1 January 1990 in a letter entitled: 'The Ecological Crisis: A Common Responsibility'.[5] In this letter, Pope John Paul asserted that humanity is under a sacred obligation both to respect the natural world, and to protect it from harm, and he concluded his epistle by presenting St Francis as a model of harmonious relations between humanity and the wider world of creation:

> As a friend of the poor who was loved by God's creatures, Saint Francis invited all of creation – animals, plants, natural forces, even Brother Sun and Sister Moon – to give honour and praise to the Lord. The poor man of Assisi gives us striking witness that when we are at peace with God we are better able to devote ourselves to building up that peace with all creation which is inseparable from peace among all peoples.
>
> It is my hope that the inspiration of Saint Francis will help us to keep ever alive a sense of 'fraternity' with all those good and beautiful things which Almighty God has created. And may he remind us of our serious obligation to respect and watch over them with care, in light of that greater and higher fraternity that exists within the human family.[6]

Although Professor White and Pope John Paul II approached the question of humanity's relationship with the natural world from radically different political, philosophical, and theological perspectives, it is striking that they both considered St Francis to be a figure who has much to teach modern society about living in peace with animals and nature.

Of course, one of the dangers of identifying Francis as an icon of the modern environmental movement is that his actions and utterances – when removed from their historical context, and viewed in terms of contemporary ecological preoccupations – may acquire meanings very different from those that the saint had originally intended.[7] Indeed, this tendency anachronistically to endow Francis with beliefs and motives that he did not in fact possess is evident in Lynn White's reaction to one

---

[5] For the official Vatican record of the declaration, see 'Apostolic Letter *Inter Sanctos*'; *AAS* 71 (1979), 1509f. See also Pope John Paul II, 'The Ecological Crisis: A Common Responsibility. Message of His Holiness Pope John Paul II for the Celebration of the World Day of Peace, January 1, 1990', in Margaret Atkins, *Must Catholics Be Green?* (London, 1995), pp. 21–32. Neither document makes any reference to White's lecture.

[6] John Paul II, 'The Ecological Crisis: A Common Responsibility', pp. 31–2.

[7] This has been pointed out by Roger D. Sorrell in his monograph, *St Francis of Assisi and Nature: Tradition and Innovation in Western Christian Attitudes toward the Environment* (Oxford, 1988), pp. 4–6, and 147–8.

of the incidents from the saint's career that has become crucially important to those who promote an ecological reading of his life: the story of
the taming of the wolf of Gubbio.

In justifying his claim that 'Francis tried to depose man of his
monarchy over creation and set up a democracy of all God's creatures',[8]
White cited the story of the wolf of Gubbio without further comment,
assuming its significance to be self-evident. As we shall see, however, the
incident is far from simple. By subjecting it to a much more searching
analysis than that undertaken by White, and placing Francis's words and
deeds vis-à-vis the wolf within the context not only of his life and
thought, but also of the wider hagiographical tradition, it will be possible
to see this event in a clearer light. This in turn will allow us to arrive at a
better understanding of the saint's relationship with creation.

The story of Francis's encounter with the wolf of Gubbio is found in
only two closely related medieval texts, both of which date from over
one hundred years after the saint's death; Ugolino di Monte Santa
Maria's *Actus Beati Francisci et Sociorum Eius* (*The Acts of Blessed
Francis and His Companions*), and its Italian derivative, *The Little
Flowers of St Francis* (*I Fioretti di San Francesco*).[9] According to
Ugolino's account of the incident, on one occasion when St Francis
was staying in the city of Gubbio, the surrounding countryside was
inhabited by a fierce and hungry wolf who killed both humans and
animals in his search for food. The people of Gubbio were so
frightened of the wolf that they armed themselves whenever they
went into the countryside, but such was the animal's ferocity that
even armed citizens were incapable of defending themselves from
attack. As a consequence, most of Gubbio's inhabitants were too
frightened to go beyond the city gate.

Taking pity on the plight of the people, St Francis went out into the
countryside in order to tame the wolf. After travelling only a short
distance he caught sight of the animal, who was running towards him
with his mouth wide open. Francis made the sign of the cross and
ordered the wolf in the name of Jesus to cease his assault. As soon as the
animal heard this command, he closed his mouth, bowed his head, and
lay down at the saint's feet. Having thus succeeded in taming the
creature, Francis then spoke to him, and condemned his terrible crimes:

[8] White, 'The Historical Roots of Our Ecological Crisis', p. 1206.
[9] Because the *Actus* and *Fioretti* are very closely related, Raphael Brown's modern
English translation of *The Little Flowers* is in fact primarily based on the Latin
text of the *Actus*. See *The Little Flowers of St Francis*, trans. Raphael Brown, in
Marion A. Habig, ed. *St Francis of Assisi, Writings and Early Biographies: English
Omnibus of the Sources for the Life of St Francis*, 4th edn (Chicago, 1991),
pp. 1267–513. For Ugolino's version of the story (on which Brown's translation is
based), see *Actus Beati Francisci et Sociorum Eius*, ed. Paul Sabatier (Paris, 1902),
Chapter 23, pp. 77–81.

Brother Wolf you have done great harm in this region, and you have committed horrible crimes by destroying God's creatures without any mercy. You have been destroying not only irrational animals, but you even have the more detestable brazenness to kill and devour human beings made in the image of God. You therefore deserve to be put to death just like the worst robber and murderer. Consequently everyone is right in crying out against you and complaining, and this whole town is your enemy. But, Brother Wolf, I want to make peace between you and them, so that they will not be harmed by you any more, and after they have forgiven you all your past crimes, neither men nor dogs will pursue you any more.[10]

After Francis had finished speaking, the wolf nodded his head, and moved his body, tail and ears so as to indicate that he understood and accepted everything that had been said. Once the animal had signalled his acquiescence in this way, St Francis addressed him yet again:

Brother Wolf, since you are willing to make and keep this peace pact, I promise you that I will have the people of this town give you food every day as long as you live, so that you will never again suffer from hunger, for I know that whatever evil you have been doing was done because of the urge of hunger. But, my brother Wolf, since I am obtaining such a favour for you, I want you to promise me that you will never hurt any animal or man.[11]

By bowing his head, the wolf once again showed that he accepted what Francis had said, and as a pledge of his good faith he placed his paw in Francis's hand. Francis then ordered the wolf to return with him to the city, and in complete obedience the wolf followed him 'just like a very gentle lamb'.[12] On reaching Gubbio, the entire population of the city gathered around St Francis, astonished at the sight of the tamed wolf. Francis then preached them a sermon:

saying among other things that such calamities were permitted by God because of their sins, and how the consuming fire of hell by which the damned have to be devoured for all eternity is much more dangerous than the raging of a wolf which can kill nothing but the body, and how much more they should fear to be plunged into hell, since one little animal could keep so great a crowd in such a state of terror and trembling.

'So, dear people', he said, 'come back to the Lord, and do fitting penance, and God will free you from the wolf in this world and from the devouring fire of hell in the next world.'[13]

---

[10] *The Little Flowers of St Francis*, Chapter 21, p. 1349.
[11] *The Little Flowers of St Francis*, Chapter 21, p. 1349.
[12] *The Little Flowers of St Francis*, Chapter 21, p. 1350.
[13] *The Little Flowers of St Francis*, Chapter 21, p. 1350.

After Francis had finished his sermon, he told the people of his pact with the wolf, and with one voice they agreed to supply the animal with all the food that he required. Once again, Francis invited the wolf to make a pledge of his good faith, and as before the creature did so by placing his paw in Francis's hand. The wolf then moved into the city, and was fed and cared for by the people until he finally died of old age two years later. The death of the wolf filled the citizens with great sorrow, for whenever they had seen the animal peacefully wandering the streets of their city, they had been reminded of the holiness of St Francis.

It is not difficult to understand why the story of the wolf of Gubbio appealed so strongly to Lynn White, for it presents St Francis as a figure of extraordinary benevolence, whose sympathy and compassion for the plight of both humans and animals not only enabled him to pacify a ravening wolf, but also inspired him to reconcile the creature to the very community that he had formerly been terrorising. By refusing to condemn the wolf out of hand – choosing instead to forgive the animal, and provide him with the means of remedying his violent behaviour – Francis would appear to have recognised that the creature was an autonomous being in his own right, who was entitled to be treated by humans with respect and understanding, and not simply an inanimate object with no independent claim to life. This apparent willingness of Francis to acknowledge the wolf's entitlement to moral consideration is further suggested by the fact that he repeatedly referred to the animal as 'Brother', a mode of address that assumes the existence of a familial bond – even an equality – between the human and animal worlds.

For White, then, the empathy and understanding that Francis so conspicuously exhibited in relation to the wolf was symptomatic of his democratic and egalitarian attitude towards animals in general, an attitude that constituted a radical rejection of the anthropocentric world-view promulgated by the medieval Church. However, as indicated above, this ecologically orientated interpretation of the incident presents only a partial, and ultimately misleading portrait of the saint. After all, Francis did not merely call upon the people of Gubbio to treat the wolf with consideration, he was also fiercely critical of the animal's bestial and savage behaviour, condemning the creature's 'horrible crimes' in explicitly moral terms: 'you even have the more detestable brazenness to kill and devour human beings made in the image of God. You therefore deserve to be put to death just like the worst robber and murderer.'[14] Moreover, having accused the wolf of criminality, Francis's forgiveness was conditional upon the animal abandoning his murderous actions, and moving into the city as an honorary member of the human community, where he was to live in accordance with society's rules. Francis's moral censure of the wolf, and his insistence that the animal curb his wolfish

---

[14] *The Little Flowers of St Francis*, Chapter 21, p. 1349.

instincts, and abide instead by the laws of human civilisation, would seem to reflect the anthropomorphic assumption that animals share with human beings a common moral sense of good and evil, an assumption that far from anticipating the opinion of modern environmentalists, was firmly rooted in the culture of the time.[15]

Therefore, rather than viewing the story of Francis and the wolf of Gubbio through the distorting lens of contemporary ecological pre-occupations, it is much more useful to try to understand the incident in terms that would have been readily comprehensible to Francis and his contemporaries. During the later Middle Ages, Francis's supernatural power over animals was interpreted as a sign of his remarkable sanctity, for such was his extraordinary holiness, innocence, and piety that he was thought to have miraculously restored to the natural world the harmonious condition that it had originally enjoyed before the Fall.[16] Thus, like countless saints before him, Francis was believed to have re-established the dominion over the animal kingdom that had once been exercised by Adam and Eve in the Garden of Eden. Writing in his commentary on the *Sentences* of Peter Lombard, St Bonaventure – Francis's official biographer, and the Minister General of the Franciscan Order from 1257 to 1273 – explained Francis's special affinity for animals in the following way:

> If you ask what is the virtue which makes a person love creatures ... I reply that it is compassion and a sort of natural affection. For example, we see that even now a person can be very fond of a dog because it obeys him faithfully. In the same way, man in his original state had a natural inclination to love animals and even irrational creatures. Therefore, the greater the progress a man makes and the nearer he approaches to the state of innocence the more docile these creatures come towards him, and the greater the affection he feels for them. We see this in the case of St Francis; he overflowed with tender affection even for animals, because to some extent he had returned to the state of innocence. This was made clear by the way irrational creatures obeyed him.[17]

[15] E. A. Armstrong has noted that Francis's denunciation of the wolf as a murderer and robber, with the assumption of moral and legal responsibility that this implies, has much in common with the many criminal prosecutions that were undertaken of animals during the late-medieval and early modern periods. See E. A. Armstrong, *Saint Francis, Nature Mystic: The Derivation and Significance of the Nature Stories in the Franciscan Legend* (Berkeley, 1973), p. 203. For a useful overview of the phenomenon of animal trials, see E. P. Evans, *The Criminal Prosecution and Capital Punishment of Animals* (London, 1906), and Gerald Carson, 'Bugs and Beasts Before the Law', *Natural History* 77 (1968), 4, 6–19.

[16] A Middle English account, written in the early fourteenth century, of the state of peace and harmony that prevailed amongst the animals before the Fall can be found in the *Cursor Mundi*. See Sarah M. Horrall, ed. *The Southern Version of Cursor Mundi* (Ottawa, 1978), lines 677–700.

[17] Quoted in Benen Fahy, trans. *Major and Minor Life of St Francis with Excerpts*

Thomas of Celano, the author of two Lives of the saint, the first of which was written within three years of his death, gave personal testimony to the fact that Francis had temporarily re-established the peaceful state of existence that had originally prevailed before the Fall. In his *Second Life of St Francis* (composed in 1246), Thomas described how Francis's benign influence had ensured that peace and plenty had reigned during his own lifetime, but that once he had died – and his beneficent protection had been withdrawn from the earth – the moral and physical corruption of the fallen world had reasserted itself, to produce terrible famine and civil strife:

> For all of us who saw it know what quiet and peaceful times passed while the servant of Christ lived and how they were filled with such an abundance of all good things. . . . But after he had been taken away the order of things was completely reversed and everything was changed; for wars and insurrections prevailed everywhere, and a carnage of many deaths suddenly passed through many kingdoms. The horror of famine too spread far and wide, and the cruelty of it, which exceeds the bitterness of everything else, consumed very many. Necessity then turned everything into food and compelled human teeth to chew things that were not even customarily eaten by animals. Bread was made with the shells of nuts and the bark of trees; and, to put it mildly, paternal piety, under the compulsion of famine, did not mourn the death of a child, as became clear from the confession of a certain man.[18]

The wars and insurrections to which Thomas refers, here, were in fact local skirmishes in the much larger conflict between Pope Gregory IX and the Emperor Frederick II that broke out intermittently in the years following Francis's death. However, it is striking that Thomas attributed both the civil unrest, and the famine and privation that it produced, not to political or diplomatic causes, but to the removal of the pre-lapsarian harmony that Francis had temporarily restored to the world.[19]

When writing of Francis's encounters with animals, then, it would appear that the interest of his biographers lay not so much in the animals themselves, but in what their peaceful and demure behaviour revealed about the holiness and purity of the saint. This was certainly true in the case of Ugolino, who claimed that the whole episode of the taming of the wolf had been ordained by God in order that Francis's sanctity might be

from Other Works, in Marion A. Habig, ed. *St Francis of Assisi, Writings and Early Biographies: English Omnibus of the Sources for the Life of St Francis*, 4th edn (Chicago, 1991), p. 849.

[18] Thomas of Celano, *The Second Life of St Francis*, trans. Placid Hermann, in Marion A. Habig, ed. *St Francis of Assisi, Writings and Early Biographies: English Omnibus of the Sources for the Life of St Francis*, 4th edn (Chicago, 1991), Book II, Chapter 23, p. 409.

[19] For a more extended discussion of this subject, see Sorrell, *St Francis of Assisi and Nature*, pp. 50–4.

made known to the citizens of Gubbio: 'But God wished to bring the holiness of St Francis to the attention of those people'.[20] However, the notion that animals were to be viewed first and foremost as signs, whose behaviour – when read symbolically – could impart to human beings important spiritual truths, was held not just by Francis's biographers, but by Francis himself. As we have seen, after Francis returned to Gubbio with the tamed wolf, he preached a sermon in which he invited the people to compare the purely physical devastation that the animal had wrought with the infinitely greater pain that they would experience if condemned to suffer the eternal torments of Hell. Therefore, like Ugolino, Francis would seem to have regarded the wolf as a symbolic object, seeing in the creature's ferocity and destructiveness a divine admonition, warning sinners of the urgent need to repent for their misdeeds.

For Francis's contemporaries, then, the taming of the wolf was not a revolutionary break with the past, as Lynn White Jr maintained, but rather a deeply traditional manifestation of the saint's holiness and piety.[21] Instead of instituting 'a democracy of God's creatures', Francis was thought to have reasserted humanity's original authority over the animal kingdom – a return to the state of primal innocence that caused the wolf to abandon his wild and savage behaviour, and adopt a life of dutiful obedience. Moreover, it would appear that Francis shared with his contemporaries a similar set of assumptions about animals, treating the wolf (at least in part), as though he were a sign that had been sent by God to alert wrongdoers to the terrible pain of damnation.

In the following chapter, I shall explore more fully the various philosophical and theological assumptions that underpin the idea of the return to Paradise by examining one of the stories from the Life of St Francis that tells how he curbed his sexual desires by beating his body – which he regarded as a metaphorical animal, and pointedly referred to as 'Brother Ass' – in the hope of re-establishing the absolute control over his physical nature that humanity had once enjoyed in the Garden of Eden, but which – like the ascendancy over the animal kingdom – had been relinquished as a consequence of the Fall.

---

[20] *The Little Flowers of St Francis*, Chapter 21, p. 1348.
[21] The traditional hagiographical motif of the saint's miraculous power over animals is also illustrated with reference to a wolf in the tenth-century *Life* of the English martyr-king, St Edmund, in which a wolf guarded the saint's severed head before its discovery by his followers. See the *Life of St Edmund* by Abbo of Fleury, in Michael Winterbottom, ed. *Three Lives of English Saints* (Toronto, 1972), pp. 65–87.

3

Dominion over Animals: The Taming of 'Brother Ass'

FRANCIS'S relationship with the animal kingdom was inextricably bound up with his complex attitude towards his own body, and nowhere is this connection more strikingly apparent than in the story of his reproof to Brother Ass, an incident that was recounted by both Thomas of Celano and St Bonaventure.[1] According to Bonaventure's account of the episode, one night while Francis was praying in his cell in the hermitage of Sarteano, he was visited by the Devil, who afflicted him with the temptation of lust. As soon as Francis felt the first stirrings of his flesh, he removed his habit, and began to whip himself, saying:

> There, Brother Ass, this is how you ought to be treated, to bear the whip like this. The habit serves the religious state and presents a symbol of holiness. A lustful man has no right to steal it. If you want to go that way, then go.[2]

Having beaten himself severely, Francis went outside and rolled around naked in the snow. After some time he made seven snowmen, and standing before them, he again addressed his body:

> Look, this larger one is your wife, those four are your two sons and two daughters; the other two are a servant and a maid whom you should have to serve you. Hurry, then, and clothe them since they are dying of cold. But if it is too much for you to care for so many, then take care to serve one master.[3]

With that, St Francis conquered his lustful thoughts, and returned triumphantly to his cell, never to be afflicted by a similar temptation again.

In the same way that the taming of the wolf of Gubbio turned out to be a deeply traditional manifestation of Francis's sanctity, whose significance

---

[1] See Thomas of Celano, *The Second Life of St Francis*, Book II, Chapter 82, pp. 458–9, and St Bonaventure, *The Major Life of St Francis*, The Classics of Western Spirituality, trans. Ewert Cousins (New York, 1979), Chapter 5, pp. 220–1.

[2] St Bonaventure, *The Major Life of St Francis*, Chapter 5, pp. 220–1.

[3] St Bonaventure, *The Major Life of St Francis*, Chapter 5, p. 221.

can only be properly understood with reference to hagiographical convention, so this incident, however idiosyncratic it may seem, has its conventional analogues. Francis was not alone in considering the human body to be essentially asinine in nature. Writing in his *Life of St Hilarion* (composed at the end of the fourth century), St Jerome told how the Palestinian monk, ascete, and virgin, Hilarion, withdrew into the desert while still in his teens, where he successfully warded off lustful thoughts by beating his body, which he also referred to as an ass:

> The Devil, consequently, tickled the boy's senses and excited the fires of passion usual in puberty. Christ's young novice was compelled to reflect upon what he knew not and to revolve in his mind processions of seductive images and scenes which he had never experienced. Enraged with himself, he beat blows upon his heart as if he could destroy the disturbing thoughts by the sheer violence of the attack. 'You ass,' he said to his body, 'I'll see that you don't kick against the goad; I'll fill you not with barley, but with chaff. I shall wear you out with hunger and thirst; I shall weigh you down with a heavy burden; through the heat and cold I shall drive you, so that you will think of food rather than lust.'[4]

Like Hilarion almost a thousand years earlier, Francis would appear to have looked upon his own nature in profoundly dualistic terms, believing that one of the functions of his rational, spiritual soul was to control – by mortifying his flesh if necessary – the wayward sexual impulses that had their origins in, and derived their energies from, his irrational, animalistic body. That Francis actually conceived of himself in these warring terms was reiterated by Bonaventure, who observed that the saint: 'used to call his body Brother Ass, for he felt it should be subjected to heavy labour, beaten frequently with whips and fed with the poorest food.'[5] For Francis, the relationship between the soul and the body was analogous to that between the human and animal worlds, and his successful conquest of Brother Ass – paralleling as it does the dominion that he was thought to have established over the animal kingdom – has important implications for our understanding of the role of animals in the Franciscan legend.

This correspondence between humanity's control over the brute

---

[4] St Jerome, *Life of St Hilarion*, trans. Sister Marie Liguori Ewald, in Roy J. Deferrari, ed. *Early Christian Biographies*, The Fathers of the Church, Vol. 15 (Washington D.C., 1952), pp. 248–9. Francis's rebuke to Brother Ass is not the only aspect of the story to call to mind an incident from an earlier saint's *Life*. According to Gregory the Great (c. 540–604), St Benedict of Niola overcame the temptation of lust by diving naked into a thick patch of nettles and briars, an action that clearly anticipated Francis's naked dive into the deep snow. See Gregory the Great, *Dialogues*, trans. Odo John Zimmerman, The Fathers of the Church, Vol. 39 (New York, 1959), Book II, Chapter 2, pp. 59–60.

[5] St Bonaventure, *The Major Life of St Francis*, Chapter 5, p. 222.

creation, and the soul's command of the body's erotic desires, was famously elaborated by St Augustine in his discussion of original sin in the *City of God*, a work written during the second and third decades of the fifth century, whose influence on the subsequent development of Western thought has been profound.[6]

Augustine believed that an anatomy of the sin of lust – which he conceived of as spontaneous and uncontrollable sexual desire – could provide a unique insight into both the nature and origins of original sin, because each lustful thought or action contained within itself the same dynamic conflict that had accompanied humanity's first act of disobedience: Adam and Eve's consumption of the forbidden fruit in the Garden of Eden. Although Augustine insisted that lust was by its very nature sinful, and that it emerged as a direct consequence of the Fall, he did not consider human sexuality to be intrinsically evil. Instead, he maintained that Adam and Eve could have conceived children in Paradise without lust, since before the Fall their sexual organs were subject not to lustful passions, but to the rational control of the human will:

> When mankind was in such a state of ease and plenty, blest with such felicity, let us never imagine that it was impossible for the seed of children to be sown without the morbid condition of lust. Instead, the sexual organs would have been brought into activity by the same bidding of the will as controlled the other organs. Then, without feeling the allurement of passion goading him on, the husband would have relaxed on the wife's bosom in tranquility of mind and with no impairment of the body's integrity. Moreover, although we can not prove this in experience, it does not therefore follow that we should not believe that when these parts of the body were not activated by the turbulent heat of passion but brought into service by deliberate use of power when the need arose, the male seed could not have been dispatched into the womb, with no loss of the wife's integrity, just as the menstrual flux can now be produced from the womb of a virgin without loss of maidenhead. For the seed could be injected through the same passage by which the flux is now ejected. Now just as the female womb might have been opened for parturition by a natural impulse when the time was ripe, instead of by the groans of travail, so the two sexes might have been united for impregnation and conception by an act of will, instead of by a lustful craving.[7]

Thus, according to Augustine, the origins of the sin of lust lay not in an innately corrupt human sexual nature, but in humanity's complete loss of conscious control over sexual feelings, a loss that Augustine believed

---

[6] For an assessment of the importance of Augustine's work, see Elaine Pagels, *Adam, Eve, and the Serpent* (Harmondsworth, 1990), p. xxvi.

[7] St Augustine, *Concerning the City of God against the Pagans*, trans. Henry Bettenson (Harmondsworth, 1984), Book XIV, Chapter 26, p. 591.

occurred as a result of the Fall, and could best be understood in terms of the changing relationship between the body, the soul, and God.

Following the opinion of classical philosophers, Augustine assumed that human nature consisted of two elements; a rational soul and an irrational body, with the former exercising a natural authority over the latter:

> For the body is undoubtedly a servant; as Sallust says, 'Our soul is appointed to command, our body to obey.' And he adds, 'One element in us we share with the gods, the other with the beasts,' for he is speaking about man, who, like the beasts, has a mortal body.'[8]

In the same way that God had granted human beings an absolute right to rule over the animal kingdom – 'He [God] did not wish the rational being, made in his own image, to have dominion over any but irrational creatures, not man over man, but man over the beasts'[9] – so Augustine believed that the soul had originally enjoyed an undisputed sovereignty over the body. According to this formulation, there was nothing egalitarian or democratic about Paradise. On the contrary, the state of harmony that existed before the Fall was founded upon the ascendancy of the rational over the irrational, whether manifested in the form of humanity's dominion over the animal kingdom, or the soul's mastery of the body.

Following the traditional Christian interpretation of the Fall, Augustine claimed that the pre-lapsarian state of harmony was shattered at the very moment that Adam and Eve disobeyed God's commandment by eating the fruit of the forbidden tree. And yet he viewed this primal act of human disobedience not just as an attack upon God's authority, but as an attempt by Adam and Eve to overthrow the hierarchical order that God had originally created. According to Augustine, the human soul – which should have remained subservient to the will of God – was filled with a perverse desire for autonomy, and as a fitting punishment for its sinful wish for independence, it was forced to contend with an analogous act of rebellion from its own servant, the body:

> The soul in fact rejoiced in its freedom to act perversely and disdained to be God's servant; and so it was deprived of the obedient service which its body had at first rendered. At its own pleasure the soul deserted its superior and master; and so it no longer retained its inferior and servant to its will. It did not keep its own flesh subject to it in all respects, as it could have kept it for ever if it had itself continued in subjection to God. This then was the time when the flesh began to 'lust in opposition to the spirit', which is the conflict that attends us from our birth.[10]

---

[8] St Augustine, *City of God*, Book IX, Chapter 9, p. 354.
[9] St Augustine, *City of God*, Book XIX, Chapter 15, pp. 874–5.
[10] St Augustine, *City of God*, Book XIII, Chapter 13, p. 522.

As Elaine Pagels has observed, Augustine conceived of Adam and Eve's sin in overtly political terms, seeing it as a revolutionary act that itself resulted in two further acts of rebellion – that of the body against the soul, and of the animal kingdom against humanity.[11] For Augustine, then, the existence of lust was intimately connected with the disobedience of the animals, and both phenomena constituted painful and shameful reminders of humanity's corrupt and fallen nature.

Having briefly considered some of Augustine's comments on both the origins and the consequences of the sin of lust, it is possible to approach St Francis's encounter with Brother Ass with more confidence and understanding. Clearly, Bonaventure considered that Francis's successful suppression of his lustful impulses, like his sovereignty over the animal kingdom, spoke of a perfect harmony that existed between his body and his soul, and his soul and God:

> Francis had reached such purity that his body was in remarkable harmony with his spirit and his spirit with God. As a result God ordained that creation which serves its maker should be subject in an extraordinary way to his will and command.[12]

Bonaventure was thus able to conclude his account of the taming of Brother Ass by claiming that Francis was never to experience a similar affliction again. For just as he had re-established the state of peace and harmony that had originally characterised relations between humanity and the animal kingdom, so within the microcosm of his own self he had succeeded in permanently restoring the natural authority of his soul, and the innate obedience of his body.

However, as indicated above, the story of Brother Ass does not merely tell us something of Francis's attitude towards his own bodily desires and impulses, it also casts light on his underlying beliefs and assumptions about the animal kingdom, and in particular the nature of its relationship (whether pre- or post-lapsarian), with the human world. Because Brother Ass was a metaphorical animal, it does not necessarily follow that Francis either treated, or considered it acceptable to treat, real asses with the same degree of severity that he showed his own body. Rather, my interpretation of the story highlights the very great extent to which Francis shared what Keith Thomas has referred to as 'the breathtakingly anthropocentric spirit' of the time.[13] After all, the saint would appear to have believed that the original condition of the animal kingdom was one of natural servility and obedience to humanity, a state that he himself was miraculously able to restore thanks to his remarkable purity and holiness. Indeed, so conscious was Francis of the instinctive yearning on

[11] See Pagels, *Adam, Eve and the Serpent*, p. 148.
[12] St Bonaventure, *The Major Life of St Francis*, Chapter 5, p. 225.
[13] Thomas, *Man and the Natural World*, p. 18.

the part of animals to serve and obey their human masters, that according to his companions Leo, Rufino, and Angelo, he once exclaimed: 'all creatures say and proclaim; "God made me for you, O man."'[14]

Francis was able to justify his belief that animals had been created solely for the benefit of humanity by appealing to the opening chapter of the Book of Genesis, which relates how God granted the first man and woman – whom He had made in His own image – dominion over the whole of the animal kingdom:

> And God blessed them, and God said unto them, Be fruitful, and multiply, and replenish the earth, and subdue it; and have dominion over the fish of the sea, and over the fowl of the air, and over every living thing that moveth upon the earth. (Genesis 1: 28).

The next chapter will explore some of the different ways in which the Bible governed Francis's perceptions of, and behaviour towards, animals, as he read events in the world around him both through and by specific biblical texts. For, as well as confirming his belief in the divinely ordained utility of the creation, alternative, sometimes contradictory ideas about the animal kingdom as a whole, and individual animal species, were suggested to him by passages from the Old and New Testaments.

---

[14] *Scripta Leonis, Rufini et Angeli*, ed. and trans. Rosalind B. Brooke (Oxford, 1970), Chapter 51, p. 179.

4

Reading The Book of Nature: St Francis, the Bible, and the Natural World

IN the spring of 1213, a mere three years after Pope Innocent III had granted him permission to establish a new religious order, St Francis suffered a major spiritual crisis brought on by uncertainty about the nature of his vocation. Deeply attached to the contemplative life, the saint questioned whether he should abandon the evangelical mission that he had been pursuing up to that point, and withdraw instead to a remote hermitage where he could devote himself entirely to prayer. Unable to decide which course to follow, he consulted two of his most trusted friends; a certain Brother Silvester, and St Clare, who both urged him to continue with his preaching ministry. Believing their pronouncements to have been inspired by the Holy Spirit, Francis – filled with a new spiritual enthusiasm immediately embarked on a preaching mission, and it was during this tour of the local Umbrian countryside that he delivered his famous sermon to the birds.[1]

According to Bonaventure's account of the sermon, while Francis and his companions were travelling through the countryside near Bevagna, a village not far from Assisi, they came across a large flock of birds:

> When God's saint saw them, he quickly ran to the spot and greeted them as if they were endowed with reason. They all became alert and turned toward him, and those perched in the trees bent their heads as he approached them and in an uncommon way directed their attention to him. He went right up to them and solicitously urged them to listen to the word of God, saying: 'Oh birds, my brothers, you have a great obligation to praise your creator, who clothed you in feathers and gave you wings to fly with, provided you with the pure air and cares for you without any worries on your part.' While he was saying this and similar things to them, the birds showed their joy in a remarkable fashion. They began to stretch out their necks, extend their wings, open their beaks and gaze at him attentively. He went through their midst with

---

[1] For the story of the sermon to the birds, see Thomas of Celano, *The First Life of St Francis*, Book I, Chapter 21, pp. 277–8, St Bonaventure, *The Major Life of St Francis*, Chapter 12, pp. 294–5, and *The Little Flowers of St Francis*, Chapter 16, pp. 1336–7.

amazing fervor of spirit, brushing against them with his tunic. Yet none of them moved from the spot until the man of God made the sign of the cross and gave them his blessing and permission to leave, then they all flew away together. His companions waiting on the road saw all these things. When he returned to them, that pure and simple man began to accuse himself of negligence because he had not preached to the birds before.[2]

Here we appear to have the archetypal vision of St Francis, the lover of nature, preaching to birds as if they were a human congregation, affording them the same rights and responsibilities as a human audience. But, it is important to recognise that the sermon was as much a summation of traditional biblical attitudes towards nature, as a spontaneous and personal response on the part of Francis to his avian audience. A number of biblical injunctions would seem to lie behind Francis's call to the birds to honour their debt of gratitude to their Creator. Christ himself commanded human beings to preach to the animal kingdom (Mark 16: 15), while non-human creatures are frequently reminded in the Old Testament of their duty to praise God.[3] Although Francis assumed that God valued humans more than animals (a belief that was explicitly sanctioned by Christ in the Gospels),[4] he nonetheless argued that all creatures, regardless of their status, were under a moral obligation to glorify God for the precious gift of life. In his sermon, he told the birds of the many blessings that God had bestowed upon them, claiming that their Creator had generously provided for their every need, and while this assertion ignores the reality of struggle and conflict that characterises the life of birds, it is nonetheless informed by one of the central tenets of the Christian religion; a belief – that can be traced back to the opening chapter of the Book of Genesis – in the essential goodness of the creation:

> And God made the beast of the earth after his kind, and cattle after their kind, and every thing that creepeth upon the earth after his kind: and God saw that it was good. (Genesis 1: 25).

While his mode of expression clearly struck his biographers as novel and idiosyncratic, Francis was not actually breaking with theological tradition in the substance of his injunctions to the birds. There were biblical precedents for treating the wider animal kingdom with something akin to

---

[2] St Bonaventure, *The Major Life of St Francis*, Chapter 12, pp. 294–5.

[3] For instance, the Book of Daniel tells of the three righteous Jews who called upon the birds of the air to glorify and exalt their Creator: 'O all ye fowls of the air, bless ye the Lord; praise and exalt him above all for ever' (Daniel 3: 58).

[4] 'Behold the fowls of the air: for they sow not, neither do they reap, nor gather into barns; yet your heavenly father feedeth them. *Are ye not much better than they?*' (Matthew 6: 26, my italics).

the respect afforded to humanity, and these could have formed the basis of a new and radical approach to the natural world. But, crucially, Francis did not exploit these texts in that way. It is important to attend to the true motivation behind his sermon, which, on closer inspection, proves to be less concerned with the nature of the birds themselves, than with the saint's wider theological preoccupations. Francis expressed in his avian sermon a belief in the goodness of the natural world; but it was a belief based not upon a sense of the intrinsic virtues of nature, but on the assumption that each and every creature reflected, and partook of, the glory of God. Francis loved and respected the birds because he saw in them a reflection of their Creator, a reflection that called to mind his own relationship with God. It was their great good fortune at having been clothed with feathers and housed in the air that reminded him of God's goodness, power, and wisdom, and it was this sense of God's generosity and bounty that prompted the saint to preach a sermon that is as much an expression of his own sense of gratitude for continued divine favour, as a statement on the real role of birds in the world.

Because no animal story from the legend of St Francis reverberates with such biblical resonance as the narrative of the sermon to the birds, it is crucially important, as we have already seen, to look beyond the words of the sermon itself, to the sacred texts upon which it draws.[5] Even the seemingly incidental detail of Francis's self-reproach – uttered for never having preached to birds before – would appear to have been inspired by a passage from the Gospel of Mark, in which Jesus instructed his apostles to preach 'to every creature.' (Mark 16: 15) And this alerts us to a second, and perhaps more important dimension to the saint's motivation, his apparent need to fulfil through his own actions a rather literal reading of biblical injunctions. Francis's sermon to the birds was a reflection of his intensely biblicist approach to life in general, an approach that, as I shall demonstrate in what follows, saw biblical texts as expressly and intensely applicable to the contemporary world, a world that in turn could be seen as a 'text' equally expressive of divine truth for those with the ability and desire to search out its deeper symbolic meaning.

Both Bonaventure and Thomas of Celano commented upon this capacity of St Francis to see beneath the surface of things, and detect the secret signature that God had imprinted on all His work. To quote Thomas of Celano: 'he discerned the hidden things of nature with his sensitive heart, as one who has already escaped into the freedom of the glory of the sons of God.'[6] For Francis, all natural objects, whether animate or inanimate, were holy by dint of their association with God,

---

[5] Roger D. Sorrell's excellent interpretation of the sermon treats its many scriptural allusions with great sensitivity. See Sorrell, *St Francis of Assisi and Nature*, pp. 59–68.
[6] Thomas of Celano, *The First Life of St Francis*, Book I, Chapter 29, p. 297.

so that he was filled with ineffable joy simply by contemplating the sun, moon, and stars, while he exhorted flowers, vineyards, cornfields, forests, and stones to thank their Creator for His goodness and liberality.[7]

Of course, the God who was revealed to Francis through his contemplation of the natural world was not an abstract or impersonal deity, but was rather the divine being whose unfolding relationship with humanity had been recorded in the pages of the Bible. However, there was no conflict for Francis between what he had learnt about God from his reading of the Scriptures, and the image of the Creator that he saw reflected in the natural world. On the contrary, he saw in the cosmos much that he associated quite specifically with Christ and his incarnation. For instance, as Bonaventure observed, the sight of young lambs being led to the slaughter would remind the saint of the image of the lamb of God, which in turn would inspire him to save the creatures from their fate: 'He often paid to ransom lambs that were being led to their death, remembering the most gentle lamb who willed to be led to the slaughter to pay the ransom of sinners.'[8] Bonaventure's comments would therefore seem to suggest that Francis loved lambs not because they were intrinsically loveable, but because they symbolised the meekness and purity of Christ. For Francis, favouring lambs was an act of religious devotion: an expression of his deep gratitude to Jesus for his sacrifice on the cross. Consequently, Francis's mystical contemplation of the natural world deepened not so much his respect and affection for animals, *qua* animals, as his personal love of Christ. To refer once again to Thomas of Celano:

> among all the various kinds of animals, he loved little lambs with a special predilection and more ready affection, because in the sacred scriptures the humility of our Lord Jesus Christ is more frequently likened to that of the lamb and best illustrated by the simile of the lamb. So, all things, especially those in which some allegorical similarity to the son of God could be found, he would embrace more fondly and look upon more willingly.[9]

There would appear to be something of a contradiction lying at the heart of Francis's vision of the natural world, for while he is said to have loved

---

[7] See Thomas of Celano, *The First Life of St Francis*, Book I, Chapter 29, pp. 296–7. Edward Armstrong (*Saint Francis, Nature Mystic*, pp. 11–12), has summarised Francis's sacramental reverence for the natural world in the following way: 'For him nature spoke of God. All created things pointed beyond themselves to their Creator . . . It was because nature revealed in sight, sound, and fragrance the handiwork and glory of God that he admired and rejoiced in things of beauty. He envisaged all Creation, man supremely, as worshipping the Creator.'

[8] St Bonaventure, *The Major Life of St Francis*, Chapter 8, p. 255.

[9] Thomas of Celano, *The First Life of St Francis*, Book I, Chapter 28, p. 293.

all creatures 'on account of their Creator',[10] he nevertheless believed that some animals – such as lambs   spoke more eloquently of God than others, and it was to these more symbolically articulate creatures that he reserved his special favour. Therefore, in addition to his general, all-embracing love of the natural world, Francis bore a particular love for those creatures that either stood as symbols for, or were conventionally associated with, Christ.

The story of Francis's encounter with the solitary lamb forced to live with a herd of goats not only highlights this inconsistency in his attitude towards creation, but also reveals just how profoundly his perceptions of, and responses to, animals and nature, were determined by his reading of the Bible. According to Thomas of Celano, while Francis was travelling through the Marches of Ancona with a certain Brother Paul, he came across a shepherd who was feeding a large herd of goats, in the midst of which was a single lamb. Deeply touched with sorrow at the sight of this solitary little sheep, Francis said to his companion:

> Do you not see this sheep that walks so meekly among the goats? I tell you that our Lord Jesus Christ walked in the same way meekly among the pharisees and chief priests. Therefore I ask you, my son, to have pity with me on this little sheep. Let us pay the price and lead her away from among these goats.[11]

Having no money with which to purchase the animal, the two friars were wondering what to do when a merchant suddenly appeared and offered to pay the shepherd the required price. After the transaction was completed, Francis removed the lamb from the field of goats, and gave it to the community of Poor Clares at San Severino where it was well looked after. Some time later, the nuns of San Severino sent St Francis a tunic that they had made using the lamb's wool.

So all-encompassing was Francis's devotion to Christ, and so deeply had he immersed himself in the pages of the Bible, that he was able to transform the seemingly unremarkable sight of a solitary sheep sur-rounded by a herd of goats into a vision of Christ wandering meekly amongst the pharisees and chief priests. For Francis, the natural world was an allegorical text in which God had cryptically concealed certain signs and symbols whose underlying meaning could be recovered or deciphered only with reference to the holy Scriptures. But, it is important to note that in addition to viewing the lamb as a living emblem, who symbolically re-enacted a scene from sacred history within the Book of Nature, Francis also responded to the creature on a much more practical, utilitarian level. By accepting a tunic made from the lamb's wool, he implicitly recognised that on one level at least the animal was simply a

---

[10] Thomas of Celano, *The First Life of St Francis*, Book I, Chapter 29, p. 295.
[11] Thomas of Celano, *The First Life of St Francis*, Book I, Chapter 28, p. 294.

domesticated, wool-producing beast, whose life was firmly rooted in the concrete, physical world of the here and now. Although there is a clear disjunction between these two responses to the lamb – the one transcendent, the other utilitarian – both reactions were informed by a similarly anthropocentric spirit, which saw the creature exclusively in terms of how its existence benefited human beings, whether in purely practical terms by providing men and women with wool for clothing, or in the spiritual sphere by encouraging individuals to mediate upon the life of Christ.

The story of Francis's encounter with the lamb and the goats is also significant because it demonstrates that there were some animals that the saint actively disliked. Prompted by the same biblical precedent that led him to bestow his special love and care on lambs, Francis felt compelled to view certain other animals – such as goats – as somehow evil or sinister. He probably derived his suspicion of goats from the twenty-fifth chapter of St Matthew's Gospel, where, in a parable on the day of judgement, Christ compared the damned sinners who would have to endure an eternity of torment, to the unwanted goats that a shepherd separates from his sheep:

> When the son of man shall come in his glory, and all the holy angels with him, then shall he sit upon the throne of his glory. And before him shall be gathered all nations: and he shall separate them one from another, as a shepherd divideth his sheep from his goats. And he shall set the sheep on his right hand, but the goats on his left. . . . Then shall he say also unto them on the left hand, Depart from me ye cursed, into everlasting fire, prepared for the devil and his angels.
>
> (Matthew 25: 31–33, & 41)

Francis's antipathy to goats illustrates with great clarity the apparent inconsistency in his vision of the natural world to which I have already referred. On the one hand, he clearly believed that all creatures shared in the goodness of their Creator, and – as he indicated in his sermon to the birds – had a duty to praise and thank God for the precious gift of life. But, on the other hand, and in seeming defiance of this all-encompassing love of creation, his implicit faith in the veracity of the Bible encouraged him to discriminate between animals, viewing some as images – almost embodiments – of Christ, while seeing others as symbols of the damned.

Of all the members of the animal kingdom, Francis probably disliked pigs most of all, a fact that would seem to reflect their especially unwholesome reputation for uncleanness and greed, a reputation that finds expression in such biblical episodes as the parable of the prodigal son, in which Jesus told of a young man who was forced to suffer the terrible indignity of becoming a swineherd after he had recklessly squandered his father's inheritance, and the story of the Gadarene swine, which relates how Jesus cast a multitude of demons into a herd of pigs, causing the animals to stampede over a cliff.[12]

Francis's moral disapproval of, and strong aversion to, pigs, is most conspicuously in evidence in the story of the wicked sow and the innocent lamb, an episode that was related by both Thomas of Celano and Bonaventure.[13] According to Bonaventure's account of this incident, while the saint was staying at the monastery of San Verecondo in the diocese of Gubbio, a newborn lamb was attacked and killed by a 'ferocious sow'.[14] The death of the lamb reminded Francis of the supreme sacrifice that had been made by the immaculate Lamb of God, and with this thought in his mind he cursed the sow for its act of murder, saying: 'Alas, brother lamb, innocent animal, you represent Christ to men. A curse on that impious beast that killed you; may no man or beast ever eat of her.'[15] As soon as he had uttered these words, the sow fell sick, eventually dying from her illness after suffering in terrible agony for three days. The sow's carcass was then thrown into the monastery moat, where – in fulfilment of St Francis's curse – it remained completely untouched by even the hungriest animal.[16]

Perhaps what is most immediately striking about this story is the sheer intensity of Francis's animosity to the sow, and his genuine sense of horror at its greed and savagery. The strength of the saint's aversion is revealed in the words of the curse that he directed against the animal, in which he accused her of committing an impious act of murder. In Francis's eyes, the sow's actions were overlaid with such religious significance that she was effectively guilty of sacrilege, having performed a deed that – in a symbolic sense at least – both recalled and repeated the crucifixion of Christ. Once again, we find that a couple of farmyard animals were transformed through the power of Francis's biblically inspired imagination into symbols of good and evil, enabling a seemingly unremarkable agricultural incident to be viewed as an allegorical confrontation between the most fundamental of cosmic forces.

But, as well as illustrating Francis's hostility to pigs, the story of the

---

[12] For the parable of the prodigal son, see Luke 15: 11–32, while the story of the Gadarene swine can be found in Matthew 8: 28–32, Mark 5: 1–13, and Luke 8: 26–33. For a more extensive discussion of Francis's aversion to pigs, see Armstrong, *Saint Francis, Nature Mystic*, pp. 113–23.

[13] See Thomas of Celano, *The Second Life of St Francis*, Book II, Chapter 77, p. 454, and St Bonaventure, *The Major Life of St Francis*, Chapter 8, p. 255.

[14] St Bonaventure, *The Major Life of St Francis*, Chapter 8, p. 255.

[15] St Bonaventure, *The Major Life of St Francis*, Chapter 8, p. 255.

[16] The reputation of pigs for savagery both to humans and to other animals was sufficiently well founded during the later Middle Ages for it to become something of a commonplace. For instance, one of the horrors depicted on the wall of the Temple of Mars in *The Knight's Tale* is: 'The sowe freten the child right in the cradel'. See Geoffrey Chaucer, *The Knight's Tale* (2019), in Larry D. Benson *et al.*, *The Riverside Chaucer* (Oxford, 1988).

lamb and the sow is also interesting for the light that it sheds on the saint's attitude towards the eating of animals. For, in the malediction that Francis uttered against the sow, not only did he condemn her to death, but he also imposed a *post mortem* injunction preventing any creature – whether human or animal – from ever eating any of her flesh. This rather curious prohibition can be explained in two different ways. On the one hand, it is possible that Francis believed that the sow had rendered herself so spiritually unclean through her act of wickedness and impiety that both humans and animals would intuitively recoil from any contact with her impure, polluted carcass. On the other hand, however, the injunction against eating the pig might be seen as yet another penalty directed against the animal, over and above the taking of her life. According to this reading of the curse, by denying the sow the opportunity of being eaten, the saint was able to compound her punishment by preventing her from fulfilling one of the purposes for which she had been created.

This interpretation of Francis's curse would seem to suggest that the saint did not simply look upon animals as sources of food, but believed that this was how they actually conceived of themselves. That Francis ate animals for food is beyond dispute, being well attested in the various sources, and yet his attitude towards meat-eating has been the subject of some confusion and controversy in recent years, with certain commentators – viewing his relationship with the animal kingdom through the filter of the modern environmental and animal rights movements – expressing surprise and disappointment at his failure to become a vegetarian. For instance, after describing the saint's great love of creation (citing as proof both the sermon to the birds and the taming of the wolf of Gubbio), Morris Bishop went on to express his puzzlement at the fact that Francis did not refrain from eating meat: 'Curiously, this brother of all life did not take the next logical, almost inevitable, step and refuse to eat meat.'[17] However, as Roger Sorrell amongst others has noted, far from opposing the killing of animals for food, Francis actually considered meat-eating to be a moral duty, basing both his own conduct, and the rule of the Franciscan Order on a literal interpretation of Christ's commandment to his apostles: 'eat such things as are set before you' (Luke 10: 8); an injunction that he incorporated into the Franciscan Rule of 1223 (the so-called *Regula Bullata*): 'Whatever house they [the friars] enter, they should first say, "Peace to this house" (Luke 10: 5), and in the words of the Gospel they may eat what is set before them (Luke 10: 8)'.[18] For Francis, then, the eating of meat was not just a matter of custom or

---

[17] Morris Bishop, *Saint Francis of Assisi* (Boston, 1974), p. 187.
[18] St Francis of Assisi, *The Rule of 1223*, trans. Benen Fahy, in Marion A. Habig, ed. *St Francis of Assisi, Writings and Early Biographies: English Omnibus of the Sources for the Life of St Francis*, 4th edn (Chicago, 1991), Chapter 3, p. 60.

necessity, it was a religious obligation that had been imposed upon humanity by no less a figure than Jesus himself.[19]

Perhaps the most interesting story about meat-eating in the Franciscan canon – and certainly the one that casts the most light on the influence that Jesus's dietary habits had on the Friars Minor – concerns not Francis himself, but St Anthony of Padua, one of Francis's earliest and most illustrious followers.[20] According to the *Actus Beati Francisci* (and its Italian derivative *The Little Flowers of St Francis*), while Anthony was staying in the city of Rimini, he was confronted by a large group of heretics who were so stubborn that they refused to be swayed by his preaching. In order to expose both their obstinacy and the falseness of their dogma, the saint went to the mouth of a river near the sea, and began to preach a sermon to the fish, saying: 'You fishes of the sea and river, listen to the word of God, since the faithless heretics refuse to hear it.'[21] As soon as he had spoken these words, a great multitude of fish gathered before him, holding their heads above the water and gazing intently at his face. Having gained the complete attention of his audience of fish, Anthony then proceeded to enumerate some of the many favours that God had bestowed upon them:

> My fish brothers, you should give as many thanks as you can to your Creator who has granted you such a noble element as your dwelling place, so that you have fresh and salt water, just as you please. Moreover He has given you many refuges to escape from storms. He has also given you a clear and transparent element and ways to travel and food to live on. Your kind creator also prepares for you the food that you need even in the depths of the ocean. When He created you at the creation of the world, He gave you the command to increase and multiply, and He gave you His blessing . . . You were chosen as food for the Eternal King, Our Blessed Lord Jesus Christ, before his resurrection and in a mysterious way afterwards. Because of all these things you should praise and bless the Lord, who has given you so many more blessings than other creatures.[22]

[19] The eating of meat also received divine sanction in the Old Testament. In God's *post diluvian* covenant with Noah, God granted Noah and his descendents the right to eat all the beasts of the earth, air, and sea: 'And God blessed Noah and his sons, and said unto them, Be fruitful, and multiply, and replenish the earth. And the fear of you and the dread of you shall be upon every beast of the earth, and upon every fowl of the air, upon all that moveth upon the earth, and upon all the fishes of the sea; into your hand are they delivered. Every moving thing that liveth shall be meat for you, even as the green herb have I given you all things' (Genesis 9: 1–3).

[20] St Anthony of Padua (1193–1231), joined the Franciscans in 1220, and was appointed to teach the friars theology, first at Bologna, and then at Padua. He also travelled widely through Southern France where he preached against heresy, eventually winning the title 'the hammer of the heretics' for the effectiveness of his preaching. In deference to St Anthony's great learning, St Francis referred to him as 'his bishop'. See *The Little Flowers of St Francis*, Chapter 39, p. 1390.

[21] *The Little Flowers of St Francis*, Chapter 40, p. 1391.

[22] *The Little Flowers of St Francis*, Chapter 40, pp. 1392–3.

All the inhabitants of the city – including the heretics – were so amazed at the sight of this miracle that they sat down at Anthony's feet and begged him to preach them a sermon. Anthony acceded to their request, and spoke with such eloquence about the Catholic religion that he succeeded in converting all of the city's heretics.

In many ways, St Anthony's sermon to the fish recalls St Francis's sermon to the birds, for in both stories the animals were told of the extraordinary generosity of their Creator, and urged to praise and thank Him for His benevolence and wisdom. Moreover, just as St Francis valued the birds not so much for their own intrinsic worth, but as creatures who were in some way touched by the glory of their Creator, so Anthony praised God by extolling the virtues of His creation. However, among the many acts of divine kindness for which Anthony expected his audience to be grateful was the somewhat dubious honour that Jesus had chosen to eat fish both before and after his resurrection. Once again, a story from the legend of St Francis highlights the profoundly anthropocentric spirit of the age, with Anthony assuming not only that his audience of fish would instinctively understand that the role or purpose of their lives was to be eaten by humans, but also that they would experience a sense of pride and gratitude in the knowledge that their Creator, Jesus, had condescended to consume fish during his time on earth.

Anthony's sermon to the fish – and the attitude towards the animal kingdom underlying it – is therefore profoundly paradoxical in character. Like St Francis before him, Anthony would appear to have believed that the lives of animals were entirely expendable, and that their worth resided in their usefulness to humanity, as well as in the fact that they reflected the glory of God, their Creator. But, at the same time (and again following the precedent of the sermon to the birds), Anthony also treated his audience of fish as though it were endowed both with intelligence, and an instinctive, spiritual awareness of the presence of God. We are confronted, then, by a tension in Anthony's sermon between two conflicting views of the animal kingdom; one anthropocentric and pragmatic, the other transcendent and spiritual, a confusion that has been noted by the historian, Colin Spencer:

> After giving the sermon to the admiring fish, St Anthony probably went back home and grilled a few of them for supper. Or if not, the fact that fish was an integral part of their diet, a necessity on fast days, was never questioned by either St Francis or by St Anthony, nor by the people who told the story. The fish might well have listened with greater attention than 'sinful heretics' but they could still be killed and eaten. The medieval mind saw the animal kingdom in a deeply complex and contradictory way.[23]

[23] Colin Spencer, *The Heretic's Feast: A History of Vegetarianism* (London, 1993), p. 174.

Francis's attitude towards the eating of meat – and the complete absence from his thinking of any moral qualms about the killing of animals – probably finds its definitive, and most graphic expression in an incident recorded by Thomas of Celano in his *Second Life of St Francis*. According to Thomas, on one occasion when Christmas happened to fall on a Friday – a day of fasting and abstinence – Francis was asked by a certain Brother Morico whether or not the friars were allowed to eat meat:

> When the question arose about eating meat that day, since the Christmas day was a Friday, he [St Francis] replied, saying to Brother Morico: 'You sin, Brother, calling the day on which the Child was born to us a day of fast. It is my wish,' he said, 'that even the walls should eat meat on such a day, and if they cannot, they should be smeared with meat on the outside.'[24]

For Francis, the duty to celebrate Christmas outweighed any obligations on the part of the friars to abstain from meat-eating on a Friday. Moreover, far from being troubled by the morality of killing animals, Francis believed that a failure to eat meat on Christmas day would itself constitute an immoral act, arguing that it could be interpreted as something of an affront to Christ, whose birthday should be an occasion of joy and festivity. Therefore, not only did Francis associate meat-eating at Christmas with celebration and thanksgiving, more importantly, he considered it to be a sacramental duty that symbolically conveyed humanity's gratitude to Jesus for his willingness to assume human form, and suffer death on the cross.[25]

Francis's moral approval of meat-eating, and his intense aversion to pigs, find further expression in one final story from the Franciscan canon, a story that concentrates on the figure not of Francis himself, but of a certain Brother Juniper, one of the saint's holiest and most humble companions.[26] According to the *Life of Brother Juniper*, while the humble Brother Juniper was living in the church of St Mary of the Angels, he asked a certain sick friar whom he was nursing if there was anything that

[24] Thomas of Celano, *The Second Life of St Francis*, Book II, Chapter 151, pp. 521–2.

[25] Roger D. Sorrell has also suggested that Francis's enthusiasm for meat-eating was in part a reaction to the fact that vegetarianism was practised by the Cathars, a sect which – although at its strongest in Southern France – was not unknown in Northern and Central Italy. Thus, Sorrell argued that Francis deliberately emphasised the importance of meat-eating both for himself, and his followers, as a way of establishing his own orthodox credentials, and distinguishing the Friars Minor from the many heretical movements that were in existence at the time. See Sorrell, *St Francis of Assisi and Nature*, pp. 77–9.

[26] This episode is recounted in an anonymous fourteenth-century *Life* of Brother Juniper. See *Vita Fratris Iuniperi*, in *Analecta Franciscana* 3 (Quaracchi, 1897), pp. 54–64. For an English translation, see the *Life of Friar Juniper*, in T. Okey, trans. *The Little Flowers of St Francis* (London, 1910), pp. 134–47.

he desired. When the friar answered that what he most wanted was to eat a pig's foot, Juniper went to a wood where he knew that some pigs would be feeding, selected an animal, and chopped off one of its feet with a knife. Juniper then returned to the church of St Mary, where he prepared the food, and gave it to his companion.

Meanwhile, the owner of the injured pig became so angry on discovering what had happened that he complained to the friars. St Francis heard the uproar that the man was causing, and humbly tried to assuage his anger, but to no avail. The man could not be pacified, and returned home, raging against the wickedness of the friars. Suspecting that Juniper was responsible for the furore, Francis asked him whether or not he had chopped off the pig's foot, and because Juniper considered the deed to be an act of charity, he blithely told Francis the whole story. Fearful of the great scandal that might ensue, Francis instructed Juniper to follow the man, humbly beg his forgiveness, and do whatever was in his power to make amends. Juniper instantly complied with Francis's command, and once he had caught up with the man, he embraced him, and told him of the charitable motive that had inspired his action. At first the man was unmoved by these protestations, but after a while he became so touched by Juniper's simplicity and humility that he acknowledged his own wrongdoing, and offered to kill the pig and give the rest of the carcass to the friars as a gift. All this was carried out, and after the animal had been delivered to the friars, Francis praised the patience and simplicity of Juniper, saying: 'Would to God, my brethren, that I had a whole forest of such Junipers.'[27]

This is one of only a handful of narratives in the canon of Franciscan literature in which the holiness of St Francis is eclipsed by the spiritual achievements of one of his companions. Despite the many criticisms levelled against him, Juniper is entirely vindicated at the end of the story, with his various actions – interpreted at first as misdeeds – being shown to be nothing more than expressions of his spiritual fervour and holy simplicity. Indeed, such was the humility of Juniper that he remained completely oblivious of, and indifferent to, the good opinion of others, with the result that even St Francis fared badly in comparison, appearing somewhat worldly in his concern for the reputation of the Order.

Of course, from the point of view of the present discussion, what is most interesting about the story is the fact that far from eliciting the opprobrium or moral condemnation of the anonymous author, the act of chopping off the pig's foot was presented as an ideal example of saintly behaviour, which eventually won for Juniper the lavish praise of St Francis himself. Significantly, neither Juniper nor Francis felt it necessary to address themselves to the subject of the compassionate treatment of animals, and at no stage did they suggest that pigs were either entitled

[27] *Life of Friar Juniper*, p. 137.

to protection from unnecessary cruelty, or even capable of experiencing pain. Rather, Juniper succeeded in persuading both Francis and the pig's owner that his charitable responsibilities towards the sick friar outweighed the claims of ownership that any individual human might have over the animal itself. As Juniper remarked:

> I tell thee this much, that considering the consolation this friar of ours felt, and the comfort he took from the said foot, had I cut off the feet of a hundred pigs as I did this one, I believe of a surety God would have looked on it as a good deed.[28]

Although Juniper's treatment of the pig is the starkest example that we have so far considered of human indifference to animal suffering, it nevertheless typifies the low status that was accorded to members of the animal kingdom by both Francis and his biographers. Indeed, as the story of Juniper and the pig all too clearly reveals, Francis and his followers tended to look upon animals first and foremost as objects that had been created by God for human use, whether for food or clothing, or as transcendent symbols, designed to remind human beings of the spiritual reality lying beyond the material world. Even on those occasions when Francis celebrated animal life, such as his sermon to the birds, he would appear to have been using animals as a way of praising and thanking God for the glory of His creation, a fact this is borne out by one further observation that Francis made on the subject of the celebration of Christmas:

> I would ask that a general law be made that all who can should scatter corn and grain along the roads so that the birds might have an abundance of food on the day of such great solemnity, especially our sisters the larks.[29]

Francis's comments would seem to have been motivated not by compassion for the plight of larks in winter, but by a feeling that human beings were under a special obligation to care for God's creation on the anniversary of Christ's birth. Once again, the question of Francis's motivation is crucially important, for as we have seen, it was his intense love of God, rather than any particular affection for the individual creatures themselves, that lay behind his acts of kindness towards such creatures as lambs and birds.

In Part 2, I shall turn from hagiography to romance, and explore how the animal themes and motifs that I have been investigating in relation to St Francis were adopted by the writers of romance literature, and used by them as a way of suggesting that holiness and piety were essential qualities of the courtly, aristocratic hero. Concentrating on the fourteenth-century

[28] *Life of Friar Juniper*, pp. 135–6.
[29] Thomas of Celano, *The Second Life of St Francis*, Book II, Chapter 151, p. 522.

Middle English romances, *Sir Isumbras*, *Sir Gowther*, *Octavian*, and *Sir Orfeo*, I shall examine through their respective depictions of the animal kingdom how the figure of the romance hero was able to reconcile such traditional saintly qualities as patience and humility, with more conventional chivalric attributes, like the love of hunting, and prowess in arms.

Part II

Knights and the Brute Creation: Nobility and Sanctity in Four Middle English Romances

Plate 2. Pisanello, *The Vision of St Eustace*. National Gallery, London.

5

Romance and Hagiography: *The Vision of St Eustace* and *Sir Isumbras*

PAINTED some time around the middle of the fifteenth century, Pisanello's *The Vision of St Eustace* (Plate 2), depicts the central and most dramatic incident from the legend of a martyr whose cult enjoyed great popularity during the later Middle Ages. St Eustace is said to have been a general in the army of the Roman Emperor, Trajan, and to have been martyred during the reign of his successor, Hadrian, although there is no supporting historical evidence to corroborate either of these claims. Indeed, the legend so abounds in fabulous incidents and implausible coincidences that it is now generally thought to have no basis in fact.[1] However, whatever the nature of Eustace's relationship to history, the saint clearly exerted a powerful hold over the imagination of the writers and artists of the later Middle Ages, as numerous versions of the legend (written in both Latin and the vernacular) survive from the period, as do a number of visual treatments of the life, most notably that undertaken by Pisanello himself.[2]

Pisanello (whose name is derived from Pisa, his father's birthplace) is believed to have died in 1455 at around the age of sixty, and is probably best remembered today for his drawings and commemorative medals. The assistant of Gentile de Fabriano (with whom he undertook a number of commissions in Venice and Rome), Pisanello travelled widely during the course of his career, working in various Italian courts for a number of aristocratic patrons. Despite the fact that much of his life remains shrouded in mystery, and that many of his compositions, particularly his paintings, have been lost, he is nonetheless regarded as one of the

---

[1] See David Hugh Farmer, *The Oxford Dictionary of Saints*, 3rd edn (Oxford, 1992), p. 171.

[2] For a brief survey of the literary versions of the *vita*, see Laurel Braswell, 'Sir Isumbras and the Legend of Saint Eustace', *Medieval Studies* 27 (1965), 128–51, pp. 128–30. Perhaps the most influential, and certainly the most widely disseminated version of the legend, is to be found in the *Legenda Aurea* of Jacobus of Voragine which was written around 1260. It is to this version that I shall be referring throughout. See Jacobus of Voragine, *The Golden Legend of Jacobus of Voragine*, trans. Granger Ryan and Helmut Ripperger (New York, 1941), pp. 555–61.

foremost Italian artists of the first half of the fifteenth century.[3] Like so much of his life, the circumstances surrounding the composition of *The Vision of St Eustace* are extremely obscure. It is not known for sure either when – or for whom – the panel was painted, although it must date from some time around the middle of the fifteenth century. The painting itself provides few clues to its provenance. The *cartellino* or scroll in the foreground of the composition bears no trace of an inscription, and while it has been suggested that the saint – who is depicted in contemporary, courtly dress – may have been a portrait of Pisanello's patron, the only inference that this conjecture allows us to draw is that he was a wealthy and fashionable nobleman with a love of hunting.[4]

The painting itself is a representation of the moment of Eustace's conversion. The legend tells how – while hunting one day deep in a forest – the virtuous pagan, Eustace, encounters a stag with a crucifix attached to its head, fixed between its antlers. On seeing the stag, we are told that Eustace hears the voice of Christ, who first reveals the mysteries of the Christian religion, and then tells him to undergo baptism with his family.

Perhaps what is most immediately striking about the painting is the way in which Pisanello invests the scene with such a strong sense of mystery, powerfully suggesting the strange, otherworldly nature of Eustace's supernatural experience. Famed both for his portraits of the contemporary Italian nobility, and for his accurate sketches of animals, Pisanello evidently took great care in realistically depicting not only Eustace and the stag, but also the other birds and beasts in the painting, namely Eustace's horse and hounds, along with the bear, hare, deer, and assorted waterfowl that inhabit the forest. But although each individual creature is portrayed in a detailed and accurate manner, the naturalistic effect is somewhat distorted by the fact that the animals are not painted to scale. (This applies equally to the many other objects, such as trees and stones, that comprise the woodland landscape.) So, while all of the constituent elements of the composition are brilliantly observed, they appear to be slightly out of alignment with one another. It is precisely this lack of perspective (along, of course, with the eerie darkness of the woodland setting), that gives the painting an almost dream-like quality, making the forest seem a profoundly mysterious place where two distinct worlds or ontological states – the known and the unknown, or the human and the divine – come together and merge.

The strange, almost ethereal quality that suffuses *The Vision of St*

---

[3] For an account of Pisanello's life and work, see Renzo Chiarelli and J. C. Pollard, 'Pisanello', in Jane Turner, ed. *The Dictionary of Art*, Vol. 24 (London, 1996), pp. 860–5.

[4] For a discussion of the painting, see Jill Dunkerton, Susan Foister, Dillian Gordon, and Nicholas Penny, *Giotto to Durer: Early Renaissance Painting in the National Gallery* (New Haven, 1992), pp. 276–7, and Erika Langmuir, *The National Gallery Companion Guide* (New Haven, 1994), pp. 83–4.

Eustace is obviously highly appropriate to the religious subject of the painting. And yet to a modern audience, unfamiliar both with the legend itself, and with the hagiographical traditions that lie behind it, the mystical atmosphere that permeates the landscape may seem to be at odds with the insistent – almost defiant – worldliness of Eustace himself. As noted above, Eustace is dressed in all of the finery of a contemporary aristocrat. In a conspicuous display of wealth, not only does he wear a golden tunic, but his hunting horn and spurs are also decorated in gold. Moreover, he is pictured with his faithful hounds, joyfully engaging in the favourite pastime of the medieval aristocracy: hunting, and there is nothing in the painting to suggest that this pursuit is sinful or should in any way be condemned. To a modern sensibility, then, used to a strict separation between the realms of the religious and the secular, the spiritual and the worldly, what might seem most strange about the painting is the emphatic way in which Pisanello portrays, even celebrates, Eustace's worldly nobility – something that could be considered to be incompatible with his calling as a saint. But just as the composition seems deliberately to disorientate the viewer by depicting the forest in such a mysterious, enchanted manner, so it also upsets modern expectations of a strict separation between the sacred and the profane, the holy and the chivalric. For, in the figure of Eustace, we see that saintliness and nobility – far from being in opposition – are fused and celebrated simultaneously. Pisanello's *The Vision of St Eustace,* then, suggests that during the later Middle Ages, there was no clear dividing-line separating the realms of religious and secular experience. For Pisanello and his audience, the chivalric values underpinning romance narratives were entirely consistent with the traditional virtues of a saint. It is these strong affinities between knights and saints, and the literary genres of which they are the chief protagonists – romance and hagiography – that I shall explore in the pages that follow.

The heroes of medieval romance – particularly when viewed from a modern perspective, far removed in time and understanding from the culture of the High Middle Ages – may seem to have very little in common with the saintly protagonists of hagiography. Romance heroes, after all, tend to be firmly rooted in the material world, and their goals and ambitions are primarily secular and temporal. They struggle to gain fame, fortune, worldly honour, and – most crucially – sexual love, which they realise either in the socially acceptable form of marriage, or (as in the well-known cases of Lancelot and Tristram), illicitly through an adulterous relationship with a mistress. The heroes of saints' lives, on the other hand, renounce the physical world, setting their sights instead exclusively on the spiritual realm. They hold in contempt all that is material, and strive to suppress the very desires and ambitions that romance heroes seek to fulfil. So, on one level at least, a huge gulf seems to separate the protagonists of romance and hagiography, with the former appearing to be almost the antithesis of the latter. And yet, there are many underlying affinities between the heroes of the two genres, and these similarities far outweigh the differences. Thus, we find that the heroes both of romance and of hagiography inhabit a magical world, suffused with mystery and enchantment. In addition, both sets of protagonists are idealised figures, capable of superhuman feats of courage and endurance. (It is worth remembering, here, that bravery is not the exclusive preserve of the romance hero. The persecuted saints of the early Church were said to have been brutally tortured before they were martyred, while confessor saints tormented themselves mercilessly through starvation and self-mortification.) Finally, and perhaps most significantly, romance heroes (like their hagiographical counterparts) are inspired by a strong sense of vocation. The protagonists of both genres are called – whether to action, to adventure, or to a life spent in the service of God – by an external force or power which they do not properly understand, over which they have no control, and which they are ultimately powerless to resist. This force is variously conceived of as fate, fortune, honour, romantic love, or divine providence, depending on the type of narrative concerned. And just as saints surrender to the will of God, ensuring that their lives are governed entirely by His judgement, so romance heroes willingly and courageously submit themselves to chance or 'aventure', refusing to shape their own destinies, but allowing the paths that they follow and the actions that they take to be determined by strange, supernatural forces to which they are mysteriously bound.[5]

The close resemblance between knights and saints (at least those knights and saints that are represented in literary narratives), suggests that the genres of hagiography and romance are much more closely related to one another than they might at first appear. Indeed, the parallels between the two genres can be so striking that at times it is difficult clearly to distinguish the one from the other. Thus, we often find examples of romance heroes who possess certain characteristics that appear to be more typical of saints than of knights, and conversely, saints – such as Eustace – whose holiness is represented in conventional, chivalric terms.[6]

---

[5] I have taken the idea of the essential passivity of romance heroes, and their vocation or calling to adventure, from Morton W. Bloomfield's seminal study of the subject. See Morton W. Bloomfield, 'Episodic Motivation and Marvels in Epic and Romance', in *Essays and Explorations: Studies in Ideas, Language, and Literature* (Cambridge, Massachusetts, 1970), pp. 96–128. On the passivity of knights, see also Jill Mann, 'Sir Gawain and the Romance Hero', in Leo Carruthers, ed. *Heroes and Heroines in Medieval English Literature* (Cambridge, 1994), pp. 105–17.

[6] The similarities between hagiography and secular romance have been the subject of much critical debate during the last thirty years. See, for example, Jennifer Fellows, 'St George as Romance Hero', *Reading Medieval Studies* 19 (1993), 27–54; Susan Crane, *Insular Romance* (Berkeley, 1986), pp. 92–133; Diana T. Childress, 'Between

The blurring of the boundaries between the two genres, and the borrowing of themes and images from one to the other, is a feature of many of the romances and saints' lives of the thirteenth and fourteenth centuries, and can be illustrated with particular clarity by comparing the legend of St Eustace to the closely related Middle English romance, *Sir Isumbras*.[7] But the popular, chivalric romances of the twelfth, thirteenth, and fourteenth centuries had such a powerful influence on the spirit of the age that they profoundly affected the way in which even the most saintly of contemporary figures – such as Francis of Assisi – conceived of their relationship to God. Before turning to St Eustace and *Sir Isumbras*, then, I should like to illustrate just how prevalent and deep rooted was the influence of romance on hagiography by considering both how and why chivalric notions of knighthood were appropriated by religious writers in order to explore spiritual truths. A number of particularly interesting examples of these borrowings can be found in the early Lives of St Francis of Assisi, as well as in William Langland's *The Vision of Piers Plowman*, an allegorical dream vision written in Middle English, and dating from approximately one hundred and fifty years after Francis's death.

In a revealing anecdote related by Francis of Assisi's three closest companions – Brothers Leo, Rufino, and Angello – the saint expressed his opinions on those friars who had abandoned the primitive simplicity that had originally been practised during the early years of the Order, and who had turned instead to the study of theology. These brothers, Francis claimed, were motivated purely by vanity, and – adopting the language of the Arthurian romances – he contrasted what he saw as their overweening pride with the holy simplicity of the faithful friars who had remained loyal to the founding principles of the Order:

> These humble and simple brothers of mine are *knights of the round table* (my italics) who conceal themselves in remote and desert places that they may the more diligently apply themselves in prayer and

Romance and Legend: "Secular Hagiography" in Middle English Literature', *Philological Quarterly* 57 (1978), 311–22; Thomas J. Heffernan, 'An Analysis of the Narrative Motifs in the Legend of St Eustace', *Medievalia et Humanistica* n. s. 6 (1975), 63–89; Valerie M. Lagorio, 'The *Joseph of Arimathie*: English Hagiography in Transition', *Medievalia et Humanistica* n. s. 6 (1975), 91–102; David N. Klausner, 'Didacticism and Drama in *Guy of Warwick*', *Medievalia et Humanistica* n. s. 6 (1975), 103–19; Margaret Hurley, 'Saints' Legends and Romance Again: Secularization of Structure and Motif', *Genre* 8 (1975), 60–73; Kathryn Hume, 'Structure and Perspective: Romance and Hagiographic Features in the Amicus and Amelius Story', *JEGP* 69 (1970), 89–107; Dieter Mehl, *The Middle English Romances of the Thirteenth and Fourteenth Centuries* (London, 1968), pp. 120–58; and L. Braswell, '*Sir Isumbras* and the Legend of Saint Eustace'.

[7] The striking affinities between the legend of St Eustace and *Sir Isumbras* have not gone unnoticed. For a very thorough investigation of the many parallels, see Braswell, '*Sir Isumbras* and the Legend of Saint Eustace', *passim*.

meditation, and weep over the sins of themselves and others. Their holiness is known to God, though it maybe unknown to the friars and to men.[8]

Ironically, the very friars whom Francis so vociferously condemned were the ones who came to dominate the leadership of the Order after his death, and so were in a position both to marginalise the three companions, and to ignore their writings.[9] My interest here, however, lies not in Francis's actual thoughts on the study of theology, but in the manner in which – or the language through which – he expressed them. That he chose to communicate his respect for, and fellowship with, his humble brothers by alluding to the tales of King Arthur and his knights, rather than to a biblical narrative or saint's legend, is a testament to the high cultural status and wide dissemination of these stories, as well as to the close connection that existed at the time between the concepts of religious and secular virtue. It would appear, then, that Francis had no difficulty in appropriating the figure of the Arthurian knight for his own religious ends, associating the penitence, humility, and simplicity of his ascetic followers, with the courtesy, nobility, and physical prowess that were the hallmarks of the knights of the round table. Although to a modern sensibility, the affinities between knights and hermits might not be immediately apparent, Francis nonetheless recognised an underlying connection between the chivalric attributes celebrated in the Arthurian romances, and the religious virtues displayed by his holy followers.

The association in Francis's mind between the aristocratic qualities of nobility and courtesy (characteristics typical of a romance hero), and the religious attributes of humility and submission, is further underlined in a story related by both of his official biographers: Thomas of Celano and St Bonaventure. Before becoming aware of his religious vocation, Francis had wanted to become a knight, an ambition that was fuelled by a dream in which he was shown 'a large and splendid palace full of military weapons emblazoned with the insignia of Christ's cross'.[10] In the dream, Francis asked to whom these riches belonged, and was told

[8] *Scripta Leonis, Rufini et Angeli Sociorum S. Francisci* (Oxford, 1970), Chapter 71, p. 213.

[9] For an account of the internal conflicts that beset the Order during its early years, see Rosalind Brooke, *Early Franciscan Government: Elias to Bonaventure* (Cambridge, 1959). See also John Moorman, *A History of the Franciscan Order from Its Origins to the Year 1517* (Oxford, 1968), pp. 83–122.

[10] St Bonaventure, *The Major Life of St Francis*, The Classics of Western Spirituality, trans. Ewert Cousins (New York, 1978), Chapter 1, p. 187. See also Thomas of Celano, *The Second Life of St Francis*, trans. Placid Hermann, in Marion A. Habig, ed. *St Francis of Assisi, Writings and Early Biographies: English Omnibus of the Sources for the Life of St Francis of Assisi*, 4th edn (Chicago, 1991), Chapter 2, pp. 365–6.

by God that they had been provided for him and his knights. However, lacking the experience of interpreting divine visions, the saint was unaware that the dream should have been read allegorically, believing instead that it was a sign that he was to win worldly honour and renown. As a result, he resolved to become a knight, and left Assisi shortly afterwards in order to enter the service of a certain count in Apulia.

Although Francis never realised his courtly ambitions – the day after he departed for Apulia he had another vision in which he was told to return to Assisi – the romantic imagery of the dream, and the underlying idea that it conveyed of entering God's service as a knight, maintained a strong hold over his imagination, and influenced the way in which both he, and his biographers, understood the nature of his relationship with God. This is borne out in a passage occurring near the end of the *Legenda Major*, where, in a discussion of Francis's various visions of the cross, Bonaventure returned to the subject of the dream. Addressing Francis directly, Bonaventure offered an allegorical interpretation of the meaning of the vision:

> Now is fulfilled the first vision which you saw, namely, that you would
> be a captain in the army of Christ and bear the arms of heaven
> emblazoned with the sign of the cross.[11]

For Bonaventure, then, the dream was fulfilled not in a literal sense, but allegorically. Through his holy life, Francis had become a captain in Christ's spiritual army, and so had acquired the rich array of weaponry – 'the arms of heaven' – that he had been promised in his vision. Bonaventure's allegorical reading of Francis's mystical dream illustrates the ease with which concepts normally associated with the secular world of the romances could be adopted by religious authors, and used in hagiographical narratives. Of course, in the process of appropriating this chivalric material, it underwent a profound transformation, so that the social world of the court described in the romances was projected by Bonaventure onto a cosmic plane, with Francis, the 'knight of Christ',[12] offering his fealty not to an earthly lord or monarch, but to the king of the court of heaven.

This vision of Christ as a feudal Lord, reigning over his celestial host of vassals, is something of a commonplace in the popular religious literature of the later Middle Ages. For instance, in Passus I of William Langland's *The Vision of Piers Plowman*, Christ, the king of kings, is said to have knighted the ten Orders of angels, giving them authority to rule over his lesser creatures:

---

[11] Bonaventure, *The Major Life of St Francis*, Chapter 13, p. 312.
[12] Bonaventure, *The Major Life of St Francis*, Chapter 13, p. 311.

But Crist, kyngene kyng, knyghted ten –
Cherubyn and Seraphyn, swiche sevene and another,
And yaf hem myght in his majestee – the murier hem thoughte –
And over his meene meynee made hem archangeles.

(Passus I. 105–1)[13]

Rather than viewing the order of chivalry as a secular institution, Langland would seem to have believed that it had originally been established by God in heaven, suggesting, perhaps, that he considered the human form of knighthood to be merely a pale reflection, or imperfect manifestation, of its ideal, celestial state. But, in addition to this picture of Christ as the overlord of the cosmos, dubbing angelic knights to act as intermediaries between himself and the more humble members of his creation, Langland – in his account of the Passion and the Harrowing of Hell (Passus XVIII of the B text) – also conceives of Christ as the chivalric hero of a romance, presenting him as a noble knight fighting the forces of evil in order to redeem the souls of fallen humanity.[14] Langland succeeds in skilfully weaving the Passion narratives of the canonical Gospels, along with the version of the story recorded in the apocryphal *Gospel of Nicodemus*, into the allegorical framework of his dream vision, using the conventions of courtly romance as a way of exploring not only Christ's noble and heroic stature, but also the paradoxical nature of his conflict with the Devil. Langland's allegorical vision of the Passion, then, is of a tournament held in Jerusalem in which Christ – cloaking his Godhead beneath the arms of Piers the Plowman – jousts with the Devil to decide the fate of humanity. In a dialogue with the allegorical figure of Faith, the dreamer, Will, learns of Jesus's forthcoming contest:

'This Jesus of his gentries wol juste in Piers armes,
In his helm and in his haubergeon – *humana natura*
That Crist be noght biknowe here for *consummatus Deus*,
In Piers paltok the Plowman this prikiere shal ryde;
For no dynt shal him dere as *in deitate Patris*.'

[13] All references to *Piers Plowman* are to A. V. C. Schmidt's edition of the B text. See William Langland, *The Vision of Piers Plowman: A Complete Edition of the B Text*, ed. A. V. C. Schmidt (London, 1987).

[14] For a discussion of Langland's treatment of the Christ-knight figure, see R. A. Waldron, 'Langland's Originality: The Christ-Knight and the Harrowing of Hell', in Gregory Kratzmann and James Simpson, ed. *Medieval English Religious and Ethical Literature: Essays in Honour of G. H. Russell* (Cambridge, 1986), pp. 66–81. Christ is also portrayed as a knight in the *Ancrene Wisse*, an early thirteenth-century devotional work written for the instruction of anchoresses. See *Ancrene Wisse: The English Text of the Ancrene Riwle*, ed. J. R. R. Tolkien, EETS OS 249 (Oxford, 1962), pp. 199–201. For an analysis of this topos, see also Rosemary Woolf, *The English Religious Lyric in the Middle Ages* (Oxford, 1968), pp. 59–60.

'Who shal juste with Jesus?' quod I, 'Jewes or scrybes?'
'Nay,' quod Feith, 'but the fend and fals doom to deye.'
(Passus XVIII. 22–8)

Clearly, Langland's treatment of this episode is greatly indebted to the conventions of courtly romance, for in common with such heroic knights as Sir Lancelot and Sir Gareth, who deliberately conceal their noble identities by engaging in combat in disguise, Jesus hides his divinity from the world by entering the tournament in Jerusalem bearing the arms of the peasant, Piers the Plowman.[15] However, the victory that Jesus achieves over the Devil is gained not through force of arms, but by humble and patient sacrifice, and the coat of armour that he bears – which according to the allegorical schema of the poem represents *humana natura*, that is, his frail and vulnerable humanity – affords him no protection against the weapons of his adversary. Thus, as James Simpson has observed, at the same time as he depicts Christ as a chivalric hero, Langland is also able to present him as a suffering human being, who, out of love for his fellow creatures, willingly accepts a painful and humiliating death.[16]

Langland further develops this image of Christ as a passive knight, who triumphs over his enemies not through violent assertion, but by willingly surrendering himself to them, in his account of the crucifixion. According to Langland, the Roman soldiers who break the arms and legs of the two criminals crucified on either side of Jesus, do not dare – in

---

[15] The two competing theories of the redemption that held sway in the Middle Ages – on the one hand, the view that Christ concealed his divinity in order to trap the Devil into abusing his rights over humanity (the so-called Devil's rights theory), and on the other hand, the idea first proposed by St Anselm of Christ's redemptive sacrifice – have been usefully explored in relation to *Piers Plowman* in C. W. Marx's recent study, *The Devil's Rights and the Redemption in the Literature of Medieval England* (Cambridge, 1995), pp. 100–13. However, my interest here lies not so much in the theology of the redemption itself, but in the fact that Langland chooses to present the topos of the deceptive nature of Christ's incarnation in explicitly chivalric terms. Countless examples can be found in the Arthurian romances of Lancelot's desire to maintain his anonymity while participating in tournaments. For instance, see Sir Thomas Malory's, 'A Noble Tale of Sir Launcelot du Lake', in Malory, *Works*, ed. Eugene Vinaver, 2nd edn (Oxford, 1971), p. 155, and 'The Book of Sir Launcelot and Queen Guinevere', in Malory, *Works*, p. 623. Malory's, 'The Tale of Sir Gareth of Orkney', in Malory, *Works*, pp. 175–226, describes how Gareth, the youngest brother of Sir Gawain, and hence the nephew of King Arthur, refused to reveal his identity when he arrived at Camelot, and so was made to work in the kitchens, where he was given the name 'Bewmaynes'. In this humble guise, he set off on an adventure in which he defeated a number of valiant opponents, winning both worldly honour, and the love of the noble lady, Lyones. Very similar implications of humility, nobility, and heroism are inherent in Langland's use of this motif in relation to Christ.

[16] See James Simpson, *Piers Plowman: An Introduction to the B Text* (London, 1990), p. 211.

deference to his knighthood – to do the same to him. Instead, they make a blind knight called Longinus strike Christ with his lance (Longinus's sight is then miraculously restored by the blood that flows from Jesus's wound). This encounter between Longinus and Jesus is presented in chivalric terms as a joust from which Jesus emerges victorious, in spite of the mortal injury that he received. For, in accordance with the principle *'Pacientes vincunt'* (Passus XIII. 172) – the patient conquer – it is only by dying that Jesus is able to triumph over his adversaries; the Devil and Death.[17]

These examples from *Piers Plowman* – when viewed alongside those I discussed earlier from the Lives of St Francis of Assisi – illustrate the degree to which the vocation of chivalric knighthood was considered to be closely related to, and entirely compatible with, the calling of a saint. Moreover, and of particular relevance to the present study, the many parallels between the genres of hagiography and romance extend to their respective treatment of the animal kingdom. For, just as we found that animals played a central role in the lives of the saints, demonstrating their holiness by helping and befriending them, so creatures fulfil an analogous function in romance, marking – through their special devotion – the hero's elevated status as a figure whom some higher power has favoured or blessed.

The close correspondences between knights and saints, and the similar ways in which animals are used either to establish or to reveal their identities, can clearly be seen when we compare the legend of St Eustace to the fourteenth-century Middle English romance, *Sir Isumbras*. As noted above, St Eustace – who is called Placidus before his conversion to Christianity – is a pagan general (*magister militum*) in the army of the Roman Emperor, Trajan. According to the legend, one day while hunting, Placidus encounters a stag. Chasing the creature deep into the forest, he becomes separated from his companions long before he finally catches up with his quarry. As he approaches the animal, he observes – as we have seen – that there is a cross attached to its head, fixed between its antlers, on which there is imprinted an image of Christ. Speaking through the stag, Christ reveals himself to Placidus, telling him to undergo baptism with his family, and then to come back to the same place in the forest on the following day. Placidus immediately returns home, is baptised alongside his wife and two sons (taking the name Eustace), and on the next day rides back into the forest as instructed. There, he once again encounters the stag, and is told by Christ that at some point he must endure great trials and tribulations, but that he is free to choose when he is to experience them; either immediately, or at the end of his life. Eustace chooses the former, and within days a series of catastrophes renders him destitute. Ashamed of his poverty, Eustace

[17] See Langland, *The Vision of Piers Plowman*, Passus XVIII 71–109.

takes his family to Egypt, but unable to pay his passage across the sea, a sailor seizes his wife, forcing Eustace and his sons to remain on shore. Eustace then travels over land, but coming to a fast-flowing river he leaves one son on the near bank while taking the other across to the far side. As he returns to carry the second child across the river, a wolf rushes out and seizes the one on the far bank. Before he can return to pick up his remaining son, a lion carries him off too.

Mourning his misfortunes, Eustace cries out in despair to God and compares himself to Job. But, unknown to him, some shepherds rescue the child who had been taken by the lion, while a number of ploughmen save the other child from the wolf. The two boys – ignorant both of their parentage and of their relationship to each other – are then bought up together in the same village, while Eustace himself settles in a neighbouring town, where he works as a farm labourer. Meanwhile, the man who had abducted Eustace's wife dies, leaving her free from harm.

After a period of fifteen years, the Emperor Trajan – threatened by a foreign enemy – searches for his erstwhile general. Eustace is eventually discovered, restored to his former dignified state, and so once again becomes the leader of the Roman legions. His two sons are recruited into the army, and Eustace is so impressed by their strength and aptitude that he gives them important positions under his command. After fighting and vanquishing the enemy, the army rests for a few days and the two boys are lodged in an inn that is kept by their mother. Recognising her two children, Eustace's wife seeks out the leader of the army to ask to be sent back to Rome. She recognises her husband, and so the family is reunited.

They finally return to Rome only to find the Emperor Trajan dead and succeeded by the notoriously dissolute Hadrian. The Emperor Hadrian celebrates Eustace's victory by sacrificing to idols in the pagan temple. He asks why Eustace refuses to offer a sacrifice, and when Eustace tells him that it is because he worships Christ, the Emperor flies into a fury and condemns the family to death. They are cast into the arena, but the ferocious lion that is let loose to kill them meekly withdraws from their presence after bowing before them. A hollow bronze bull is then heated at the Emperor's command, and the family is placed inside it. They are removed after three days, and – miraculously – their lifeless bodies are found to be perfectly intact and completely unblemished. Their remains are then buried by the local Christian community, and a church is consecrated in their memory.

This brief summary of the legend not only illustrates the central role played by animals in the unfolding story of Eustace's life, but also highlights the many different narrative functions that they fulfil. At the very centre of the legend, and the immediate and direct cause of Eustace's conversion, we have the mysterious stag that acts as an agent of divine providence. But the stag is not the only animal to be closely associated with the supernatural realm. The lion that the Emperor lets loose in the arena to kill Eustace and his family, but that meekly withdraws from their presence after paying them homage, is (as we have already seen in relation to a number of saints' lives) a familiar figure from hagiographical narratives. In addition, the wolf and the lion that are responsible for carrying off Eustace's two sons into the forest can also be seen as instruments of God's will, as the abduction of his children constitutes the ultimate test of his faith, the moment at which – reduced to a totally abject state – he cries out to God in despair. Moreover, in accordance with the logic of romance and fairytales, it is evident that the wolf and the lion fulfil an important narrative function, for it is only by losing his children so traumatically that their eventual restoration can be presented in such a marvellous, almost miraculous light. The final group of animals to figure in the legend is Eustace's hunting hounds. While these creatures do not perform a key role in terms of the narrative, their importance to the legend is apparent from the prominence that they are given in Pisanello's painting. It should be remembered that during the later Middle Ages, hunting was the preserve of the aristocracy, which developed a considerable body of lore and ritual to mark out this pastime as its exclusive domain. This sense of social exclusivity extended to the hounds that participated in the chase, and these creatures came to be seen both as noble in themselves, and as the fitting companions of noblemen. The hunting hounds that Eustace takes with him into the forest should thus be viewed not as symbols of his holiness, but as emblems of his nobility and social refinement. (I shall explore in more detail the social symbolism of the hunt, and the noble, aristocratic connotations that came to be attached to those predatory animals – whether hounds, hawks, or falcons – that were used in hunting, in the chapters on *Sir Gowther*, *Octavian*, and *Sir Orfeo*, below.)

This capacity of animals to symbolise the two sides of Eustace's identity – both his saintliness, and his knightly, chivalric nature – is also a feature of the hero's relationship to the animal kingdom in *Sir Isumbras*. Dating from the middle of the fourteenth century (although reproduced in manuscripts and early printed books for a further two hundred years), the Middle English romance, *Sir Isumbras*, is so similar to the legend of Eustace that it is often viewed as a secularised version of the saint's narrative.[18] Indeed, even the most cursory comparison of the

---

[18] Believed to have been composed in the northeast Midlands some time around the middle of the fourteenth century, fragments of *Sir Isumbras* can be found in nine manuscripts and five printed editions dating from the fourteenth, fifteenth, and sixteenth centuries. However, the full text of the romance is preserved in only four manuscripts: British Library, MS Cotton Caligula A.ii; Lincoln Dean and Chapter Library, MS 91 (the Lincoln Thornton manuscript); National Library of Scotland, Advocates MS 19.3.1; and Bodleian Library, MS Ashmole 61. Madwyn Mills's edition of the romance is based on the Cotton Caligula text. See *Sir Isumbras*, in

two reveals their underlying structural affinities. Moreover, while they are not insignificant, those few differences that do emerge tend to involve incidental details, rather than important matters of substance.

The poem opens with Isumbras, (a Christian nobleman rather than a pagan general), hunting in a forest. There, he is told by God – who appears in the form of 'a fowle' (47) – that he must suffer great hardships as a punishment for his pride, but that he is free to choose when he is to endure this reversal of fortune: either in youth or in old age. Like Eustace, he chooses the former option, and immediately on making this choice his hawks fly away and his horse and hounds drop dead. He returns home to find his estates in ruin, and his wife and three sons running naked from his burning house. Recognising his own sinfulness, Isumbras embarks with his family on a pilgrimage to the Holy Land, although his two eldest sons are carried off in a forest by a lion and a leopard. Coming to the coast, Isumbras sees a ship which he approaches in order to ask for help. Unfortunately, it belongs to a sultan, who proceeds to abduct Isumbras's wife (giving Isumbras some gold in payment for her). Isumbras's misfortunes, however, are not at an end: his third son is carried off by a unicorn, while a griffin seizes the gold (which Isumbras had wrapped up in a cloak).

Just as Eustace spends many years working as a labourer, so Isumbras humbles himself by becoming a blacksmith. But after a period of seven years, the Sultan – who has installed Isumbras's wife as his queen – launches an attack on Christendom. Isumbras enters the battle between the heathen and Christian forces, and wins the day by fighting heroically and killing the Sultan. Isumbras refuses to reveal his true identity, but continues on his pilgrimage to the Holy Land. It is only when he eventually achieves his goal seven years later, that he is finally told by an angel that his sins are forgiven.

Isumbras is reunited with his wife when he comes to her castle seeking alms. However, as he is still dressed as a poor pilgrim, his wife fails to recognise him. One day while out walking, Isumbras sees a bird's nest in which he finds the gold (wrapped up in his cloak) that had been carried off by the griffin fourteen years earlier. Isumbras's wife recognises these objects, and through them she comes to recognise her husband. Isumbras then becomes king, although the rulers of the two neighbouring Saracen kingdoms decide to dispossess him of his new realm. Deserted by his heathen subjects, Isumbras takes to the battlefield alone with his wife. But they are delivered from what seems like an inevitable and violent

Madwyn Mills, ed. *Six Middle English Romances* (London, 1973). For an edition of the romance based on Cambridge, Gonville and Caius MS 175 (of which lines 35 to 197 are missing), see *Sir Isumbras*, in Harriet Hudson, ed. *Four Middle English Romances: Sir Isumbras, Octavian, Sir Eglamour of Artois, Sir Tryamour* (Kalamazoo, 1996). I shall refer throughout to Mills's edition of the Cotton Caligula manuscript.

death by three young knights, the first riding a lion, the second a leopard, and the third a unicorn. These knights, who identify themselves as Isumbras's three lost sons, gain a glorious victory over their father's enemies. After the heathen armies are so resoundingly defeated, all of Isumbras's subjects agree to be baptised, while Isumbras himself rewards his three sons with kingdoms of their own. Finally, after leading a good life, the souls of Isumbras and his family are taken up into heaven.

In the same way that the authors of religious works borrowed elements and ideas taken from secular literature, so we can see from *Sir Isumbras* that the writers of romance were able to adopt hagiographical motifs, and an overtly pious tone, as a way of investing their stories with moral authority, and exploring the religious duties, as well as the ethical responsibilities, expected of a knight. *Sir Isumbras*, then, like the legend of St Eustace, offers us a blend of the secular and the spiritual, the chivalric and the hagiographic. And once again, animals function as markers of the two sides of the hero's identity: the aristocratic and the saintly. (It is particularly significant in this regard to note that the loss of Isumbras's horse, hounds, and hawks, which – as we have seen – are signs of his nobility and elevated social status, seems both to foreshadow and symbolise all of the subsequent deprivations that he suffers.) Of course, the key difference between the two narratives is that Eustace is ultimately martyred for his faith, while the more worldly Isumbras – having been punished for his sins – is eventually restored to his former high station, and so seems to be rewarded with happiness in this life before enjoying bliss in the next. But, as noted above, it is the similarities between the two tales that are more compelling than the differences. While the narratives vary slightly in points of detail (for instance, Isumbras has three children whereas Eustace has twins), they nonetheless share a common underlying structure.

Breaking down the two narratives into their constituent parts, Laura Braswell has identified those structural elements that are common to both, which she has labelled: 'The Choice', 'The Loss of Fortune', 'The Separation of Family', 'The Trial', 'The Lost Treasure', 'The Recognition', and 'The Reunion'.[19] This model enables us to appreciate just how closely the two tales resemble one another, and although an examination of each of these six elements lies beyond the scope of this discussion, it is worth noting how animals perform a central function in at least two of them: 'The Choice' and 'The Separation of Family'. Thus, in both the legend of St Eustace and *Sir Isumbras*, God speaks to the two heroes through an animal (a stag and a bird respectively), while the two sets of children are also taken away from their fathers by wild beasts (a lion and a wolf in the case of Eustace; a lion, a leopard, and a unicorn in that of Isumbras). It is also worth noting that in *Sir Isumbras*, the same animals

---

[19] See Braswell, '*Sir Isumbras* and the Legend of Saint Eustace', p. 135.

that are responsible for separating the hero's family are instrumental in bringing about its reunion. With no explanation offered to account for the fourteen years in which they are missing, Isumbras's three lost sons are transported (as if by magic) to the battlefield on which their parents appear to be facing certain death, by the very creatures that abducted them.

Laura Braswell has noted that both the legend of St Eustace and *Sir Isumbras* belong to a group of thematically linked stories that variously relate the tale of the 'Man Tried by Fate', or its female counterpart: the 'Calumniated Wife'.[20] While differing from one another in important points of detail, each of the narratives within this group tells the story of a hero (or heroine) of noble birth, who – for one of a number of reasons – is exiled from his or her homeland. During this period of exile, the hero or heroine experiences intense physical and spiritual hardships due to isolation and separation from family, material deprivation, loss of social status, general confusion of identity, and so on. The protagonists of these tales are frequently exiled in a forest or wilderness, where they either live in close proximity to animals, or are reduced by circumstances to an almost beast-like state. Moreover, this period of exile often assumes a strongly religious tone, with the hero or heroine compared (either implicitly or explicitly), to a whole host of biblical or hagiographical figures (such as Nebuchadnezzar), who are said to have undergone analogous sufferings in the wilderness. But the heroes and heroines of romance are eventually able to break free from this purgatorial world of penance and suffering, and on their return from exile are triumphantly restored to their former elevated state.

Of the romances that are included in this group, a number employ the same animal motifs that we have observed in both the legend of St Eustace and *Sir Isumbras*. In these tales, the various friendships and encounters between humans and animals demonstrate the multifaceted nature of the hero's identity, which – as we have seen – encompasses both aristocratic and saintly elements.[21] The crucial importance of animals in

---

[20] See Braswell, '*Sir Isumbras* and the Legend of Saint Eustace', p. 133. This collection of romances and saints' lives – known as the 'Eustace–Constance–Florence–Griselda' group, was first described by John Edwin Wells in 1916. See John Edwin Wells, *A Manual of the Writing in Middle English, 1050–1400* (New Haven, 1916), pp. 112–24.

[21] A very interesting text in regard to this tradition is the twelfth-century Old French, *Guillaume d'Angleterre*, often attributed to Chrétien de Troyes. The romance tells of Guillaume, the pious king of England, who – accompanied by his pregnant wife, Gratienne – exiles himself from his own kingdom after experiencing a divine vision. Guillaume and Gratienne undergo a very similar set of trials to those endured by Eustace, Isumbras, and their wives. After giving birth to twins, Gratienne is taken away by merchants, eventually to find herself betrothed to an old Lord (who thankfully dies before he is able to consummate the relationship). Meanwhile, Guillaume is separated from his twin sons (one of whom is carried off

establishing and defining the nature of romantic heroism is revealed with particular clarity in three Middle English romances that are affiliated to this group: *Sir Gowther*, *Octavian*, and *Sir Orfeo*. I shall examine the distinct yet related uses to which animals are put in these narratives in the following three chapters.

by a wolf). The two boys are rescued and raised by merchants, but such is their natural nobility that they soon find their way into aristocratic circles. After enduring physical hardships and spiritual anguish for twenty-four years, the family is finally reunited, and Guillaume resumes his rightful place on the throne of England. See *William of England*, in *The Complete Romances of Chrétien de Troyes*, trans. David Staines (Bloomington and Indianapolis, 1990), pp. 450–91.

6

Sir Gowther

ALTHOUGH it refers to itself as both a Breton lay and a romance, and contains all of the secular elements of love and adventure that are conventionally associated with such a designation, *Sir Gowther* (which was written anonymously at the end of the fourteenth century) is nonetheless steeped in the pious religious spirit of the late Middle Ages, and reverberates with biblical and hagiographical echoes. Moreover, it self-consciously concludes in the manner of a saint's legend with a description of the eponymous hero's holy death, as well as an account of how his grave becomes a place of pilgrimage where many miracles are performed.[1]

The hybrid nature of *Sir Gowther* – encompassing as it does themes and motifs drawn from the two genres of romance and hagiography – is the aspect of the poem that has attracted most critical comment, a fact that is reflected in the different generic classifications that have been formulated to describe the work. For instance, Dieter Mehl labelled the narrative a 'homiletic romance', Andrea Hopkins preferred the term 'penitential romance', while E. M. Bradstock chose to call it a 'secular hagiography'.[2] Furthermore, as these various designations suggest (and

---

[1] *Sir Gowther*, which is believed to have been written at the end of the fourteenth century in the North Midlands, survives in two manuscripts dating from the late fifteenth century: Edinburgh, National Library of Scotland, MS Advocates 19.3.1, and London, British Library, Royal MS 17.B.43. For a discussion of the date and provenance of the poem, see J. Burke Severs, *A Manual of Writing in Middle English, 1050–1500*, Vol. 1 (New Haven, 1967), p. 141. Although no direct source for *Sir Gowther* has been identified, it is closely related to the legend of *Robert the Devil*, which survives in many different forms – romance, chronicle, exemplum, and drama – and in a number of different languages – French, Latin, Dutch, Spanish, and Portuguese. For a discussion of *Sir Gowther*'s relationship to *Robert the Devil*, see Shirley Marchalonis, '*Sir Gowther*: The Process of a Romance', *Chaucer Review* 6 (1971), 14–29. On *Sir Gowther* and animals, see Jeffrey Jerome Cohen, *Of Giants: Sex, Monsters, and the Middle Ages* (Minneapolis, 1999), pp. 120–41. All references to *Sir Gowther* will be to the text of the Advocates manuscript, edited by Anne Laskaya and Eve Salisbury. See Anne Laskaya and Eve Salisbury, ed. *The Middle English Breton Lays* (Kalamazoo, 1995), pp. 263–307. For an edition of the text of Royal MS 17.B.43, see Thomas C. Rumble, ed. *The Breton Lays in Middle English* (Detroit, 1965), pp. 179–204.

[2] See Mehl, *The Middle English Romances of the Thirteenth and Fourteenth Centuries*,

as we observed in relation to *Sir Isumbras*), far from being a superficial or incidental detail, the fusion of religious and secular elements is fundamental to the meaning of the poem, and is woven into the very fabric of its narrative structure. But before embarking upon an analysis of the story's constituent parts, it will perhaps be helpful to provide a brief outline of its rather complex plot.

Sir Gowther opens with the story of the eponymous hero's demonic birth. After ten years of marriage in which she fails to produce an heir, and having been informed by her husband that he intends to abandon her, the Duchess of Austria (Estryke) prays to God and the Virgin Mary for a child. Shortly afterwards, the Duchess is approached in her orchard by the Devil, who perfectly assumes the physical appearance of her husband, the Duke. And so – acting under the mistaken belief that it is her husband – the Duchess has sex with the Devil beneath a chestnut tree, and becomes pregnant. Then, with his wicked deed accomplished, the Devil casts aside his human form, and in the guise of a shaggy fiend [a 'felturd fende' (74)], tells her that she will give birth to a diabolical child who will become a wild and ungovernable youth.

When the boy is born, he is taken by the Duke to church and christened Gowther. But even in his infancy his demonic nature is apparent, for such is the voraciousness of his appetite that he suckles nine wet-nurses to death, and when his mother is eventually obliged to feed him (because no more nurses can be found), he bites off her nipple. He grows prodigiously fast, and at the age of fifteen forges a falchion ['fachon' (142)], which he alone is strong enough to wield.[3] Realising that Gowther cannot be controlled, the Duke makes him a knight, but this completely fails to curb his excesses. The Duke then dies of sorrow, and the Duchess withdraws to the safety of a strong castle, leaving Gowther free to terrorise the land. Although violent towards everyone, Gowther's malign nature is chiefly directed against the Church, and he expresses his antipathy for all things sacred by forcing friars to leap off cliffs, hanging parsons, killing other priests, and burning hermits. His hatred of the Church culminates in an attack upon a convent, in which he first rapes all of the nuns, and then kills them by setting fire to the building.

Amid this mayhem, an old earl approaches Gowther and tells him that his unnatural behaviour suggests that he is the son not of a man, but a fiend. Unsure whether or not to believe this, Gowther confronts his

pp. 127–8; Andrea Hopkins, *The Sinful Knight: A Study of Middle English Penitential Romances* (Oxford, 1990), pp. 144–78; and E. M. Bradstock, '*Sir Gowther*: Secular Hagiography or Hagiographical Romance or Neither?', *AUMLA* 59 (1983), 26–47.

[3] *The Middle English Dictionary* defines faucŏun (fachoun) as: 'A large, broad sword with a curved blade, a falchion: also, a short stabbing-sword or dagger.' According to the *OED*, a falchion is 'A broad sword more or less curved with the edge on the convex side. In later use and in poetry: a sword of any kind.'

mother, whereupon she reveals all the details of his conception. In a sudden act of conversion, Gowther begins to cry, and in the hope of saving himself from his devilish father, he leaves his castle in the care of the old earl, abandons all of his possessions except for his falchion, and sets off for Rome to seek absolution from the Pope. On arriving in Rome, Gowther fully confesses his past misdeeds, and as a penance he is told by the Pope that – until he receives a sign indicating that his sins have been forgiven – he must remain completely silent, and eat nothing but food taken from the mouths of dogs.

Leaving Rome, Gowther in time comes to a hill, where, on three successive nights, a greyhound brings him food. When the greyhound fails to appear on the fourth night, Gowther continues on his way, coming at last to the castle of the Emperor of Germany. Gaining admittance to the main hall, he sits on the floor under the head table, and is granted permission to stay on account of his exceptional beauty. Gowther refuses the fine food that he is offered, but begins to eat a bone which he takes from the mouth of a spaniel. Seeing this, the Emperor and Empress, along with the assembled knights and ladies, feed the hounds, and Gowther takes his place beside them and shares their food.

The Emperor has a beautiful but mute daughter whom the Sultan of Persia wishes to carry off by force and marry against her will. The Sultan brings his army to the Emperor's castle, and on the morning on which the two adversaries are due to engage in battle, Gowther prays for a horse and coat of armour so that he might assist the Emperor, his lord. Miraculously, a black horse and coat of armour suddenly appear before him, enabling him to join the battle, in which he kills many Saracens with his falchion, and so wins the day for the Christians. In the evening, Gowther secretly returns to the castle, his horse and armour disappear, and he resumes his place under the table in the hall. The mute Princess is the only person to realise that Gowther is the heroic knight in black, and she washes the mouth of a greyhound with wine, places a loaf of white bread between its teeth, and then sends the dog over to him. The following day, having been given a red horse and coat of armour, Gowther again performs valiant deeds on the battlefield, and in the evening is once again sent food in the mouth of a greyhound by the Princess. On the third and final day, with a white horse and coat of armour, Gowther rides out to battle, rescues the Emperor who has been taken captive, kills the Sultan, but is wounded in the shoulder in the process. When he receives his wound, the Princess, who is watching proceedings from the castle, falls out of her tower from shock and sorrow. Believing her to be dead, the Emperor sends for the Pope to officiate at the funeral. However, the Princess wakes up not only fully recovered from her fall, but also miraculously cured of her dumbness. Addressing Sir Gowther, she tells him that God has absolved him of his sins, so that he is now free both to eat normally and to speak. The Pope confirms that Gowther had indeed atoned for his crimes, and it is decided that he should marry the Princess. Returning briefly to his own land, Gowther gives his mother to the old earl in marriage, and builds a monastery, endowing it with great wealth so that the monks can pray for the souls of all those whom he has killed. Soon afterwards, the Princess's father dies, and Gowther succeeds him as Emperor of Germany. He reigns for many years, discharging his duties as a perfect knight and monarch. He defends the Church against its enemies, the Saracens, cares for the poor, and is just to the rich. When he eventually dies, he is venerated as a saint, and is buried in the monastery that he built, which in time becomes a shrine to his cult.

As indicated above, perhaps what is most interesting about *Sir Gowther*, at least from the point of view of its generic characteristics, is the seamless way in which it integrates hagiographical elements into the broader framework of a chivalric romance. By presenting its eponymous hero as not only an exemplary knight whose chivalrous deeds are worthy of celebration, but also a saint who performs many miracles after his death, the poem – like the legend of St Eustace and *Sir Isumbras* – refuses to recognise a clear division between the genres of romance and hagiography. Indeed, Sir Gowther's status as a knight is absolutely central to his role as a saint, and the poem admits of no conflict between these two aspects – the one secular, the other religious – of his identity.[4]

The centrality of Gowther's knighthood both to the integrity of his personality, and to the wider meaning of the poem, has been recognised by Andrea Hopkins, who has observed that it is the medium through which the hero expresses first his sinful, and then his saintly, nature.[5] Hopkins goes on to note that Gowther's identity as a knight is symbolically bound up with his falchion, the curved broad sword which he forges at the age of fifteen, and with which he initially persecutes, but subsequently defends, the Church. Throughout the poem, the sword is presented as an essential adjunct to Gowther's character, and hence it comes to assume something of the significance of a personal talisman. The importance of the sword is indicated by the Devil himself, when, at the time of Gowther's conception, he tells the Duchess that their son will wield a mighty weapon in his youth:

> He seyd, 'Y have geyton a chylde on the
> That in is yothe full wylde schall bee,
> And weppons wyghtly weld.' (76–8)

Gowther's identity is mystically entwined with his falchion, for not only is he responsible for forging the sword, but he alone is strong enough to use it:

---

[4] It is significant that the text of British Library, Royal MS 17.B.43 concludes with the rubric: '*Explicit Vita Sancti*' (Here ends the life of the saint).

[5] See Hopkins, *The Sinful Knight*, p. 159.

He made a wepon that he schuld weld,
No nodur mon myght hit beyr;
A fachon bothe of stylle and yron   (140–2)

Although dubbed a knight by his 'stepfather', the Duke, Gowther
remains under the spell of his true father, the Devil, and continues to
do his evil bidding by using the falchion to terrorise the Church.
However, after his conversion, the sword is the one possession that
Gowther refuses to abandon, in spite of its association with his evil past.
Indeed, such is Gowther's deep attachment to it, that he is even prepared
to ignore the commandment of the Pope, who instructs him to cast the
weapon aside:

'Lye down thi fachon then the fro;
Thou schallt be screvon or y goo,
And asoylyd or y blyn.'
'Nay holy fadur,' seyd Gwother,
'This bous me nedus with me beyr,
My frendys ar full thyn.'   (289–94)

After travelling to Rome solely for the purpose of submitting himself to
the will of the Pope, and having promised the Pontiff to observe his
judgement to the full – 'Y schall the truly swere / At thi byddyng beyn to
be' (285–6) – Gowther's act of defiance seems, on the face of it, quite
remarkable. Shirley Marchalonis has argued that the knight's insistence
on retaining his falchion – the emblem of his knighthood – indicates that
he recognises that his salvation is to be accomplished not by penance
alone, but through the pursuit of the chivalric ideal.[6] With this interpretation in mind, it is worth noting that it is not until he has fought
valiantly against the Sultan, who is the enemy of the Church as well as
the Emperor, that he is finally absolved of his sins. The redemptive
nature of Gowther's armed combat is further suggested by the fact that
not only is he miraculously supplied by God with the means of fighting
the Saracens, but on the three successive days on which the battle rages,
the colour of his horse and armour change from black to red to white, a
transition that would seem to symbolise the internal transformation
within Gowther himself, from his initial, sinful condition, to a state of
purity and grace.[7]

Moreover, it is significant that the saintly life that Gowther leads after
becoming emperor is presented almost exclusively in terms of his role as
an exemplary knight and monarch. He is said to be the flower of chivalry,

---

[6] See Marchalonis, 'Sir Gowther: The Process of a Romance', p. 19.
[7] According to Shirley Marchalonis, 'Black, in fairly generalized terms, seems to
represent the initial, germinal stage of all processes . . . Red can indicate blood, fire,
purification, activity, passion, and the lifegiving principle; white denotes innocence
and purity.' See Marchalonis, 'Sir Gowther: The Process of a Romance', p. 20.

and to perform all of the duties required of a just king – he is always willing to do whatever is asked of him in God's name; he is charitable to the poor, just to the rich, and uses his power to defend the Christian faith:

> And he lord and emperowr,
> Of all Cryston knyghttus tho flowre . . .
> What mon so bydus hym for Godys loffe doo
> He was ey redy bown thertoo,
> And stod pore folke in styd,
> And ryche men in hor ryght,
> And halpe holy kyrke in all is myght;   (712–13 & 715–19)

Thus, not merely does the poem claim that there is no conflict between Gowther's dual roles as knight and saint, it actually seems to imply that God grants him a place in heaven as a reward for so conscientiously discharging the morally burdensome obligations expected of a knight. The belief that chivalry was a religious vocation, which was almost a guarantee of sanctity, was famously expressed by the Spanish Franciscan martyr, Ramón Lull, in his enormously influential treatise on knighthood, *Le Libre del Orde de Cauayleria*, written in Catalan during the closing years of the thirteenth century, and translated into English two hundred years later by William Caxton under the title *The Book of the Ordre of Chyualry*.[8] According to Caxton's translation of Lull's text, the first duty of every knight is to protect and uphold the Christian faith: 'The offyce of a knyght is to mayntene and deffende the holy feyth catholyque / by the whiche god the fader sente his sone in to the world to take flesshe humayne in the gloryous vyrgyn oure lady saynt Mary.'[9] To this end, the role of the knight is analogous to that of the priest, for just as God instituted the priestly office to preach Catholic doctrine, thereby ensuring that the claims of unbelievers could be disproved, so the order of chivalry was designed with the intention of physically suppressing the enemies of the Church:

---

[8] According to Maurice Keen, Lull's *Le Libre del Orde de Cauayleria* is the classic account of knighthood written during the later Middle Ages. See Maurice Keen, *Chivalry* (New Haven, 1984), pp. 10–11. For Caxton's text, which was translated from a French version of Lull's work, see William Caxton, *The Book of the Ordre of Chyualry*, ed. A. T. P. Byles, EETS OS 168 (London, 1926). Although not as influential as Lull's tract, Geoffroi de Charny's chivalric handbook, *Le Livre de Chevalerie* was written in the middle of the fourteenth century, and so is much closer in date to *Sir Gowther* than either Lull's text or Caxton's translation. Geoffroi's work is also deeply pious in tone, and expresses the same unshakeable belief in the essentially religious nature of knighthood that we can observe in Lull. See *The Book of Chivalry of Geoffroi de Charny: Text, Context, and Translation*, ed. and trans. Richard W. Kaeuper and Elspeth Kennedy (Philadelphia, 1996).

[9] Caxton, *The Book of the Ordre of Chyualry*, p. 24.

Thene in lyke wyse as our lord god hath chosen the clerkes for to mayntene þe holy feith catholike with scripture & resons ayest the mescreauts & not bileuyng / In lyke wise god of glory hath chosen knyʒtes / by cause þat by force of armes they vaynquysshe the mescreautes, whiche daily laboure for to destroye holy chirche / & suche knyʒtes god holdeth them for his frendes honoured in this world / & in that other when they kepe and mayntene the feith by the whiche we entende to be saued.[10]

Lull's vision of the responsibilities and rewards of knighthood is entirely consistent with the view outlined in *Sir Gowther*. As Maurice Keen has observed, Christian romances (such as *Sir Gowther*) do not distinguish between worldly honour and the service of God, but rather assert that 'the knightly life, with all its violence and with all the richness and decor of its aristocratic trappings, is within its own terms a road to salvation'.[11] This interpretation is borne out in the final stanza of the romance, when the poet concludes the story by stating that Gowther's devotion to the ideals of chivalry have won him not only wealth and happiness in this world, but also eternal bliss in the next:

> Thus Syr Gwother coverys is care,
> That fyrst was ryche and sython bare,
> And effte was ryche ageyn,
> And geyton with a felteryd feynd;
> Grace he had to make that eynd
> That God was of hym feyn.   (745–50)

It is significant that the restoration of Gowther's earthly wealth and social status should be considered as noteworthy as the salvation of his soul, highlighting once again the way in which knighthood is treated as a calling that straddles the realms of both secular and religious culture.

Of course, before he is able to follow the active path of Christian knighthood, Gowther first has to atone for his past misdeeds by enduring the penance that is imposed upon him by the Pope, and it is in its treatment of this initial, passive stage of Gowther's repentance that the narrative draws most heavily upon hagiographical conventions, and so comes closest to resembling a traditional saint's legend. Moreover, it is significant that these conventions are most obviously invoked through the use of animals. Thus, when he arrives in Rome, Gowther is told by the Pope that until he receives a sign from God indicating that his sins have been forgiven, he is to remain completely mute, and is to eat nothing but food taken from the mouths of dogs:

[10] Caxton, *The Book of the Ordre of Chyualry*, p. 25.
[11] Keen, *Chivalry*, p. 62.

> 'Wherser thu travellys, be northe or soth,
> Thu eyt no meyt bot that thu revus of howndus mothe
> Cum thy body within;
> Ne no worde speke for evyll ne gud,
> Or thu reyde tokyn have fro God,
> That forgyfyn is thi syn.'   (295–300)

The connection between dogs and penitential suffering has biblical precedent. In the parable of *Dives* and *Pauper* (Luke 16: 19–31), the poor man, Lazarus, who lies at the rich man's gate, and who desires to be fed with the scraps of food that fall from his table, is comforted before his death by the dogs who come and lick his sores, while the Book of Tobit describes how Tobias, Tobit's son, accompanied both by his dog and the angel, Raphael, undertakes the long and strenuous journey from Nineveh to Media in order to redeem his father's ten talents of silver (Tobit 5: 16 & 11: 4). Of course, while it is quite possible that the poem draws on this generalised association between dogs on the one hand, and arduous toil and purgative suffering on the other, it should be noted that Gowther's experience of dogs is much more all-encompassing than that of either Lazarus or Tobias. For, unlike these two biblical figures, the extremely degrading nature of the penance that Gowther has to endure means that he actually comes close to losing his identity as a human being. Indeed, he can be said to have symbolically joined the ranks of the beasts, such is his enforced intimacy with them.[12]

Gowther's close affinity with dogs, and the grave affront to his human dignity that this implies, is particularly evident in the passage which describes how – on first entering the Emperor's castle – he removes a bone from the mouth of a spaniel, and eagerly begins to eat it:

> Ther come a spanyell with a bon,
> In his mothe he hit bare,
> Syr Gwother hit fro hym droghhe,
> And gredely on hit he gnofe,
> He wold nowdur curlu ne tartte.
> Boddely sustynans wold he non
> Bot what so he fro tho howndus wan,
> If it wer gnaffyd or mard.   (353–60)

This motif of the human hero reduced to the level of the beasts by having to share his food with animals, calls to mind another biblical story: that of the madness of the Babylonian king, Nebuchadnezzar. According to the Book of Daniel, Nebuchadnezzar was driven from human society for a period of seven years as a punishment for his pride, during which time he lived with the beasts of the field, and ate grass in the manner of an ox

---

[12] For a discussion of Gowther's metaphorical transformation into a dog, see Cohen, *Of Giants*, pp. 120–41.

(Daniel 4: 29–37).[13] It is interesting to note that Nebuchadnezzar's regression to a bestial, sub-human state – like the experience of Sir Gowther – was penitential in nature, for it resulted in both the forgiveness of his sins, and the eventual restoration of his social position. Gowther's degrading sense of kinship with dogs would therefore seem to echo the madness of Nebuchadnezzar, signalling that like his biblical forebear, he is to be allowed to return to his rightful place at the apex of human society after undergoing a period of harsh atonement for his crimes.[14]

However, Gowther's close association with animals is symbolic of more than just his penitential suffering, for as well as experiencing the indignity of having to eat bones that he has removed from the mouths of dogs, he is also – on three successive evenings following his departure from Rome – miraculously supplied with food by a greyhound:

---

[13] Penelope Doob has drawn attention to the underlying affinities between Gowther's predicament and the fate of Nebuchadnezzar. See Penelope B. R. Doob, *Nebuchadnezzar's Children: Conventions of Madness in Middle English Literature* (New Haven, 1974), pp. 162–3. The story of the madness of Nebuchadnezzar is also recounted in the late-fourteenth-century Middle English religious poem, *Cleanness*, which is generally believed to have been written by the author of *Sir Gawain and the Green Knight*. See *Cleanness* (1658–1704), in *The Poems of the Pearl Manuscript: Pearl, Cleanness, Patience, Sir Gawain and the Green Knight*, ed. Malcolm Andrew and Ronald Waldron (London, 1978). Significantly, in his description of Nebuchadnezzar's madness, the *Cleanness*-poet made much of the king's bestial appearance, and the fact that he considered himself to be an animal: 'His hert heldet vnholc; he hoped non oþer / Bot a best þat he be, a bol oþer an oxe' (1681–2).

[14] The striking analogy between Nebuchadnezzar's madness and Gowther's penance is further suggested by another fourteenth-century Middle English romance, *King Robert of Sicily*, whose eponymous hero suffers a similar fate to that of Sir Gowther. Because of his sinful pride, Robert's position as King of Sicily is usurped by an angel who has perfectly assumed his physical appearance. Deprived of his regal office, and unrecognised by any of his subjects, Robert is forced by the angel to endure the further punishment of having to eat his meals on the floor with the dogs. Robert rails against his fate for three years, until, finally giving up all hope of regaining his crown, he reflects upon the figure of Nebuchadnezzar, whose predicament he recognises as identical to his own. The example of the Babylonian king teaches Robert that he must submit himself to the will of God, and humbly accept his fate. Thus reconciled to his lowly condition, Robert's sins are forgiven, whereupon he is restored by the angel to his former position, and so reigns as a just and pious king for the rest of his life. For an edition of *King Robert of Sicily*, which is preserved in ten manuscripts dating from the fourteenth and fifteenth centuries, and which is believed to have been written some time before 1370, probably in the South Midlands, see, *Robert of Sicily*, in Walter Hoyt French and Charles Brockway Hale, ed. *Middle English Metrical Romances*, Vol. 2 (1964), 933–46. For commentary and bibliography, see Lillian Hornstein's two articles, '*King Robert of Sicily*: A New Manuscript', *PMLA* 78 (1963), 453–8, and '*King Robert of Sicily*: Analogues and Origins', *PMLA* 79 (1964), 13–21.

He seyt hym down undur a hyll,
A greyhownde broght hym meyt untyll
Or evon yche a dey.
Thre neythtys ther he ley;
Tho grwhownd ylke a dey
A whyte lofe he hym broghht;
On tho fort day come hym non,
Up he start and forthe con gon,
And lovyd God in his thoght.   (310–18)

This incident is reminiscent of the many episodes from sacred biography in which – as a sign of divine favour – holy men and women are miraculously fed by animals. For instance, Elijah was given bread and meat by ravens in the wilderness (1 Kings: 17, 6), St Paul the hermit was supplied with bread every day for sixty years, also by a raven,[15] while St Cuthbert was fed with a fish brought to him by an eagle.[16] It would thus appear that the poet consciously used the widely recognised hagiographical motif of the helpful animal as a way of indicating that Gowther enjoys God's special love and protection, in spite of his demonic father and the many heinous crimes that he has committed against the Church. Indeed, Gowther himself seems to recognise that the greyhound is an instrument of divine providence, for he interprets the animal's failure to appear on the fourth day as a sign that he should continue on his journey.

In addition to the hagiographical connotations attached to the figure of the greyhound, the animal can also be viewed as an emblem of Gowther's noble nature, drawing attention to his role as an aristocratic hero of romance, as well as his identity as a saint. As Jean-Claude Schmitt has observed, unlike other dogs, who tended to be somewhat disparaged during the Middle Ages, greyhounds were prized for their innate nobility, and came to be regarded as symbols of 'the chivalric virtues (faith), occupations (hunting) and, more generally, the whole aristocratic way of life.'[17] It is this secular, chivalric aspect of the greyhound's symbolic identity that is emphasised in the two further scenes from the poem in which the animal makes an appearance. At the end of both of the first two days of fighting between the Christian and Saracen armies, the Emperor's daughter employs a couple of greyhounds – whose mouths she has washed with wine – to deliver bread and meat to Gowther as a way of rewarding him for the valiant

[15] See St Jerome, *The Life of St Paul the First Hermit*, trans. Sister Marie Liguori Ewald, in Roy J. Deferrari, ed. *Early Christian Biographies*, The Fathers of the Church, Vol. 15 (Washington D.C., 1952), p. 233.
[16] See Bede, *Life of Cuthbert*, trans. J. F. Webb, in J. F. Webb, ed. *Lives of the Saints* (Harmondsworth, 1965), p. 87.
[17] Jean-Claude Schmitt, *The Holy Greyhound: Guinefort, Healer of Children since the Thirteenth Century*, trans. Martin Thom (Cambridge, 1983), p. 59.

deeds that he has performed on the battlefield against her father's enemies:

> Tho meydon toke too gruhowndus fyn
> And waschyd hor mowthus cleyn with wyn
> And putte a lofe in tho ton;
> And in the todur flesch full gud;
> He raft bothe owt with eyggur mode,
> That doghty of body and bon.   (445–50)

In a sense, this incident can be viewed as the secular equivalent of, or counterpart to, the previous religious scene, for just as the greyhound's miraculous appearance in the wilderness signalled God's love of Gowther, so the Princess demonstrates her sympathy for the knight by using the two animals to send him food. Of course, by borrowing something of the symbolism of hagiography in order to illustrate the awakening of the Princess's human love for Gowther, the poet once again blurs the boundary between the realms of the religious and the secular, and the saintly and the heroic. Fittingly, then, the hybrid nature of both Sir Gowther himself, and the poem to which he gives his name, is emblematically reflected in the broad range of encounters that are depicted between the human and animal worlds.

The use to which animals are put in *Sir Gowther* is typical of the kind of representations that are to be found in the wider romance canon, and this is certainly borne out in the two other Middle English romances that I shall be examining in the following chapters. While neither *Octavian* nor *Sir Orfeo* is as overtly religious as *Sir Gowther*, the protagonists of the two romances nonetheless exhibit the religious characteristics of the saint as well as the aristocratic qualities of the knightly hero – and this combination of hagiographical and secular elements is reflected in the way in which the animal kingdom is represented in the two texts. For, in much the same way that the various dogs in *Sir Gowther* draw attention both to the hero's religious virtues and to his secular attributes, so animals in *Octavian* and *Sir Orfeo* function as markers, indicating not only the social status of the different human protagonists, but also the extent to which they can be said to be favoured by God.

7

Octavian

DATING from the middle of the fourteenth century, the Middle romance, *Octavian*, survives in two different versions, both of which are believed to derive independently from the same Old French source. The northern version, which is regarded as the more artistically successful of the two, and to which I shall be referring throughout this chapter, is thought to have been composed either in the North East Midlands or slightly further to the north, and survives in two manuscripts dating from the fifteenth century; Lincoln, Dean and Chapter Library, MS 91 (the Lincoln Thornton MS), and Cambridge, University Library, MS Ff.2.38.[1]

The title of *Octavian* can be viewed as something of a misnomer, since the poem is concerned not so much with the character and actions of Octavian himself – the Roman Emperor whose history the romance claims to narrate – as with the stoical suffering of his calumniated wife, and the heroic adventures of their twin sons. Although the opening rubric of the poem quite explicitly identifies Octavian as the hero – 'Here Bygynnes the Romance off Octovyane' – it is interesting to note that the Emperor enjoys the somewhat unusual distinction of being a rather marginal figure in his own story, appearing only twice in the narrative, first at its very beginning when he sets the plot in motion by banishing his family in the mistaken belief that his wife is an adulteress, and his children illegitimate, and then near the end of the romance, when, with the cloud of suspicion having been removed, all the members of the family are once again happily reunited. This lack of a clearly identifiable hero means, as Dieter Mehl has noted, that the poem has a very diffuse

---

[1] A useful discussion of the language and provenance of the northern *Octavian*, along with a consideration of the poem's relationship both to its probable source, and to the southern version of the romance, can be found in Frances McSparran's parallel edition of the Lincoln and Cambridge manuscripts. See *Octavian*, ed. Frances McSparran, EETS OS 289 (Oxford, 1986), pp. 21–53. (Unless otherwise stated, all references will be to the text of the Lincoln manuscript.) Frances McSparran has also edited the southern version of the romance, which is preserved in just the one manuscript, London, British Library, MS Cotton Caligula A. ii, and which was probably composed in the London / Essex area. See *Octovian Imperator*, ed. Frances McSparran, Middle English Texts 11 (Heidelberg, 1979).

plot, which is further complicated by the fact that it ranges across a number of different countries, and spans a period of almost two decades.[2] A summary of the poem's extremely intricate story line will therefore act as a useful prelude to a discussion of its various motifs and narrative elements.

After seven years of loving marriage in which she fails to produce an heir, the Roman Empress's fervent prayers for a child are finally answered when she gives birth to twin sons, much to the delight of her husband, Octavian. However, Octavian's mother, motivated by sheer malice, is able to convince Octavian that he is not the father of the two boys, and so, in the erroneous belief that his wife is guilty of sexual treason, he condemns her, along with their twin sons, to be burnt to death, a sentence that he commutes to banishment from feelings of compassion. Therefore, at Octavian's command, his wife and two children are escorted to the boundary of his kingdom and abandoned in a dense forest full of wild beasts.

Having thus been left in the wilderness to fend for herself, the Empress suffers the further misfortune of having one of her children carried off into the forest by an ape. Then, while she is lying in a swoon, incapacitated from the shock, her other child is abducted by a lioness, who in turn is attacked by a griffin. The lioness (who is still holding the child in her mouth), is lifted into the air by the griffin and carried off to an island. However, as soon as the lioness is placed on the ground, she fights and kills the monstrous beast, and then immediately lies down next to the child, and begins to suckle him.

The Empress, distraught at the loss of her two children, resolves to go on a pilgrimage to Jerusalem, to which end she boards a ship that happened to sail past the island on which her child and the lioness are living. She asks to be taken ashore to retrieve her son, and when she comes to the lioness's den, the animal meekly ['Full debonorly' (465)] allows her to reclaim the child. Then, accompanied by the lioness, and carrying the boy in her arms, the Empress returns to the boat and continues on her journey to the Holy Land. When she arrives in Jerusalem she is recognised by the King of that city, who invites her to join his household. There, living with the lioness who has become her child's constant companion, she is treated with all the dignity that her royal status demands. Her son is duly christened Octavian, and in the fullness of time is made a knight by the King.

Meanwhile, the Empress's other child, having been abducted by an ape, is rescued by a knight, who is in turn attacked and killed by a band of robbers. This group of outlaws, unable to kill the boy because of his innate nobility, decide to sell him instead. They come across a Parisian

---

[2] See D. Mehl, *The Middle English Romances of the Thirteenth and Fourteenth Centuries* (London, 1968), p. 112.

merchant called Clement who is returning from a pilgrimage to the Holy Land, and sell him the child for twenty pounds. When Clement returns home, he tells his wife, Gladwin, that he is the father of the boy, and that the child was born in the Holy Land of a Saracen woman. Gladwin immediately offers to adopt the boy, and they christen him Florent.

When he is old enough to earn a living, Clement and Gladwin decide that Florent should become a butcher, so one day they send him out with a couple of oxen to learn the butchery trade. However, while travelling through the city streets, he happens to pass a squire who has a falcon which he wishes to sell, and which Florent buys in exchange for his two beasts of burden. Clement is extremely angry about this, but after beating his son for his profligacy, he is persuaded by Gladwin that the boy is not suited to be a butcher. On another occasion, Clement asks Florent to deliver forty pounds of gold to his step-brother, a money changer, but once again he is distracted on the way, this time buying a fine, milk-white steed with his father's gold. Again he is beaten by Clement, yet his love of noble beasts, and his complete inability to learn a trade, convince Gladwin that Florent cannot be her husband's son, but must rather be descended from aristocratic parents.

The Sultan of the Saracen kingdom then invades France, and besieges Paris with his large army. The most fearsome of the Saracen warriors is a giant who is twenty-two feet tall, and who is in love with the Sultan's beautiful daughter, Marsabele. The giant promises to bring Marsabele the head of the King of France as a token of his love, and he leans over the city wall and threatens to kill every man, woman, and beast in Paris unless the King comes out to fight him. After five French knights who answer the challenge are defeated, Florent, riding his milk-white steed and wearing Clement's rusty coat of armour, fights and kills the giant, and brings his severed head to Marsabele, thereby winning her love. Marsabele agrees to convert to Christianity, and is able, with Florent's help, to escape from her father's camp and enter Paris.

Back inside the besieged city, Florent is lauded by both the King of France and his own father, Octavian – who has come to lend his aid in the fight against the Sultan – neither of whom believe that such a brave and courteous youth could be the son of a merchant. Octavian therefore asks Clement how he came by the child, and on hearing that the boy had originally been taken from a woman in a forest, he weeps, and claims him as his own. In the fighting that ensues between the Christian and Saracen armies, Florent, Octavian, and the King of France are all taken captive, despite performing heroic deeds on the battlefield. However, they are soon released from captivity by young Octavian, who has travelled to France with his mother, the lioness, and a host of knights for the express purpose of fighting the Saracens. The family is thus joyfully reunited; Florent marries the newly baptised Marsabele, and the Emperor's wicked mother – much to everyone's delight – cuts her throat.

In her edition of *Octavian*, Frances McSparran has argued that the complexity of the poem's plot is due in part to its composite nature, for it combines in the one apparently seamless narrative two commonly occurring, but normally quite separate, story-elements; that of the unjustly persecuted wife who is ultimately vindicated after enduring much suffering (the so-called Constance story, versions of which are to be found in Chaucer's *Man of Law's Tale* and Gower's *Confessio Amantis*), and the motif of the dispossessed hero whose noble identity is eventually acknowledged as a result of his prowess in arms (the basic plot of such romances as *Sir Degaré*, *Lybeaus Desconus*, and *Sir Perceval of Galles*).[3] Moreover, McSparran has also noted that each of these two story-elements draws on a different set of literary conventions. Thus, the Empress's narrative, with its emphasis on the heroine's innocence, patient endurance, and selfless resignation to God's will, has strong hagiographical overtones, while the parts of the story that are concerned with the character and development of her two sons are primarily secular, heroic, and (particularly in the case of Florent), social in tone. As in the case of *Sir Gowther*, this combination of hagiographical and romance elements is reflected in the poem's treatment of the animal kingdom, so that whether attesting to the Empress's sanctity, or revealing the nobility of the two royal children, the various animals that appear in the narrative occupy an absolutely central position, and perform a crucial function within its symbolic world.

Clearly, the animal that figures most prominently in the romance is the lioness, the creature who is at first responsible for abducting young Octavian, but who subsequently suckles him after they are both transported to the island by the griffin, and who then comes to live with him and his mother in Jerusalem. Although she eventually becomes the faithful companion and protector of both the Empress and young Octavian, the lioness is initially presented as a hostile, threatening beast, who is said to have abducted the child in order to feed him to her whelps. According to the poet, while the Empress is lying in a swoon, distraught at the loss of her first son, her second child is taken away by the lioness:

> And in all þe sorow þat scho [the Empress] in was,
> Ryghte so com rynnande a lyones,
> Of wode als scho wolde wede.

---

[3] See *Octavian*, ed. McSparran, p. 62. See also, Geoffrey Chaucer, *The Man of Law's Tale*, in Larry D. Benson *et al.*, ed. *The Riverside Chaucer* (Oxford, 1987), pp. 87–104; John Gower, *Confessio Amantis* (2: 587–1598), in G. C. Macaulay, ed. *The Complete Works of John Gower: The English Works*, Vol. 1, EETS ES 81 (Oxford, 1901); *Sir Degaré*, in Anne Laskaya and Eve Salisbury, ed. *The Middle English Breton Lays* (Kalamazoo, 1995), pp. 89–144; *Lybeaus Desconus*, ed. M. Mills, EETS OS 261 (London, 1969); and *Sir Perceval of Galles*, in *Sir Perceval of Galles and Ywain and Gawain*, ed. Mary Flowers Braswell (Kalamazoo, 1995), pp. 1–76.

> In swonynge als þe lady laye,
> Hyr oþir childe scho bare awaye,
> Hir whelpes with to feede. (340–5)

However, despite her evil intent, the lioness is incapable of harming the child because he is of royal blood:

> Bot for it was a kynge sone jwysse,
> The lyones moghte do it no mys,
> Bot forthe þerwith scho ȝede. (349–51)

The belief that lions are physically unable to injure those of royal descent also finds expression in another fourteenth-century Middle English romance, *Sir Beues of Hamtoun*, which describes how Josian, the daughter of King Ermin, is not harmed by a couple of lions whom she encounters in a cave because she is both a royal princess, and a virgin:

> Iosian into þe caue gan shete,
> And þe twoo lyouns at hur feete,
> Grennand on hur with much granne,
> But þey ne myȝt do hur no shanne,
> For þe kind of lyouns, y-wys,
> A kynges douȝter, þat maide is,
> Kinges douȝter, quene and maide both,
> þe lyouns myȝt do hur noo wroth. (2387–94)[4]

Underlying these two examples from *Octavian* and *Sir Beues of Hamtoun* is the assumption that lions and lionesses – as the kings and queens of the animal world – are not only able to recognise humans of royal descent, but are actually physically incapable of doing them any harm, presumably on the grounds of their shared royal kinship.[5] Therefore, despite wanting to feed young Octavian to her whelps, the lioness's intuitive or unconscious awareness of their common nobility has the effect of suppressing her normal, predatory instincts.

However, the lioness's initial feelings of animosity towards young Octavian are metamorphosed into an attitude of loving, maternal

---

[4] *Sir Beues of Hamtoun*, ed. Eugen Kölbing, EETS ES 46, 48, 65 (London, 1885–94). There is also a comic allusion to this tradition in Shakespeare's *Henry IV Part 1*, when Falstaff claims that his reason for running away from Prince Hal when threatened by him at Gads Hill is because, like a lion, his instinct prevented him from attacking a royal prince: 'Why, thou knowest I am as valiant as Hercules, but beware instinct. The lion will not touch the true prince. Instinct is a great matter. I was now a coward on instinct. I shall think the better of myself and thee during my life – I for a valiant lion, and thou for a true prince.' William Shakespeare, *Henry IV Part 1*, ed. David Bevington (Oxford, 1987), Act II, Scene 4, 260–5.

[5] This point has been made by Frances McSparran in her edition of the text. See *Octavian*, ed. McSparran, p. 59.

protection after she kill and eats the griffin who is responsible for carrying them both off to the island:

> The gryffone thurgh Goddis grace scho [the lioness] sloghe,
> And of þat fewle scho ete ynoghe
> And layde hir by þat childe.
> The childe sowkyde þe lyones,
> Als it Goddis will was,
> When it þe pappes felide.
> The lyones gan it wake
> And lufe it for hir whelpes sake,
> And was þerwith full mylde.   (367–75)

The motif of the dispossessed child who is suckled by a wild animal recurs with great frequency in legend and romance. For instance, Romulus, the mythical founder of Rome, is said to have been suckled – along with his twin-brother Remus – by a she-wolf after they were both exposed as newly born infants,[6] while the fourteenth-century alliterative romance *Cheuelere Assigne*, a legendary account of the ancestry of Godfrey of Bouillon, the first Crusader King of Jerusalem, describes how Helyas (the putative grandfather of Godfrey), is suckled by a hind with his six brothers when they are abandoned in the wilderness as children.[7] The heroic credentials of young Octavian are therefore considerably enhanced not just by his association with the lioness, the animal that best symbolises his royal identity, but also by the poem's use of the suckling-animal motif, which places the child in the company of such august figures as Romulus and Helyas.

The poem makes much of the contrast between the lioness's savage, bestial nature – which under normal circumstances is violently antagonistic towards human beings – and the benevolent feelings that she harbours for young Octavian and his mother. For instance, when the Empress's ship sails past the island on which the lioness and young Octavian are stranded, a couple of sailors are sent ashore to replenish the boat's water supply, only to be attacked and killed by the lioness:

> The lyones laye in hir dene
> And was full blythe of þo two men,
> And full sone scho had þam slayne.   (433–5)

A further party of twelve men then land on the island in order to discover the whereabouts of their missing comrades, but quickly return to the ship after witnessing the incongruous sight of the lioness

---

[6] See Livy, *The Early History of Rome: Books I–V of The History of Rome From Its Foundations*, trans. Aubrey de Sélincourt (Harmondsworth, 1960), Book I, p. 38.

[7] See *Cheuelere Assigne* (113–19), ed. Henry H. Gibbs, EETS ES 6 (London, 1868, rpt. 1932).

peacefully playing with young Octavian near the remains of her two human victims:

> Thay [the twelve sailors] tolde þe wondir þat þay seghe,
> And þat þay fonde on þe roche on heghe
> A lyones in hir den;
> A knauechilde þerin laye,
> Therewith þe lyones gan hir playe.
> And dede were bothe þaire men.   (448–53)

The striking antithesis between the lioness's savage and ferocious treatment of the two sailors, and the maternal care that she lavishes on young Octavian, once again underlines the impression – deliberately cultivated by the poet – of the child's inherent superiority to the mass of common humanity, a point that further reinforces his status as an innately royal and heroic figure.

The lioness also reacts in a similarly reverential way to the child's mother, although in the case of the Empress it is her holiness rather than her royal blood that is said to give rise to the animal's meek and submissive response. According to the poet, on being told by the party of twelve sailors that a lioness is playing with a child on the island, the Empress asks to be taken ashore, whereupon she immediately rans towards the animal's den with all the strength that she can muster:

> When scho com on þat roche on heghe,
> Scho ran ywhils þat scho myght dreghe,
> With full sory mode,
> The lyones, thurgh Goddis grace,
> When scho sawe þe lady face,
> Full debonorly vp scho stode.
> Thurgh þe myghte of Mary mylde
> Scho suffered þat lady to tak hir childe,
> And scho forthe with hir ȝode.   (460–8)

Clearly, by attributing the lioness's deferential behaviour to the direct intervention of both God and the Virgin Mary, the poet – through the use of the hagiographical motif of the acquiescent animal – sought to highlight not so much the Empress's royalty [although she is earlier identified as the daughter of the king of Calabria (190–1)], as her sanctity. However, as in the case of *Sir Gowther*, holiness and nobility are presented in *Octavian* as overlapping, almost synonymous characteristics, making it impossible to disentangle the Empress's saintliness from her royal identity as the daughter of a king and the wife of an emperor. This intermingling of the sacred and the profane, and the saintly and the aristocratic, is reflected in the actions of the lioness, who completely fails to distinguish between the religious virtues of the mother, and the secular attributes of the son – treating the holy Empress with exactly the same degree of honour and respect that she has previously shown the heroic figure of young Octavian.

This blurring of the boundaries between romance and hagiography is further evident in the poem's subsequent portrayal of the lioness. Frances McSparran has observed that as the story unfolds, the animal increasingly comes to resemble the grateful lion of St Jerome, assuming the role of a faithful, domestic beast by first joining the Empress and her son on their journey to the Holy Land (472–83), and then living with them as a member of their household in the castle of the King of Jerusalem:[8]

> The kyng aftir hir [the Empress] sente;
> He bad scho solde lett for nothynge,
> And þe lyones with hir brynge.
> To þe castelle es scho went.   (501–4)

Within the confines of the Empress's domestic circle, the lioness completely abandons her wild and savage nature – 'The lyones þat was so wilde / Belefte with þe lady and þe childe:' (521–2) – and thus stripped of her erstwhile bestiality, she comes to be treated like a domesticated family pet. However, despite this dramatic change to both her living conditions and behaviour, the animal retains the characteristically royal attributes of nobility, fidelity, and courage, attributes that she has the opportunity of exhibiting at the very end of the romance, when, out of loyalty to young Octavian, she bravely follows him into battle against the Saracens:

> The lyenas þat was so wyght,
> When she sawe þe yong knyght
> Into the batell fownde,
> Sche folowed hym wyth all her myȝt
> And faste fellyd þe folke yn fyȝt:
> Many sche made onsownde;
> Grete stedys downe sche drowe
> And many heþen men sche slowe,
> Wythynne a lytull stownde.   (1609–17)[9]

It is significant that the lioness should be depicted on the battlefield displaying the very qualities of strength, faithfulness, and courage that are conventionally associated with the figure of the romance knight, and which young Octavian himself exhibits during the same skirmish with the Saracens: ['Octauyon þe yong knyght, / Thorow þe grace of God almyght, / Full faste he fellyd ther pryde.' (1606–8)]. Therefore, the

---

[8] See *Octavian*, ed. McSparran, p. 59.
[9] Because of a lacuna in the Thornton manuscript at this point in the narrative (caused by a torn page), this quotation has been taken from McSparran's parallel text of Cambridge, University Library, MS Ff. 2. 38.

strong sense of affinity that connects young Octavian to the lioness – an affinity that is of such symbolic importance in the construction of the child's identity as a royal hero, and that is so heavily emphasised throughout the poem – is given concrete expression in their shared acceptance of, and adherence to, this aristocratic, fighting code.[10]

However, in contrast to young Octavian, whose royal and heroic nature is both acknowledged and validated by the lioness, Florent, his twin brother, receives no such recognition from any member of the animal kingdom. Indeed, the ape – the animal that is responsible for Florent's abduction – has traditionally been interpreted as a symbol not of nobility, but folly, since its appearance, which more than any other animal resembles that of a human being, was thought to represent or embody the absurdity, futility, and arrogance of an irrational beast attempting to imitate (ape) the behaviour of rational men and women.[11] It thus follows that rather than symbolising Florent's status as a royal prince, the ape – with its connotations of low foolishness – emblematically prefigures the humble, bourgeois, and occasionally comic environment into which the child is delivered by providence, and to which he is so constitutionally incapable of adapting.[12]

Whereas the fabulous adventures of young Octavian and his mother – which draw heavily on themes and motifs taken from legend, romance, and hagiography – take place in the strange, 'fairy-tale' world of the wilderness, where the laws of nature have been partially suspended, the

[10] The assistance that young Octavian receives from the lioness on the battlefield recalls the scenes from Chretién's *Yvain*, when the lion helps to defeat his master's enemies. See Chretién de Troyes, *Yvain*, in *Arthurian Romances*, trans. D. D. R. Owen (London, 1987), p. 338 (4219–48), and p. 342 (4533–66).

[11] Because of the ape's association with foolishness, it was not only a widely recognised symbol of folly, but – as in the case of *King Robert of Sicily* – was also thought to be the appropriate animal companion for the figure of the court fool. A comprehensive discussion of ape symbolism in the art and literature of the late-medieval and early modern periods can be found in H. W. Janson's classic study of the subject. See H. W. Janson, *Apes and Ape Lore in the Middle Ages and the Renaissance* (London, 1952).

[12] On a number of occasions, Clement and Gladwin, and the mercantile world that they represent, are presented as comic or clownish objects to be laughed at by their social superiors. For instance, when Florent returns to Paris after killing the giant, the King of France prepares a great celebration in his honour. However, Clement – fearing that he will have to meet the cost of the entertainment – steals the cloaks ['mantills' (1069)] of all the lords that are present, and refuses to return them until they agree to pay all the expenses themselves. The King laughs indulgently at Clement's antics, and – as befits one of royal blood – generously offers to pay for everything himself: 'Thereatt all þe kynges loghe; / There was joye and gamen ynoghe / Amonges þam in the haulle. / The kynge of Fraunce with hert full fayne / Said: "Clement, brynge þe mantils agayne, / For I sall paye for alle."' (1077–82). An analogous scene occurs at the end of *Guillaume d'Angleterre*. See *William of England*, trans. David Staines, pp. 489–90.

narrative of Florent's humble upbringing is set in the much more quotidian, workaday environment of the city. Reflecting this very different location, Florent's royal and heroic nature manifestes itself not through prodigious or supernatural occurrences, but rather, as Frances McSparran has observed, through his predilection for traditional, knightly pursuits, and his incompetence and lack of interest in the bourgeois occupations of business and trade.[13] As is the case with young Octavian, the poet takes every opportunity of asserting Florent's nobility, although in this instance the child's aristocratic nature is defined almost exclusively in terms of its opposition to the mercantile, commercial values of his adoptive father, Clement, for whom trading and bartering are so deeply ingrained into his personality that – on his return from the Holy Land – he cannot prevent himself from haggling with the band of outlaws over the price to be paid for Florent, eventually managing to purchase the boy for only half the sum that the thieves originally demanded (577–88).

Just as the lioness performs a pivotal role in confirming that young Octavian is of royal descent, so animals occupy a central position, and fulfil a key function, in Florent's narrative. However, in this latter case it is the hero's characteristically aristocratic attitude towards the animal kingdom, rather than the reverential response that his presence elicits from the various animals themselves, that helps to identify him as a person of noble origin. The first important incident involving an animal occurs when Florent is sent out into the city by his adoptive parents with two oxen in order to learn the butchery trade, only for him to meet a squire on a bridge with whom he exchanges his two beasts of burden for a 'gentill' and 'fre' falcon:

> Als Florent ouir þe brygge gan go,
> Dryvand on his oxen two,
> A semely syghte sawe he:
>
> A sqwyere bare, als I ȝow telle,
> A gentill fawcon for to selle,
> That semely was to see.
>
> Florent to þe sqwyere ȝede,
> And bothe his oxen he gan hym bede
> For þat fowle so fre;
> þe sqwyere þerof was full glade,
> He toke þe oxen als he hym bade:
> Florent was blythe in ble. (652–663)

Florent's enthusiasm for the noble, aristocratic falcon – which elsewhere in the romance is identified by the poet as a hawk (665 and 670) – is not shared by Clement, who beats his adopted son severely for squandering

---

[13] See, *Octavian*, ed. McSparran, p. 65.

the family's financial resources.[14] But, just as Clement completely fails to understand why Florent is so appreciative of, and animated about, the falcon, so Florent finds not only his father's anger, but also his indifference to the bird's qualities, equally baffling:

> The chylde þoght wondur thore
> That Clement bete hym so sore,
> And mekely he can pray:
> 'Syr,' he seyde, 'for Crystys ore,
> Leue, and bete me no more,
> But ye wyste well why,
> Wolde ye stonde now and beholde
> How feyre he can hys fedurs folde,
> And how louely they lye,
> Ye wolde pray God wyth all your mode
> That ye had solde halfe your gode,
> Soche anodur to bye.' (685–96)[15]

On one level, then, the falcon can be viewed as a focal point around which the class differences between Florent and Clement – differences which according to the poet are innate and not acquired – are able to crystallise. Thus, it would appear that Florent, completely oblivious of the commercial and utilitarian considerations that are uppermost in Clement's mind, instinctively recognises that the falcon is a fellow noble creature, and so, motivated by feelings of sympathetic kinship, feels compelled to buy the bird in exchange for his adoptive father's two humble, plebeian beasts of burden.

In the romance literature of the later Middle Ages, there are countless references to both the nobility of hawks and falcons, and their natural kinship with knights. For instance, in Marie de France's lay, *Yonec*, written in Old French during the second half of the twelfth century, a young and beautiful lady is imprisoned by her rich, elderly husband in a tower to prevent her from taking a lover. One day a hawk flies into the lady's room through an open window, and is suddenly transformed into

---

[14] Although the anatomical differences between hawks and falcons were recognised by the compilers of contemporary hunting manuals, the author of *Octavian* failed to distinguish between the two species of bird, effectively treating the word 'fawcon' as a synonym of 'hawk'. Both species were used in falconry and prized for their nobility (hence the confusion between the two), but the hawk, with its rounded, comparatively short wings, chases its prey near the ground, while the falcon has long pointed wings and soars high into the air, from which lofty position it dives to dispatch its prey. For a discussion of medieval falconry – as it was both practised in the field and portrayed on the page – see John Cummins, *The Hound and the Hawk: The Art of Medieval Hunting* (London, 1988), pp. 187–233.

[15] Because the Lincoln Thornton MS is damaged at this point in the narrative, this, and all subsequent quotations, have been taken from McSparran's text of the Cambridge manuscript.

a 'fair and noble knight'. According to Marie: 'The knight was extremely courtly and spoke to her first: "Lady, do not be afraid! The hawk is a noble bird." '[16] ('*Gentil oisel ad en ostur*').[17] The two become lovers, but the lady's jealous old husband, discovering the existence of the knight-hawk, attaches a set of spikes to her window, thus impaling him as he flies to his beloved.

If we approach this story from the point of view of the supposed social symbolism of birds, it is significant that – of all the avian forms that were available to Marie – she should consider the hawk to be the one that best embodies the nobility and courtliness of her exemplary, knightly hero.[18]

In a discussion of the symbolism of falconry, John Cummins argues that one of the reasons why hawks and falcons were viewed as noble creatures is because they provided the figure of the knight with an idealised image of himself:

> The peregrine . . . riding the wind, looking down on the world from above, or gentled and caressed on the falconer's wrist with its finely worked hood, its crest of feathers, its distinctive plumage, with those curved, cruel weapons which destroy inferiors at a blow, is almost a physiological extension of its master; an image, conscious or unconscious, of the knight, helmeted and armed in the panoply of the late-medieval passage of arms.[19]

To return to *Octavian*, then, Florent's innately royal nature, which is completely unaffected by his life-long exposure to the environment of Clement's household, asserts itself not only through his complete ignorance of, and indifference to, the commercial interests of his adoptive father, but also through his aesthetic, almost narcissistic admiration for his fellow noble creature, the falcon. Therefore, the radically different responses of Florent and Clement to the bird demonstrate the extent to which they – and by extension the two social classes that they represent – are separated by a gulf of understanding that neither is capable of bridging.

This deeply hierarchical view of human society – which holds that it is nature and not nurture that is responsible for the formation of character and personality – is further propounded when Florent yet again incurs the anger of his adoptive father by purchasing another 'noble' animal: a

---

[16] Marie de France, *Yonec*, in *The Lais of Marie de France*, trans. Glyn S. Burgess and Keith Busby (Harmondsworth, 1986), p. 87.

[17] Marie de France, *Yonec* (122), in *Lais*, ed. Alfred Ewert (Oxford, 1960).

[18] The knight's many noble qualities are enumerated at the end of the narrative by the inhabitants of the country of which he was the king: 'the inhabitants began to weep and said amidst their tears that it was the best knight, the strongest and the fiercest, the fairest and the most beloved, who had ever been born.' *The Lais of Marie de France*, p. 92.

[19] Cummins, *The Hound and the Hawk*, p. 190.

horse. Having recognised that Florent lacks the necessary skills to become a butcher, Clement, as we have seen, instructs the boy to deliver forty pounds of gold to his step-brother (who is a money changer), only for Florent to spend it instead on a fine, milk-white steed:

> Florent to the stede can gone,
> So feyre an hors sye he neuyr none
> Made of flesche and felle.
> Of wordys þe chylde was wondur bolde,
> And askyd whedur he schoulde be solde;
> The penyes he wolde hym telle.
> The man hym louyd for thyrty pownde,
> Eche peny hole and sownde:
> No lesse he wolde hym selle.
> Florent seyde: 'To lytull hyt were!
> But neuyr þe lees þou schalt haue more.'
> Fowrty pownde he can hym telle.   (721–32)

William Caxton, in his translation of Ramón Lull's, *Le Libre del Orde de Cauayleria*, attests to the nobility of the horse by claiming that when God instituted the Order of Chivalry, He chose this most noble of beasts to serve those noble, loyal, and courageous men whom He had appointed as knights:

> And after was enquyred and serched / what beest was moost couenable moost fayre / most couragyous and moost stronge to susteyne trauaylle / and moost able to serue the man / And thenne was founden / that the Hors was the moost noble / and the moost couenable to serue man / And by cause that emong alle the beestes the man chaas the hors / & gaf hym to this same man that was soo chosen amonge a thowsand men / For after the hors whiche is called Chyual in Frensshe is that man named Chyualler whiche is a knyght in Englyssh / Thus to the moost noble man / was gyuen the moost noble beest.[20]

For both Caxton and the author of *Octavian*, then, the internal organization of the animal kingdom reflects the hierarchical structure of feudal society, with the horse occupying a position in the natural order that is analogous to the place of the knight in the social world. Therefore, Florent's acquisition of the horse – an action that is motivated by a sense of sympathetic kinship with the animal – can be interpreted as yet another sign of his innate nobility and knightly destiny.[21] Indeed,

---

[20] William Caxton, *The Book of the Ordre of Chyualry*, ed. A. T. P. Byles, EETS OS 168 (London, 1926), pp. 15–16.

[21] It is also worth mentioning that when purchasing the horse, Florent displays the characteristically aristocratic virtue of largesse, paying forty pounds for the animal even though the man selling the creature only asks for thirty. Once again, Florent's beliefs and actions are shown to be diametrically opposed to those of his adoptive father, Clement.

Florent's strong affection for noble beasts constitutes such incontrovertible proof of his aristocratic origins that Gladwin, his adoptive mother, becomes convinced that he cannot be her husband's son, and it is for this reason that she implores Clement not to beat him:

> The burges wyfe felle on kne þore:
> 'Syr, mercy,' sche seyde, 'for Crysys ore,
> Owre feyre chylde bete ye noght!
> Ye may see, and ye vndurstode,
> That he had neuyr kynde of þy blode,
> That he þese werkys hath wroght.'   (751–6)

In many respects, the sense of sympathetic kinship that draws Florent to both the horse and falcon is similar to the unconscious or intuitive feeling of affinity that connect the lioness to young Octavian and his mother. For, although Florent is unaware of the circumstances of his own exalted birth, he is instinctively able – like the lioness – not only to recognise his fellow aristocratic creatures (whatever their species), but also to communicate his understanding of their shared nobility by responding to them in an affectionate manner. Moreover, the poem also suggests that the ties of common nobility that extend across the animal kingdom are stronger and more meaningful than the connections that exist between humans of different social classes. Thus, despite living together for years as members of the same household, the profound differences between Florent and his adoptive father, Clement, mean that the two men continually misunderstand one another, while the relationship that exists between young Octavian and his adoptive mother, the lioness, is based upon a deep sense of affinity and mutual affection.

In conclusion, it should be noted that the poet conceives of animals as more than just literary devices whose role or purpose in the narrative is – like the various dogs in *Sir Gowther* – to act as instruments of divine providence and markers of human nobility or saintliness. For, as well as performing these symbolic functions, the lioness, falcon, and horse are also endowed by the *Octavian*-poet with innately noble, aristocratic characteristics, which make it possible for them to forge companionable relationships with the different men and women – whether royal or holy – whom they happen to encounter. The bonds of sympathy and kinship that variously connect the Empress and her twin sons to the three noble beasts that feature in the poem, and which at least hint at the possibility of friendship between the human and animal worlds, are all the more remarkable because they provide a contrast to the early Lives of St Francis of Assisi, in which (as I sought to demonstrate in Part 1), sentiments such as friendship and empathy for animals are conspicuous by their absence. These benign, companionable, almost empathic attitudes towards the animal kingdom that are implicit in *Octavian*, are also evident in *Sir Orfeo*, the text to which I shall now turn.

8

Sir Orfeo

IN the Preface to his monumental study, *Animals in Art and Thought to the End of the Middle Ages*, Francis Klingender argues that beneath the enormous variety of different ways in which animals have been depicted in art and literature during the course of human history, it is possible to discern two fundamental but contradictory psychological impulses. On the one hand, Klingender claims that artists and writers – reflecting the reality of humanity's gradual yet remorseless conquest of the natural world – have sought to celebrate men and women's hard-won ascendancy over, and brutal subjugation of, the animal kingdom. On the other hand, however, he notes that it is also possible to detect an equally important tendency pointing in the opposite direction, a tendency that is neither aggressive nor triumphalistic, but that expresses the wish that the violent conflict that so characterises relations between humans and animals might eventually be brought to an end. According to Klingender, this desire, which manifests itself particularly strongly in the near-universal legend of the golden age, as well as in post-apocalyptic millennial fantasies, 'made men ignore the realities of struggle and exploitation altogether, thus transplanting them into a dream-world of wish-fulfilment where all creatures are friends.'[1] In the Western cultural tradition, the figure who probably best embodies this desire for peace and harmony between the human and animal worlds is Orpheus, the mythical Thracian musician who was able to charm even the wildest of beasts with the enchanting power of his music, and who – despite the antiquity of his legend – has continued to exert a strong hold over the imagination of writers and artists into modern times.[2]

---

[1] Francis Klingender, *Animals in Art and Thought to the End of the Middle Ages*, ed. Evelyn Antal and John Harthan (London, 1971), p. xxv.

[2] Evidence of the enduring potency and popularity of the Orpheus legend can be found in the work of Rainer Maria Rilke, one of the most celebrated of twentieth-century poets. In 1904, Rilke recounted the story of Orpheus's descent into the underworld in his verse narrative *Orpheus, Eurydike, Hermes*, and such was his fascination with the myth that he returned to the figure of the Thracian musician almost two decades later in *The Sonnets to Orpheus*, which A. Poulin Jr. – in the Preface to his English translation of the *Sonnets* – has described as 'Rilke's greatest achievement and one of the most fully realized artistic statements of the twentieth century.' See Rainer Maria Rilke, *Orpheus, Eurydike, Hermes*, in J. B. Lieshman, ed. and trans. *Rainer Maria*

It was not until the reign of the Roman emperor, Augustus, that Orpheus's fame as a musician and association with animals were combined to produce the version of the legend that was transmitted to the Middle Ages, principally through the work of Virgil, Ovid, and Boethius.[3] According to this version of the legend, Orpheus – distressed at the loss of his wife, Eurydice – journeys to the underworld in order to plead for her return. Moved by the mournful beauty of Orpheus's music, the king and queen of Hades grant his request, and allow him to lead his wife out of the underworld on condition that he does not look back at her until he reaches the surface of the earth. But, such is Orpheus's love for Eurydice that he is unable to prevent himself from casting a backward glance at her just as he is about to emerge into the light of day. And so, having broken his agreement with the infernal gods, he loses his wife for a second time. Overcome with grief, Orpheus withdraws into the wilderness where he enchants all of nature with his music. In memory of his wife he shuns the company of women [according to Ovid he sought consolation in the love of boys, thereby introducing homosexuality to Thrace (*Metamorphoses* X, 82–5)], and it is because of his renunciation of feminine love that the women of Thrace – believing themselves to be snubbed – tear him to pieces while inflamed in their Bacchanalian revels. Ovid, whose account of Orpheus's death is not only longer than that of Virgil, but also seems to be more intent on evoking pathos, memorably cemented the hero's identification with his animal audience by describing how they share the same violent fate at the hands of the wild and furious Thracian women:

> The first victims were the countless birds, still spellbound by the voice of the singer, the snakes and the throng of wild animals, the audience which had brought Orpheus such renown. The frenzied women began by seizing upon these; then, with bloodstained hands, they turned to Orpheus himself, flocking together just as birds do, if they see the bird of night abroad by day.[4]

For Ovid, then, although Orpheus's many sufferings lend a kind of tragic grandeur to his life, the source of his fame, and hence the characteristic

---

Rilke, New Poems (London, 1964), pp. 142–7; and *The Sonnets to Orpheus*, in A. Poulin Jr. ed. and trans. *Duino Elegies and The Sonnets to Orpheus* (Boston, 1977).
[3] See Virgil, *Georgics* IV (453–527), trans. L. P. Wilkinson (Harmondsworth, 1982), pp. 139–42, Ovid, *Metamorphoses* X (1–85), and XI (1–66), trans. Mary M. Innes (Harmondsworth, 1955), pp. 225–7 and pp. 246–7, and Boethius, *The Consolation of Philosophy*, ed. and trans. H. F. Stewart and E. K. Rand (London, 1918), Book III, Metre 12, pp. 294–7. For a discussion of the representation of Orpheus in the earlier Greek literature of the Hellenic period, see W. K. C. Guthrie, *Orpheus and Greek Religion: A Study of the Orphic Movement* (London, 1934, rpt. 1952), pp. 1–68; John Block Friedman, *Orpheus in the Middle Ages* (Cambridge Massachusetts, 1970), pp. 1–12; and Emmet Robbins, 'Famous Orpheus', in John Warden, ed. *Orpheus: The Metamorphoses of a Myth* (Toronto, 1982), pp. 3–23.
[4] Ovid, *Metamorphoses* XI (20–5), p. 246.

or defining feature of his mythological identity, is the hypnotic power that he exerts over his animal audience.

The anonymous fourteenth-century Middle English romance, *Sir Orfeo*, is ultimately derived from this version of the Orpheus legend. However, as a summary of the plot of *Sir Orfeo* will show, in the hands of an unknown English poet of the late Middle Ages, the story of Orpheus's tragic love for Eurydice is transformed almost beyond recognition, with only the hero's reputation as a lover, and his power to enchant the animal kingdom with his music (along, of course, with his name), to connect him directly to his classical forebear.[5]

According to its author, the romance of *Sir Orfeo* was originally composed as a lay by Breton minstrels, and it tells of the great love of King Orfeo of England for his wife Queen Heurodis, of the suffering that he endures after they are forcibly separated, and of the joy that they both experience when they are finally reunited. Set in the city of Winchester (which we are told was once known as Thrace), the poem opens one morning in the beginning of May when Heurodis, accompanied by two of her ladies, lies down to sleep in her orchard under a grafted fruit tree ['ympe-tre' (70)], only for her to wake up that afternoon in a mad frenzy. Tearing at her face and clothes, and crying out in terror, it takes over sixty knights and ladies to carry her back to the palace and restrain her. Orfeo, pitifully beholding the bloody wounds that Heurodis has inflicted on herself, begs her to reveal the cause of her unhappiness, and in great distress she tells him that they must part, for she has been visited in her dream by the king of the fairies who has forced her to accompany him and his entourage to the fairy-realm, and who then, after restoring her to her orchard, warns her that he will return on the following day to take her away with him again, this time for ever. The next morning, determined to oppose the fairy king, Orfeo surrounds his wife with a guard of a thousand knights, but in spite of this precaution he is powerless to prevent her abduction. Devastated at the loss of Heurodis, Orfeo renounces all of his possessions except for his harp, and entrusting the government of the kingdom to his steward, and donning a 'sclauin' (228) or pilgrim's mantle, he leaves the city to live with the beasts of the forest.

For ten years Orfeo suffers incalculable pain as he wanders alone in the wilderness, sleeping in the open and eating nothing but wild fruit, berries, roots, and grasses. Occasionally he plays his harp and produces such

---

[5] *Sir Orfeo*, which is thought to have been composed at the beginning of the fourteenth century in the London area, is preserved in three different manuscripts: Edinburgh, National Library of Scotland, MS Advocates' 19.2.1 (the Auchinleck MS); London, British Library, MS Harley 3810, and Oxford, Bodleian Library, MS Ashmole 61. For a discussion of the date, provenance, and language of the poem, see *Sir Orfeo*, ed. A. J. Bliss. 2nd edn (Oxford, 1966), pp. ix–xxvii. All references to *Sir Orfeo* will be taken from Bliss's text of the Auchinleck manuscript.

melodious music that he is able to charm the birds and animals of the forest. One day, he comes across a group of sixty ladies hunting water-fowl with falcons by a river, and caught up in the excitement of the chase he rushes towards them only to find that one of the members of the party is his wife. He follows the ladies through a tunnel in a rock that leads to the land of the fairy king, in the middle of which stands a castle so richly decorated with precious stones and metals that it resembles the court of paradise. In the guise of an itinerant minstrel he gains admittance to the castle, where he sees imprisoned within its walls a vast number of deranged or mutilated people who are thought to be dead but who have actually been taken by the fairies, among whom he recognises his own wife, Heurodis, still sleeping beneath her 'ympe-tre' (407).

Orfeo then approaches the king and queen and tells them that it is the custom of wandering minstrels to perform their music in the houses of great lords. He thus plays before them, and his music casts such a powerful spell over the court that everyone in the palace is involuntarily drawn towards it. Moved by the performance, the king instructs Orfeo to name his reward, and Orfeo asks to be given Heurodis, a request that the king reluctantly grants. Orfeo then returns with Heurodis to Winchester, where – disguised as a beggar – he plays his harp before his own court. Although the steward is unable to see through Orfeo's disguise, he does recognise his sovereign's harp, and in response to his enquiry Orfeo tells him that he found the instrument in the wilderness by the body of a man who had been eaten by lions and gnawed by wolves. Hearing this, the steward bursts into tears, bitterly mourning what he believes to be news of the death of his king. Having thus tested the steward's love and loyalty, Orfeo reveals his true identity, rewards the steward for his fidelity, and is welcomed back to court with much rejoicing.

As this somewhat lengthy recapitulation of the plot reveals, *Sir Orfeo* bears only the most perfunctory resemblance to its classical sources. In the process of transforming a legendary story of antiquity into a romance, the setting is moved from ancient Greece to medieval England, the hero and heroine are reincarnated as a noble and courtly king and queen, the underworld of classical mythology is replaced by the fairy-otherworld of Celtic legend, and most significantly of all, rather than ending with the tragic death of the two lovers, the story concludes with the joyful and triumphant return of Orfeo and Heurodis to their king-dom. Moreover, *Sir Orfeo* is framed by a prologue and epilogue in which the poet – instead of citing the Greek myth of Orpheus as the source of the romance – claims that the work was originally composed as a lay by Breton minstrels, and as G. V. Smithers has usefully pointed out, it is with this tradition of the Breton lay, and not with its classical ante-cedents, that the poem has most in common.[6]

[6] See G. V. Smithers, 'Story-Patterns in Some Breton Lays', *Medium Aevum* 22

Amidst these radical changes not only to the form and content of the narrative, but also to the identity of the hero and heroine, it is interesting to note that the one episode that the poet faithfully preserves from the classical legend is the hero's charming of the animals with his music, suggesting that for the author of *Sir Orfeo* at least, the essential characteristics of the Orpheus–Orfeo figure are his skill as a musician and his association with the animal kingdom. The first intimation of the hero's special relationship with animals comes when Orfeo announces to the assembled nobles of his realm, that because of the great sadness that he feels at the loss of his wife, he intends to abandon his kingdom in favour of a life of exile in the wilderness:

> He cleped to-gider his barouns,
> Erls, lordes of renouns,
> & when þai al y-comen were,
>
> 'Lordinges' he said, 'Bifor ʒou here
>
> Ich ordainy min heiʒe steward
> To wite mi kingdom afterward;
> In mi stede ben he schal
> To kepe mi londes ouer-al,
> For now ichaue mi quen y-lore,
> þe fairest leuedi þat euer was bore,
> Neuer eft y nil no woman se,
> In-to wilderness ichil te,
> & liue þer euermore
> Wiþ wilde bestes in holtes hore;
>
> & when ʒe vnder-stond þat y be spent,
>
> Make ʒou þan a parlement,
>
> & chese ʒou a newe king
>
> – Now doþ ʒour best wiþ all mi þinge. (201–18)

Orfeo's determination to abjure the company of women and live instead 'Wiþ wilde bestes in holtes hore' (214), mirrors the actions of the classical

(1953), 61–92. Breton lays have proved to be very difficult to define generically, since they are virtually indistinguishable from conventional medieval romances. However, as in the case of both *Sir Orfeo* and *Sir Gowther*, Breton lays purport to be literary versions of traditional songs that were originally sung by the people of Brittany in their ancient Breton language. The genre only emerged (as a literary form at least), in the second half of the twelfth century with the appearance of the Old French lays of Marie de France (which are generally believed to have been written between 1170 and 1189). There are nine poems in Middle English, all of which date from the fourteenth and fifteenth centuries, that are designated as Breton lays: *Sir Orfeo*, *Lay le Freine*, *Sir Degaré*, *Emaré*, *Sir Launfal*, *Sir Gowther*, *The Erle of Tolous*, and Chaucer's *Franklin's Tale*. For a general introduction to the Breton lay in both Old French and Middle English literature, see Mortimer J. Donovan, *The Breton Lay: A Guide to Varieties* (Notre Dame, 1969).

Orpheus – related in the accounts of Virgil and Ovid – after he fails to recover his wife from the underworld.[7] But, beyond the fact of this literary parallel, Orfeo's actual motives for relinquishing his temporal power and abandoning human society remain obscure, and have been the subject of considerable critical debate.[8] For instance, it has been argued that Orfeo is subject to the same kind of love-madness that besets Lancelot and Tristram, both of whom – like Orfeo – withdraw from human society into the wilderness after being deprived of the love of their respective mistresses, Guenevere and Isolde.[9] However, rather than spontaneously losing his reason and violently running off naked into the forest (the sequence of events enacted by Lancelot and Tristram), Orfeo freely chooses to forsake the civilised world, and in so doing he not only displays sufficient presence of mind to announce his intention of abdicating in advance, but he also has the foresight to stipulate before an assembly of his vassals the manner in which his kingdom is to be governed after his departure.

In contrast to the love-madness of the two Arthurian heroes, the poet's account of Orfeo's sojourn in the wilderness is couched in religious language and imagery, and seems to owe more to the hagiographical tradition of the saintly hermit than to the romance convention of the forlorn lover. On losing Heurodis, Orfeo renounces his position in society, assumes the appearance of a religious figure by putting aside his secular garments in favour of a 'sclauin' or pilgrim's mantle, abandons all of his possessions (except for his harp), and finally passes barefoot through the city gates:

> Al his kingdom he for-soke,
> Bot a sclauin on him he toke.
> He ne hadde kirtel ne hode,
> Schert no no noþer gode,
> Bot his harpe he tok algate
>
> & dede him barfot out atte ȝate;
>
> No man most wiþ him go.
> O, way! What þer was wepe and wo

---

[7] See Virgil, *Georgics* IV (507–20), pp. 141–2, and Ovid, *Metamorphoses* X (76–7), p. 227.

[8] A summary of the various critical positions that have been adopted on the subject can be found in Anne Laskaya and Eve Salisbury's note on lines 227–71, in their edition of the text. See *Sir Orfeo*, in Laskaya and Salisbury, ed. *The Middle English Breton Lays*, p. 50.

[9] See Dean R. Baldwin, 'Fairy Lore and the Meaning of *Sir Orfeo*', *Southern Folklore Quarterly* 41 (1977), 129–42. According to Baldwin, p. 137, by choosing to withdraw into the wilderness, Orfeo is 'unconsciously following the tradition of lovers generally and romance lovers in particular'. A description of the love-madness of both Lancelot and Tristram can be found in Thomas Malory's 'The Book of Sir Tristram de Lyones'. See Malory, *Works*, pp. 487–500, and pp. 303–8.

> When he þat hadde ben king wiþ croun
> Went so pouerlich out of toun!
> þuirth wode & ouer heþ
> in-to þe wildernes he geþ.
> Noþing he fint þat him is ays,
> But euer he liveþ in gret malais.   (227–40)

As well as willingly accepting a life of poverty and physical hardship, Orfeo's newly acquired identity as a humble and penitent saint also manifests itself through his relationship with the animal kingdom. On the most basic level, his decision to live with the beasts of the forest might be seen as a deliberate echo of Jesus's forty-day retreat in the wilderness, during which time, according to St Mark's Gospel: 'he was . . . with the wild beasts; and the angels ministered unto him' (Mark 1: 13). More significantly, however, it is while he is living in the wilderness that Orfeo charms the birds and beasts with his music, an episode which – despite its classical, pagan origins – contains clear echoes of many of the *Lives* of the saints:

> His harp, where-on was al his gle,
> He hidde in an holwe tre,
>
> & when þe weder was clere & briȝt
>
> He toke his harp to him wel riȝt
> & harped at his owhen wille.
> In-to alle þe wode þe soun gan schille,
> þat all þe wilde bestes þat þer beþ
> For ioie abouten him þai teþ,
> & alle þe foules þat þer were
> Come & sete on ich a brere,
> To here his harping a-fine
> – So miche melody was þer-in;
> & when he his harping lete wold,
> No best bi him abide nold.   (267–80)

The picture of the barefooted Orfeo, dressed in religious raiment and peacefully surrounded by a group of birds and beasts, inevitably calls to mind those saintly figures – such as the desert fathers and Francis of Assisi – whose extraordinary purity and holiness made it possible for them to restore to the natural world the harmony that it had originally enjoyed before the Fall. Through the melodious power of his music, then, Orfeo is momentarily able to re-establish amongst his audience of animals the peaceful condition that prevailed in the garden of Eden – a miraculous power that is earlier alluded to in the prologue, when the poet compares the beauty of Orfeo's harping to the joys of paradise:

> In al þe warld was no man bore
> þat ones Orfeo sat bifore
>
> (& he miȝt of his harping here)
> Bot he schuld þenche þat he were
> In on of þe ioies of Paradis,
> Swiche melody in his harping is.   (33–8)

This ability of Orfeo metaphorically to transport his audience of animals to paradise – a power that enables him to create, in the words of Seth Lerer, 'an Eden in the wilderness'[10] – lasts only for the duration of his musical performance, for the birds and beasts immediately disperse as soon as his playing comes to an end: '& when he his harping lete wold, / No best bi him abide nold' (279–80). Once the brief, paradisal interlude of Orfeo's harping is over, then, the post-lapsarian discord between humans and animals is instantly restored.

Although the peaceful and harmonious relationship that Orfeo establishes with his animal audience is only fleeting, his encounter with the birds and beasts nonetheless points to an underlying connection in the poem between the human and animal worlds. For, it is clear that the various wild creatures who gather round Orfeo in the wilderness have the ability – generally thought to be the exclusive preserve of human beings – to experience delight in music. Indeed, it would appear that the melodious strains of Orfeo's harping has the effect not so much of lulling the animals into a state of non-violent passivity, but of actively awakening within them feelings of joy: 'all þe wilde bestes þat þer beþ / For ioie abouten him þai teþ' (273–4). Thus, Orfeo – who both seeks and finds in the playing of his harp consolation from the rigours of his life in the wilderness – is able to unite with his audience of beasts and birds in a shared moment of musical enjoyment.

The power of music to forge connections across the animal kingdom is also in evidence at the very beginning of the poem, when Heurodis – accompanied by two of her ladies – withdraws into her orchard in order to listen to the birds sing:

> þis ich quen, Dame Heurodis,
> Tok to maidens of priis,
> & went in an vndrentide
> To play bi an orchard-side,
> To se þe floures sprede & spring,
> & to here þe foules sing.   (63–8)

Just as the birds gather in the wilderness to hear the music of Sir Orfeo, so Heurodis and her ladies seek out the birds for their song.

---

[10] See Seth Lerer, 'Artifice and Artistry in *Sir Orfeo*', *Speculum* 60 (1985), 92–109, p. 102.

Thus, a kind of reciprocity between humans and animals is suggested in the poem, with each able to take pleasure and delight in the music of the other.

However, a very different incident involving animals, and one that casts light on the complex and multi-faceted nature of Orfeo's identity, occurs at the end of his ten years of exile in the wilderness, when, wandering alone through the forest, he comes across a party of sixty ladies hunting water-fowl with falcons:

> And on a day he seiȝe him biside
> Sexti leuedis on hors ride,
> Gentil & iolif as brid on ris;
>
> Nouȝt a man amonges hem þer nis;
> & ich a faucoun on hond bere,
> And riden on haukin bi o riuere.
> Of game þai founde wel gode haunt,
> Maulardes, hayroun & cormeraunt;
> þe foules of þe water ariseþ,
> þe faucons hem wele deuiseþ;
>
> Ich faucoun his pray slouȝ.
>
> þat seiȝe Orfeo, & louȝ:
> 'Parfay!' quaþ he, 'þer is fair game;
> þider ichil, bi Godes name!
> Ich was y-won swiche werk to se.'
> He aros, & þider gan te.   (303–18)

Unlike Orfeo's previous encounter with the animal kingdom, which is marked both by its harmoniousness, and its fabulous, other-worldly atmosphere, this episode is rooted not only in the reality of everyday human experience, but also in the natural conflict and struggle for survival that characterises relations between animal predators and their prey.[11] For, although it subsequently transpires that the sixty ladies have come from the realm of the fairy-king, their falcons, and the three species of water-fowl on which the falcons prey – the mallards, herons, and cormorants – are all unmistakably native to England. But even more significant than the portrayal of the birds themselves is the poet's description of Orfeo's reaction to them, because through his typically aristocratic and courtly response to the spectacle of the hunt, he reveals a completely different side to his character from the one that he has earlier displayed while enchanting the animals with his music.

In contrast to the peaceful and contemplative mood that surrounds the previous scene, Orfeo greets the violent sight of the falcons hunting and killing the water-fowl with a spontaneous and uninhibited expression of

---

[11] This point has been made by A. J. Bliss in the introduction to his edition of the text. See *Sir Orfeo*, ed. Bliss, pp. xlii–xliii.

joy, first laughing, and then running towards the ladies in order to gain a better view of the proceedings. Of course, the pleasure that Orfeo experiences – which is all the more powerful (and poignant) coming as it does after the long description of his travails in the wilderness – is due at least in part to the fact that the hunt reminds him of his former, happier life at court: 'Ich was y-won swiche werk to se' (317). However, as well as triggering memories of his past, it would seem that the sight of the falcons hunting their prey actually enables Orfeo to recover or rediscover within himself his own aristocratic identity. For, in the same way that his peaceful, musical encounter with the birds and beasts somehow accords with, or is a manifestation of, the spiritual side of his nature, so his delight in falconry can be seen as a trait that corresponds to, or is indicative of, his identity as a noble king.

Hunting in one form or another constituted the principal leisure activity of the medieval aristocracy, and proficiency in its various arts was considered a necessary courtly accomplishment.[12] Moreover, just as Florent's love of falcons in *Octavian* draws attention to his royal origins, so a knowledge of the esoteric rules and rituals of hunting and falconry – when displayed by a hero in romance – is a sure sign of his nobility. For instance, in *Sir Tristrem*, an anonymous thirteenth-century Middle English romance (the only copy of which is preserved in the Auchinleck manuscript), the eponymous hero comes across a party of huntsmen in a forest inexpertly breaking up a stag. Appalled by their ignorance of hunting lore, Tristram intervenes and performes the task with great dexterity, thereby revealing himself to all present as a man of noble birth.[13] In much the same way, Orfeo's enthusiasm for falconry confirms that, despite his wild, grizzly, and decidedly uncourtly appearance, his nature is essentially noble.

One of the reasons why falconry appealed so greatly to the medieval aristocracy was because it offered those of noble birth a reassuringly familiar and comforting view of the natural world, with the divisions within the animal kingdom between the predatory falcons and their prey seeming to reflect, and in a sense vindicate, the hierarchical structure of feudal civilisation. As John Cummins has noted, the falconer saw in his activity:

> a confirmation of the structure of human society, with certain natural and ineradicable divisions; he accepts that there are beings inherently superior to others, over which they have the power of life and death; beings stronger, abler, cleaner and more refined; in a word, more 'gentle'.[14]

---

[12] For a discussion of the importance of hunting in aristocratic life, see Cummins, *The Hound and the Hawk: The Art of Medieval Hunting* (London, 1988), pp. 1–11.

[13] See *Sir Tristrem* (445–539), ed. George P. McNeill, STS 8 (Edinburgh, 1886).

[14] Cummins, *The Hound and the Hawk*, pp. 189–90.

Possibly then, Orfeo's pleasure and excitement at the sight of the birds is an expression of his affinity for, and identification with, his fellow aristocratic creature, the falcon. It follows from this that he may have regarded the bird's successful slaying of its prey as an example of a noble creature exercising its natural – almost feudal – prerogative over the plebeian mallards, herons, and cormorants.

The changing nature of Orfeo's relationship with the animal kingdom reflects the two tendencies within his character – the one religious and penitential, the other regal and courtly – that I have identified. When, at the beginning of the poem, Orfeo is prompted by an overwhelming sense of grief to withdraw into the wilderness, his peaceful commune with the birds and beasts symbolises his rejection of human society and renunciation of the world, while his joyful reaction to the sight of the falcons – marking as it does the end of his self-imposed exile in the wilderness, and the overcoming of his despair – signals the re-emergence of the royal, courtly, and assertive side of his character. However, it is interesting to note that in contrast to *Sir Isumbras*, *Sir Gowther*, and *Octavian*, in which there is a considerable overlap between the realms of religious and secular culture, with the attributes of the knight merging imperceptibly with those of the saint, these two aspects both of Orfeo himself, and the poem to which he gives his name, are never fully integrated. Whereas Isumbras and Gowther achieve sainthood through their pursuit of the chivalric ideal, and the religious virtues of the Empress in *Octavian* are virtually indistinguishable from her attributes as a noblewoman, Orfeo completely abandons his quasi-religious persona when he returns to Winchester with his wife, Dame Heurodis, and re-assumes his identity as a king.

Sir Orfeo's distinctive use of hagiographical and romance convention can perhaps be better understood if it is approached through the kind of archetypal criticism pioneered by Northrop Frye. According to Frye, romance narratives typically describe the metaphorical descent of a hero or heroine into a nightmare world of suffering and confusion (sometimes represented by a wilderness, labyrinth, or prison), in which he or she experiences either terror, grief, or awe, and suffers a profound loss of identity. However, Frye claims that in romance, this tragic mood of confinement and enchantment is eventually broken, allowing the hero or heroine to recover his or her former identity, and so return (ascend) to the world from which he or she has originally come.[15]

An archetypal reading of *Sir Orfeo*, then, would emphasise the cyclical nature of the narrative, with its symmetrical themes of descent and ascent, loss and restoration, and exile and return. Such an interpretation would therefore regard Orfeo's ten years of exile in the wilderness as a

---

[15] Frye's theory of romance is outlined in his book: *The Secular Scripture: A Study of the Structure of Romance* (Cambridge Massachusetts, 1976).

metaphorical descent into a subterranean world of grief and suffering, and his adoption of a saintly, hagiographical persona simply as a manifestation of the sense of alienation, confusion, and loss of identity that is conventionally associated with such a state. Furthermore, and with striking relevance to our current concerns, Frye also notes that the moment at which the romance hero recovers his former identity is often marked on his part by a spontaneous release of laughter, which signals a change in the prevailing narrative tone from tragedy to comedy.[16] As we have already observed, Orfeo greets the sight of the falcons – which, of course, is the point in the narrative where he recalls his past life and rediscovers his former self – by laughing: 'Ich faucoun his pray slouȝ. / þat seiȝe Orfeo, & louȝ' (313–14).

Frye's critical method is founded on the assumption that, although superficially different in regard to their content, all literary works, regardless of when or where they were produced, make use of a small number of recurring narrative patterns, which embody the deepest wishes and anxieties of humanity. Frye claims that it is only by accepting the existence of such universal or archetypal structures that one can explain how stories are able to travel across the barriers of language, custom, and religious belief, and so take root in cultures remote from one another in terms of both their geographical location and historical setting. But, specifically in relation to romance, Frye further notes that the pattern of descent and ascent that describes the trajectory of the romance hero is itself derived from the structure of vegetation and solar myths, myths that acquire their meaning and significance from the fact that they reflect, and give expression to, on the one hand the different rhythms of the natural world (for instance, the cycle of the seasons, with the annual disappearance of plant life in the autumn, and its re-emergence in the spring), and on the other hand the cyclical movements of the celestial bodies (such as the daily setting and rising of the sun).

When considered in the light of Frye's theory, then, *Sir Orfeo*'s origins in, and close connection to, the world of both classical and Celtic mythology becomes all the more apparent. From the point of view of an archetypal critic, Orfeo's ten years of exile in the wilderness can be seen as a kind of symbolic death, and it is perhaps for this reason that the saintly persona that he assumes during this period is so disconnected from the royal identity that he renounces at the beginning of the story, and which he rediscovers at its end. However, it should be noted that in contrast to *Sir Orfeo*, Frye's cyclical pattern does not apply quite so neatly to *Sir Isumbras*, *Sir Gowther*, and *Octavian*. Of course, the eponymous hero of both *Sir Isumbras* and *Sir Gowther*, as well as the Empress and her two children in *Octavian*, undergo a period of exile in the wilderness, from which – like Orfeo – they are eventually able to

---

[16] See Frye, *The Secular Scripture*, pp. 129–31.

emerge renewed (or in Frye's terms, out of which they are able to ascend, symbolically reborn). But, unlike *Sir Orfeo*, whose plot is almost perfectly cyclical (so that Orfeo and Heurodis find themselves at the end of the narrative in a virtually identical position to the one that they originally occupied at its beginning), the protagonists of *Sir Isumbras*, *Sir Gowther*, and *Octavian* grow, develop, and change. For instance, we find that Gowther leaves his kingdom as an unmarried sinner, but ends his days as a married saint, while young Octavian and his brother, Florent, are sent into exile as newly born babies, only finally to be re-united with their father as fully grown men. In both *Sir Gowther* and *Octavian*, then, the cyclical motif of descent and ascent is used in conjunction with a linear narrative, and it is this combination of linear and cyclical elements that enables the themes of courtliness and saintliness – themes that are treated in *Sir Orfeo* as alternative, mutually exclusive categories – to be seamlessly integrated. Frye's model, then, while helpful, takes full account of just the one variety of romance experience, only touching tangentially upon the other kinds of narrative structure that we have been considering.

Even amongst the romances that borrow from, and have affinities with, hagiography, then, individual works employ hagiographical themes and motifs – especially those associated with animals – in their own distinct ways. However, there is a further category of Middle English romance – best exemplified by the legendary tales of Alexander the Great – that draws upon, and is closely connected to, not the Lives of the saints, but the genres of chronicle and history. I shall be examining this tradition of pseudo-historical romance narrative, and exploring the different symbolic and narrative uses to which it put the animal kingdom, in the third and final part of this book.

Part III

Nature and Supernature:
The Middle English Romances of
Alexander the Great

9

Alexander: Romance and History

OF all the historical figures from classical antiquity whose lives were known during the Middle Ages, none could rival the fame and popularity enjoyed by Alexander the Great. Writing at the end of the fourteenth century, Geoffrey Chaucer – in a much-quoted passage from *The Monk's Tale* – attested to Alexander's extraordinary renown:

> The storie of Alisaundre is so commune
> That every wight that hath discrecioun
> Hath herd somwhat or al of his fortune.[1]

The reasons why the story of Alexander appealed so strongly to a medieval audience are not difficult to understand, for his life – like that of a romance hero – was packed full of fabulous incident and dramatic adventure. He was born in 356 BC, the son of Queen Olympias and King Philip II of Macedon, and in his youth he came under the influence of the philosopher Aristotle, who had been appointed by Philip to act as his tutor. Alexander succeeded to the Macedonian throne at the age of twenty (after the assassination of his father), and as soon as he had ensured the security of his realm by putting down a series of rebellions in Greece and the Balkans, he led an army across the Hellespont into Asia on a campaign against the Persian emperor, Darius III. Despite the vast numerical superiority of the Persians, Alexander achieved three decisive military victories at the battles of Granicus (334 BC), Issus (333 BC), and Gaugamela (331 BC), as a result of which he found himself – at the age of twenty-five – the ruler of a vast territory that stretched from Libya in the west to Bactria (modern Afghanistan) in the east. But, not content with simply preserving the boundaries of Darius's empire, Alexander pressed on into India, only ending his eastward march at the banks of the River Beas in the Punjab, when his troops – seeing no end to the campaign, and exhausted after their years of toil and fighting – refused to advance any further. Therefore, unable to conquer the whole of India as he had intended, Alexander reluctantly returned to Babylon, the administrative

---

[1] Geoffrey Chaucer, *The Monk's Tale*, Fragment VII, *The Canterbury Tales* (2631–3), in Larry D. Benson *et al.*, ed. *The Riverside Chaucer*.

centre of his empire, where he unexpectedly died of a fever in 323 BC, at the age of thirty-two.[2]

It would appear from this brief biographical sketch that Alexander owes his enduring fame to a number of different factors, the most obvious of which are his seeming invincibility in battle, the unprecedented size of the territory that he conquered, and the very young age at which he achieved his victories.[3] However, while the scale and historical significance of Alexander's accomplishments have never been in dispute, the nature of his personality and the morality of his actions were the subject of a fierce debate that raged throughout the Hellenistic, Roman, and medieval periods. On the one hand, he was regarded by some as a heroic figure whose stupendous achievements set the standard of military excellence that all subsequent kings and generals sought to follow.[4] Conversely, he was believed by others to have been a cruel tyrant whose character contained all that was most evil in human nature, and who was responsible – during the course of his campaigns – for causing untold human misery and suffering.[5] As an historical figure, then,

[2] Numerous biographies of Alexander have appeared in recent years, among the most highly regarded of which are W. W. Tarn's *Alexander the Great*, 2 Vols (Cambridge, 1948); Robin Lane Fox's *Alexander the Great* (London, 1973); and A. B. Bosworth's *Conquest and Empire: The Reign of Alexander the Great* (Cambridge, 1988).

[3] An anecdote from the life of Julius Caesar recorded by the Roman historian Suetonius reflects precisely these aspects of Alexander's posthumous reputation. According to Suetonius, while Caesar held the rank of quaestor – the most junior of all the Roman offices of state – he was sent on a mission to Further Spain, where: 'he saw a statue of Alexander the Great in the Temple of Hercules, and was overheard to sigh impatiently; vexed it seems, that at an age when Alexander had already conquered the whole world, he himself had done nothing in the least epoch making.' See Suetonius, *The Twelve Caesars*, trans. Robert Graves (Harmondsworth, 1979), p. 16.

[4] Alexander's inclusion in the list of the nine worthies – the catalogue of the nine noblest men in history that was first drawn up at the beginning of the fourteenth century by Jacques de Longuyon in his verse romance, *Les Voeux de Paon*, and which was frequently repeated in the popular literature of the fourteenth, fifteenth, and sixteenth centuries – reflects the Macedonian emperor's status as an exemplary, chivalric hero. The nine worthies consisted of three pagans: Hector, Alexander, and Julius Caesar; three Jews: Joshua, David, and Judas Maccabeus; and three Christians: Arthur, Charlemagne, and Godfrey of Bouillon. The most notable Middle English treatments of this theme can be found in two alliterative poems of the late-fourteenth and earlyfifteenth centuries; *The Parlement of the Thre Ages* (300–583), and the *Morte Arthure* (3223–455). See *The Parlement of the Thre Ages*, ed. M. Y. Offord, EETS OS (Oxford, 1959), and *The Alliterative Morte Arthure*, in Larry D. Benson, ed. *King Arthur's Death: The Middle English Stanzaic Morte Arthure and Alliterative Morte Arthure* (Indianapolis, 1974).

[5] Alexander was condemned for just this reason by Paulus Orosius in his *Seven Books of History Against the Pagans*, written in the early years of the fifth century at the request of Orosius's friend and mentor, St Augustine, and which became a standard textbook on the history of the classical period during the Middle Ages. Orosius portrayed Alexander as a ruthless sadist who was impelled ever onwards by

Alexander impressed himself so forcibly on the world that not even his most vehement critics could deny the importance of his accomplishments, yet his deeds elicited violently opposing responses in the work of poets, philosophers, theologians, and preachers.[6]

Although Alexander's place in medieval culture's pantheon of great and famous men was not in doubt, the path by which knowledge of his life was passed down to posterity was far from straightforward. None of the accounts of his career that were written by his contemporaries has survived; and their descriptions of his actions and assessments of his character are now only known at second or third hand through the work of Greek and Roman historians of the first and second centuries AD, such as Arrian, Plutarch, and Quintus Curtius Rufus.[7] However, the work of Arrian and Plutarch was not available in Western Europe during the Middle Ages; which meant that the principal historical sources that shaped medieval perceptions of Alexander's reign were Curtius Rufus's *History of Alexander*, Orosius's *The Seven Books of History Against the Pagans*, and its source, Marcus Julianus Justinus's *Epitome* of the lost *Historiae Philippicae* of Pompeius Trogus.[8]

But, in addition to these historical works, medieval knowledge of Alexander was also derived from an alternative, legendary tradition, which was ultimately based on a highly romanticised biography of the Macedonian emperor that is thought to have been written by a Greek inhabitant of Alexandria some time between 200 BC and AD 200, and which is known as *Pseudo-Callisthenes* because of an erroneous attribution to the Peripatetic philosopher, Callisthenes, in one of the manuscripts.[9]

---

his love of cruelty. For instance, in his account of the subjugation of Bactria, Orosius claimed that: 'Alexander, insatiable for human blood, whether of enemies or even allies, was always thirsting for fresh bloodshed. So with a stubborn heart, he received in surrender the Chorasmi and Dahae, a tribe which had not been conquered.' See Paulus Orosius, *The Seven Books of History Against the Pagans*, Book III: 18, p. 105, trans. Roy J. Deferrari (Washington, 1964).

[6] For a detailed consideration of the wide range of different attitudes towards Alexander that can be found in the literature of the Middle Ages, see George Cary, *The Medieval Alexander* (Cambridge, 1956), *passim*.

[7] See Arrian, *The Campaigns of Alexander*, trans. Aubrey de Sélincourt (Harmondsworth, 1971); Plutarch, *Life of Alexander*, trans. Ian Scott-Kilvert, in Plutarch, *The Age of Alexander* (Harmondsworth, 1973), pp. 252–334; and Quintus Curtius Rufus, *The History of Alexander*, trans. John Yardley (Harmondsworth, 1984). For a brief discussion of the problems faced by modern historians of Alexander because of the loss of the primary sources for his life, see Lane Fox, *Alexander the Great*, pp. 499–500.

[8] The medieval reception of these texts is examined at some length by both George Cary and David Ross. See Cary, *The Medieval Alexander*, pp. 62–70; D. J. A. Ross, *Alexander Historiatus: A Guide to Medieval Illustrated Alexander Literature* (London, 1963), pp. 67–83; and Gerrit H. V. Bunt, *Alexander the Great in the Literature of Medieval Britain* (Groningen, 1994), pp. 3–13.

[9] *Pseudo-Callisthenes* – derivatives of which are known as far afield as Iceland,

Two Latin translations of *Pseudo-Callisthenes* were of particular importance for the reception of the romance in Western Europe during the Middle
Ages. The first, known as the *Res Gestae Alexandri Magni,* was undertaken
in the early fourth century by a certain North African called Julius
Valerius, and it achieved considerable popularity from the ninth century
onwards in an abridged version (known as the *Zacher Epitome*). However,
the *Zacher Epitome* was itself superseded in the later Middle Ages by the
Historia de Preliis Alexandri Magni, a translation of *Pseudo-Callisthenes*
which was made in the mid-tenth century by Archpriest Leo of Naples, and
which was widely known in three different versions (the so-called J¹, J², and
J³ interpolated recensions). Together, the works of Julius Valerius and Leo
of Naples spawned hundreds of derivatives in the different vernacular
languages of Western Europe, including all of the Middle English
romances of Alexander the Great, of which the most coherent and
artistically successful is *Kyng Alisaunder*.[10]

Because it is so conspicuously lacking in reliable historical and
biographical detail, modern critics have tended to look rather dispara-
gingly on the tradition of the medieval Alexander romance. For instance,
David Ross began his study of the illustrated Alexander literature of the
Middle Ages by describing *Pseudo-Callisthenes* as 'a work of . . .
excessive mediocrity', and he further noted (somewhat dismissively),

Ethiopia, and China – was pivotal in disseminating the fame of Alexander far
beyond the boundaries of his empire, and the extremely wide diffusion of the
romance has made it, as Robin Lane Fox has noted, possibly the most widely read
tale 'in world history to have spread without a religious message'. See Robin Lane
Fox, *The Search for Alexander* (London, 1980), p. 40. The complex process by
which *Pseudo-Callisthenes* was translated into Latin and the vernacular languages
of Western Europe has been exhaustively documented by George Cary. See Cary,
The Medieval Alexander, pp. 9–16, and pp. 24–61. For a modern English
translation of *Pseudo-Callisthenes,* see *The Greek Alexander Romance,* trans.
Richard Stoneman (Harmondsworth, 1991).

10 *Kyng Alisaunder* is in fact a translation of Thomas of Kent's *Le Roman de Toute
Chevalerie,* written in Anglo-Norman at the end of the twelfth century, and which
in turn was derived from the *Zacher Epitome* of Julius Valerius. *Kyng Alisaunder* is
believed to have been composed at the beginning of the fourteenth century in the
London area, and is the only Middle English version of the Alexander story to
survive as a complete text. It is preserved in three manuscripts: Edinburgh,
National Library of Scotland, MS Advocates' 19.2.1 (the Auchinleck MS);
Oxford, Bodleian Library, Misc 622; and London, Lincoln's Inn 150. All
references will be to G. V. Smithers's edition of the Laud MS. See *Kyng Alisaunder,*
ed. G. V. Smithers, EETS OS 227, 237 (1952–1957). For an edition of *Le Roman de
Toute Chevalerie,* see Thomas of Kent, *The Anglo-Norman 'Alexander' (Le Roman
de Toute Chevalerie),* ed. B. Foster, ANTS 29, 31 (London, 1976). The two other
surviving full-length treatments of Alexander's career that were written in Middle
English – *The Wars of Alexander* and *The Thornton Prose Life of Alexander* – both
date from the fifteenth century, and are translations of the J³ recension of the
Historia de Preliis. See *The Wars of Alexander,* ed. H. N. Duggan and Thorlac
Turville-Petre, EETS ES 10 (Oxford, 1989), and *The Prose Life of Alexander from
The Thornton Manuscript,* ed. J. S. Westlake, EETS OS 143 (1913).

114

that it was the ultimate source from which 'the average illiterate or semieducated man from late Antiquity to the Renaissance gleaned his knowledge of Alexander the Great'.[11] However, while to a modern sensibility, the medieval adaptations of *Pseudo-Callisthenes* might appear to be works of frivolous entertainment, suitable only for the 'illiterate or semieducated', this was certainly not the view that was held by those – such as the author of *Kyng Alisaunder* – who were actually responsible for producing the romances. Indeed, in the prologue to *Kyng Alisaunder*, the Middle English poet insists upon the seriousness of the work. To this end, the poet cites a collection of popular sayings attributed to the Roman moralist Cato (the *Dicta Catonis*), to claim that much needed comfort ['solas' (15)], can be gained by reflecting upon the deeds of others:

> Bysynesse, care and sorouȝ
>
> Js myd man vche morowȝe,
>
> Somme for sekenesse, for smert,
> Somme for defaut oiþer pouert,
> Somme for þe lyucs drede
> þat glyt away so floure in mede.
>
> Ne is lyues man non so sleiȝe
>
> þat he ne þoleþ ofte ennoyȝe
> Jn many cas, on many manere,
> Whiles he lyueþ in werlde here.
> Ac is þere non, fole ne wys,
>
> Kyng, ne duk, ne kniȝth of prys,
> þat ne desireþ sum solas
> Forto here of selcouþe cas;
> For Caton seiþ, þe gode techer,
> Oþere mannes lijf is ouer shewer.   (3–18)

This tone of moral and intellectual seriousness is evident throughout the poem, but it is particularly to the fore in the sections concerned with the wonders of the East, those marvellous human, animal, and plant forms that Alexander is said to have observed in the eastern lands through which he travelled. According to the poet, these phenomena were originally recorded by the philosopher, Aristotle, who (so the poet claims), actually accompanied his former pupil on the journey to India:

> þoo Alisaunder went þorouȝ desert,
>
> Many wondres he seiȝ apert,
> Whiche he dude wel descryue
> By gode clerkes in her lyue –

---

[11] See Ross, *Alexander Historiatus*, p. 5.

By Aristotle, his maister þat was.
Better clerk siþen non nas –
He was wiþ hym, and sei3 and wroot
All þise wondres, God it woot.   (4763–70)

As Dieter Mehl has noted, the pseudo-scientific tone used to describe the many curious phenomena – whether botanical, zoological, or anthropological – encountered by Alexander in India, sets the poem apart from the more conventional courtly romances of the later Middle Ages, and gives it something of the character of an academic treatise.[12]

It could be argued, then, that the claims to historical authenticity and scientific authority that were made by the author of *Kyng Alisaunder* have the effect of blurring the boundary between the genres of history and romance. Similarly, the line dividing history and legend occasionally becomes unclear in those historical accounts of Alexander's life that were written during the classical period, with the result that the Macedonian emperor was at times portrayed by such eminent historians as Plutarch and Quintus Curtius Rufus more in the manner of a romance hero than a genuine historical figure. For instance, Plutarch began his biography of Alexander by asserting that his subject was descended from Hercules on his father's side, and Aeacus the grandfather of Achilles on his mother's, and he went on to assure his readers that those facts at least were beyond dispute, as they were universally accepted by all the authorities.[13] But, as well as tracing Alexander's ancestry back to the mythological past, both Plutarch and Quintus Curtius Rufus also embellished their narratives of his life by describing encounters that he is said to have had with legendary peoples from far off lands. One such story famously describes Alexander's supposed meeting with Thalestris, the queen of the Amazons, who is said to have come to his camp in order to conceive his child, and whose sexual appetite was so prodigious that it took Alexander thirteen days fully to satisfy her desires.[14] However, although the classical histories of Alexander's reign contain clear traces of legend and romance, while the romances aspire to the status of history, the two types of writing are nonetheless distinct from one another, and one of the ways in which the formal differences between the two can be drawn out is by comparing their respective treatments of Alexander's relationship with the animal kingdom, a relationship that is encapsulated in the story of how – while still a child – he succeeded in taming his horse, Bucephalas.

---

[12] See Dieter Mehl, *The Middle English Romances of the Thirteenth and Fourteenth Centuries* (London, 1968), p. 231.

[13] See Plutarch, *Life of Alexander*, 1, pp. 252–3.

[14] See Quintus Curtius Rufus, *The History of Alexander*, Book VI, pp. 127–8. Plutarch was slightly more circumspect in his account of this episode, reporting that many years after Alexander's death, his one-time bodyguard, Lysimachus, on hearing the story, 'smiled and asked quietly, "I wonder where I was then."' See Plutarch, *Life of Alexander*, 46, pp. 302–3.

Knowledge of Bucephalas – the horse on whom Alexander was eventually to ride to India – spread far and wide along with the fame of his master, and such was the extent of the animal's renown that in legend and popular folklore he came to be regarded as the archetypal great horse, a creature whose strength, courage, and nobility were comparable to those of his heroic rider.[15] The only surviving historical account of the taming of Bucephalas – which was the occasion on which Alexander first encountered his horse – is contained in Plutarch's *Life*, and is one of a series of anecdotes concerning Alexander's childhood and adolescence that were recorded by the Greek historian:

> There came a day when Philoneicus the Thessalian brought Philip a horse named Bucephalas, which he offered to sell for thirteen talents. The king and his friends went down to the plain to watch the horse's trials, and came to the conclusion that he was wild and quite unmanageable, for he would allow no one to mount him, nor would he endure the shouts of Philip's grooms, but reared up against anyone who approached him. The king became angry at being offered such a vicious animal unbroken, and ordered it to be led away. But Alexander, who was standing close by, remarked, 'What a horse they are losing, and all because they don't know how to handle him, or dare not try!' Philip kept quiet at first, but when he heard Alexander repeat these words several times and saw that he was upset, he asked him, 'Are you finding fault with your elders because you think you know more than they do, or can manage a horse better?' 'At least I could manage this one better', retorted Alexander. 'And if you cannot,' said his father, 'what penalty will you pay for being so impertinent?' 'I will pay the price of the horse', answered the boy. At this the whole company burst out laughing, and then as soon as the father and son had settled the terms of the bet, Alexander went quickly to Bucephalas, took hold of his bridle, and turned him towards the sun, for he had

---

[15] Striking proof of the endurance of the Bucephalas legend was provided by the Venetian traveller, Marco Polo, whose journey to China during the latter part of the thirteenth century took him through many of the lands that Alexander had conquered over sixteen hundred years earlier. When passing through Badakhshan (a province located in modern-day Afghanistan), Marco Polo heard of a local breed of horses which was said to have been descended from Bucephalas, and which had only recently died out: 'And Messer Marco was told that not long ago they possessed in that province a breed of horses from the strain of Alexander's horse Bucephalus, all of which had from their birth a particular mark on their forehead. This breed was entirely in the hands of an uncle of the king's; and in consequence of his refusing to let the king have any of them, the latter put him to death. The widow then, in despite, destroyed the whole breed, and it is now extinct.' See Marco Polo, *The Book of Ser Marco Polo the Venetian Concerning the Kingdoms and Marvels of the East*, Vol. 1, ed. and trans. Henry Yule (London, 1903), p. 158. For a general discussion of the representation of Bucephalas in history and romance, see Andrew Runni Anderson, 'Bucephalas and His Legend', *American Journal of Philology* 51 (1930), 1–21.

noticed that the horse was shying at the sight of his own shadow, as it fell in front of him and constantly moved whenever he did. He ran alongside the animal for a little way, calming him down by stroking him, and then, when he saw he was full of spirit and courage, he quietly threw aside his cloak and with a light spring vaulted safely on to his back. For a little while he kept feeling the bit with his reins, without jarring or tearing his mouth, and got him collected. Finally, when he saw the horse was free of his fears and impatient to show his speed, he gave him his head and urged him forward, using a commanding voice and a touch of the foot.

At first Philip and his friends held their breath and looked on in an agony of suspense, until they saw Alexander reach the end of his gallop, turn in full control, and ride back triumphant and exalting in his success. Thereupon the rest of the company broke into loud applause, while his father, we are told, actually wept for joy, and when Alexander had dismounted he kissed him and said, 'My boy, you must find a kingdom big enough for your ambitions. Macedonia is too small for you.'[16]

Although Bucephalas is the ostensible subject of this story, it is interesting to note that Plutarch showed relatively little interest in the horse himself. There is no physical description of the animal, and beyond the fact that Philip and his friends at first thought him to be wild and unmanageable, but that once he had been freed from his fears by Alexander he showed himself to be full of spirit and courage, no further mention is made of either his temperament or demeanour. Indeed, the only indication to suggest that Bucephalas was in any way exceptional has to be inferred from the fact that Alexander considered him to be worth thirteen talents, a sum which – according to Robin Lane Fox – was more than three times the amount ever known to have been paid for a horse in antiquity.[17] Consequently, the real subject of this anecdote, and the figure on whom all the attention is directed, is not Bucephalas, but Alexander. After all, he alone recognised that Bucephalas was not wild, but merely fearful of his own shadow, and this insight did not simply allow him to ride a horse considered by everyone else to be unbroken, it also revealed him to be an astute and observant figure who was capable of assessing a situation from more than one point of view, and then acting boldly on his conclusions. In short, by taming Bucephalas, Alexander displayed in miniature the very qualities of courage, intelligence, and imagination that he was subsequently to demonstrate on a much grander scale during his career as a great general and conqueror. Therefore, as well as being a charming tale in its own right, Plutarch's account of the taming of Bucephalas suggests that Alexander's successes

---

[16] Plutarch, *Life of Alexander*, 6, pp. 257–8.
[17] See Lane Fox, *Alexander the Great*, p. 47.

on the battlefield could have been predicted from the flamboyant and daring behaviour that he exhibited as a child.

Turning from Plutarch's *Life* to the version of the incident found in *Kyng Alisaunder*, it becomes immediately apparent that the Middle English poet employed a completely different mode of representation from that used by the Greek historian. According to the author of *Kyng Alisaunder*, one day while King Philip is out with his men, he is presented with a wild and ferocious horse called Bulcyfal who has been captured in a forest:

> Jn þis tyme fel a chaunce;
> Kyng Philippe pleyed in a pleyne.
>
> His man hym brouȝth by a cheyne
> A grisely beest, a rugged colt,
>
> He had ylauȝth in an holt.
> He presented it to þe kyng.
>
> Jt þouȝth hym a selkouþ þing.
> Jt had a croupe so an hert,
> An heued so a bole, cert,
> An horne in þe forehede amydward
> þat wolde perce a shelde hard.
> Jt was more þan any stede,
>
> And rede wete me miȝth it fede,
> Ac mannes flesshe leuere hym was
> þan hay-rek oiþer corne-tas.
> Jn an out-hous jn yrnen bende,
> Jt stood, and no man it hende.
> All þeues þat shulden ben ylore
>
> Men brouȝtten þat hors bifore.
> He had soner y-eten a man
> þan two champyons a han.
> Bulcyfal þat hors hete;
> Many man in his lyue he frete.
> No-man ne durst þere-on ycome
> Bot Alisaundre þe gode gome.
> Ne most noman it bistride
> Bot Alisaundre, ne on hym ride.
> To hym he wolde wel obeye –
> He most on hym ride and pleye.   (682–710)

Unlike the historical Bucephalas, the medieval Bulcyfal is presented as no ordinary horse, but a freak of nature – a hybrid creature whose monstrous body consists of the hind-quarters of a hart, the head of a bull, and a unicorn's single horn, and whose savage temperament (and penchant for human flesh), makes him uniquely qualified to perform the role of official executioner. Although Alexander is barely mentioned in the passage, his identity is inextricably bound up with the temperament and appearance of the horse, for the more vicious and savage the portrait of Bulcyfal, and the greater the sense of terror that the animal arouses in Philip's subjects, the more exceptional becomes Alexander's achievement in subduing him. Moreover, it should be noted that in this instance the act of taming the horse cannot be put down to human ingenuity – as in the case of Plutarch's Alexander – but is rather the result of the hero's innate, supernatural powers. In striking contrast to Plutarch's historical account of the episode, then, the romance version of the story describes a miracle performed by a figure of such superhuman stature, that his status is comparable to that of a god.

This incident has a sequel in *Kyng Alisaunder* that further highlights the supernatural aspect of the narrative, and provides yet more clarification of those elements that distinguish the Middle English poet's treatment of the episode from Plutarch's. King Philip, unsure as to which of his two sons should succeed him to the throne, consults an oracle on the subject and is told that whichever of the two is able to ride Bulcyfal should be declared the rightful heir. The king therefore sends for his two children, but whereas his second son, who also happens to be called Philip, is so fearful of the horse that he does not dare to approach him, Alexander proves himself the lawful successor by leaping upon Bulcyfal's back with ease:

> A voice ansuered in an ymage,
> 'Kyng, þou hast a colt sauage.
> Who so may þere-on skippe,
> Be it Alisaunder, be it Philippe,
> He shall of Corinthe toun
> After þee bere coroun.' . . .
> þe kyng in to court wendeþ.
> þe children sone he ofsendeþ.
>
> Bulcyfal nayȝeþ so loude
> þat it shrilleþ in to þe cloude.
> þai wenten alle to þe stable
> þere it was tyed jnne, saun fable –
> For a þousande pounde of golde
>
> Phillippoun it neiȝen wolde,
> Ac Alisaundre lep on his rygge
> So a goldfynche dooþ on þe hegge . . .
>
> Nys he bot of twelue ȝer olde –
> His dedes weren stronge and bolde.
>
> Fele weren at his liȝttyng þare
> þat reuerence gret hym bare,
> And seiden it was worþi þing
> He were þe nexte crouned kyng.   (765–70, 773–82, and 78–794)

Thus, as well as being a monstrous freak of nature, Bulcyfal is also an instrument of divine providence, a creature who – by allowing himself to be ridden by Alexander – is able to demonstrate beyond any doubt which of the two young princes is the rightful heir to the throne. In a sense, the meaning of Bulcyfal's existence is only fulfilled once he has consented to be tamed and ridden by Alexander. It is for this reason that in contrast to the guile, ingenuity, and courage shown by Alexander in Plutarch's account, the hero of the medieval romance does not have to do anything exceptional to tame the horse, he merely has to be himself.

Therefore, it is the presence or absence of a supernatural component to the story that most obviously distinguishes the way in which it was depicted in the two literary works. On the one hand, Plutarch's Alexander is presented as an exceptional individual who applied his remarkable intelligence to controlling a seemingly unmanageable horse, while on the other hand his medieval counterpart simply draws on his store of miraculous power to tame a beast of unnatural savagery. One useful way of approaching these very different conceptions of Alexander is through the use of Northrop Frye's theory of fictional modes, a theory that Frye outlined in his seminal work, the *Anatomy of Criticism*. Borrowing an idea from Aristotle's *Poetics*, Frye argued that fictional narratives can be classified in terms of the hero's power of action over his environment. Thus, Plutarch's Alexander, who succeeds in taming Bucephalas through human genius alone, corresponds to what Frye has called the hero of the high mimetic mode, as he is a figure

> superior in degree to other men but not to his natural environment . . . He has authority, passions, and power of expression far greater than ours, but what he does is subject both to social criticism and the order of nature.[18]

In *Kyng Alisaunder* on the other hand, it is possible to detect within Alexander himself the presence of a superhuman force that places him above the natural world, and gives him power over it. Frye's description of the hero of the romance mode succinctly delineates the powers that are at the disposal of the medieval Alexander. According to Frye, the romance hero is superior in degree both to other men and his environment, and he

> moves in a world in which the ordinary laws of nature are slightly suspended, prodigies of courage and endurance, unnatural to us, are natural to him, and enchanted weapons, talking animals, terrifying ogres and witches, and talismans of miraculous power violate no rule of probability once the postulates of romance have been established.[19]

---

[18] Northrop Frye, *Anatomy of Criticism* (Princeton, 1957), pp. 33–4.
[19] Frye, *Anatomy of Criticism*, p. 33.

Thus, the story of the taming of Bucephalas offers an interesting point of comparison from which to assess the differences between the historical and romance narratives of Alexander the Great. In *Kyng Alisaunder* and the wider romance tradition to which it belongs, we repeatedly find that the biographical facts of Alexander's life – such as his taming of Bucephalas – are enlarged upon and embellished with legendary material, thereby transforming the recognisably human figure of the histories into a hero of destiny. As in the case of the story of Bucephalas, this process of romantic exaggeration and elaboration frequently pertains to Alexander's relationship with the animal kingdom, and in chapter 11 I shall examine how the Macedonian emperor's scientific interest in the zoology, botany, and geography of the East (an interest that was fostered by Aristotle, and which is well documented in the historical sources), was the inspiration behind fantastic tales that appear in the romances telling of his encounters with fabulous beasts, and his dealings with monstrous and exotic peoples. However, the next chapter – while continuing with the general animal theme – explores not Alexander's relationship with the animal kingdom as such, but the various ways in which animals were used in the romances to symbolise the mysterious story of his conception and birth. Although ultimately based on legend, the romance accounts of his conception took their inspiration from certain rumours that were circulating during Alexander's own lifetime; rumours that would seem to indicate that he actually believed himself to be the son of the Libyan god, Zeus Ammon.

10

Alexander's Miraculous Conception and Birth

IN the spring of 331 BC, after his unopposed invasion and occupation of Egypt, Alexander travelled to the oasis of Siwah in the Sahara desert in order to consult the oracle of the god, Ammon. Although originally a Libyan deity, Ammon – who was depicted in the form of a man with a ram's head – had been known and worshipped in the Greek world for over a century, having been identified as a local North African manifestation of the Olympian god, Zeus. The oracle of Ammon at Siwah was widely respected throughout Greece and Greek Asia Minor, and it enjoyed a reputation for truthfulness and infallibility that was comparable to the oracle of Apollo at Delphi.[1] Alexander's motives for embarking on the long and arduous journey to Siwah are not altogether clear, but according to Arrian – whose account of the episode is fuller than those found in any of the other ancient sources – he 'had a feeling that in some way he was descended from Ammon . . . [and] he undertook this expedition with the deliberate purpose of obtaining more precise information on this subject'.[2] Alexander questioned the oracle in private, never making known what was revealed to him, but despite the secrecy that surrounded the incident it is reported that he was publicly greeted by the chief priest of the temple, who addressed him as 'son of Zeus'.[3]

The extent to which Alexander actually believed himself to be the son of a god, and the effect that this had on his attitude towards Philip, as well as his understanding of his own nature, remains unclear, but his visit to Siwah, and the rumours of his divine lineage that resulted from it,

---

[1] For a discussion both of the cult of Zeus Ammon, and the shrine to the god at Siwah, see H. W. Parke, *The Oracles of Zeus: Dodona – Olympia – Ammon* (Cambridge Massachusetts, 1967), pp. 194–241. Useful discussions of Alexander's visit to Siwah, and his claims to divine parentage can be found in Fox, *Alexander the Great*, pp. 194–218, and Bosworth, *Conquest and Empire*, pp. 278–90.

[2] Arrian, *The Campaigns of Alexander*, Book III, p. 151.

[3] According to Plutarch, the divine honour that the Libyan priest paid Alexander was in fact unintentional, resulting from his poor command of Greek: 'Others say that the priest, who wished as a mark of courtesy to address him with the Greek phrase "*O, paidion*" (O, my son) spoke the words because of his barbarian origin as "*O, pai dios*" (O, son of Zeus), and that Alexander was delighted at the slip of pronunciation, and hence the legend grew up that the god had addressed him as "O, son of Zeus".' See Plutarch, *Life of Alexander*, 27, pp. 283–4.

irrevocably altered the way in which he was perceived by both his contemporaries and posterity. Amongst Alexander's troops, his claim to divine parentage was at times treated with ridicule and contempt. For instance, on one occasion shortly before Alexander's death, his relationship with his soldiers had become so strained that they sarcastically called on him to dismiss them all, and continue his campaigns with his father, Ammon.[4] The derision of his troops was later to be echoed in the work of such historians as Quintus Curtius Rufus, Paulus Orosius, and Marcus Julianus Justinus, who all viewed his willingness to entertain a belief in his own divine origins as evidence – along with his adoption of the barbaric customs of the Persians – of the degeneration of his personality, which was ultimately brought about by the corrupting influence of good fortune. Thus, Quintus Curtius Rufus's account of the visit to Siwah is strongly censorious in tone:

> the king . . . was addressed as 'son' by the oldest of the priests, who claimed that this title was bestowed on him by his father Jupiter. Forgetting his mortal state, Alexander said he accepted and acknowledged this title, and he proceeded to ask whether he was fated to rule over the entire world. The priest, who was as ready as anyone else to flatter him, answered that he was going to rule over all the earth . . . Alexander thereupon offered sacrifice, presented gifts both to the priests and to the god, and also allowed his friends to consult Jupiter on their own account. Their only question was whether the god authorised their according divine honours to their king, and this, too, so the priest replied, would be agreeable to Jupiter.
>
> Someone making a sound and honest judgement of the oracle's reliability might well have found these responses disingenuous, but fortune generally makes those whom she has compelled to put their trust in her alone more thirsty for glory than capable of coping with it. So Alexander did not just permit but actually ordered the title 'Jupiter's son' to be accorded to himself, and while he wanted such a title to add lustre to his achievements he really detracted from them.[5]

Amongst those classical historians who wrote about Alexander's life, his assumption of divine honours tended to provoke a mixture of embarrassment, scepticism, and ridicule. However, the disdainful attitude that is so evident in many of the histories did not influence the way in which the episode was treated in the romance tradition: the principal medium through which Alexander's association with Ammon came to be transmitted to the world.[6]

---

[4] See Arrian, *The Campaigns of Alexander*, Book VII, pp. 359–60.
[5] Quintus Curtius Rufus, *The History of Alexander*, Book IV, 7, 25–30, p. 68.
[6] Alexander's connection to Ammon was certainly known to the Jewish author (or authors) of the Book of Daniel, which is thought to have been written in the middle of the second century BC, for it is in the guise of the 'ram with two horns', a clear allusion to his putative father, the ram-headed, Ammon, that Alexander appears in

Although ultimately derived from the historical accounts of Alexander's journey to Siwah, the story that is recorded in the romances of his miraculous conception and birth was further complicated by a local Egyptian legend which identified the conquering Macedonian king as the son of the last indigenous Egyptian pharaoh, Nectanebo II.[7] Nectanebo fled Egypt in 343 BC before the advancing armies of the Persian emperor, Artaxerxes III, but while it is now generally believed that he took refuge in Ethiopia (where he entirely vanishes from the historical record), an alternative destiny is ascribed to him by a nationalist Egyptian legend (which would seem to have been circulating as early as the third century BC), according to which he actually travelled to Macedonia where he became first the lover of Olympias, Philip's wife, and then in due course the father of Alexander, her son.[8] This legend enabled the Egyptian people of the third century BC to claim Alexander as a native hero, and to view his invasion of their land not as an inglorious foreign conquest, but as a great patriotic victory over their hated enemies, the Persians.[9]

This Egyptian account of Alexander's conception, while seemingly incompatible with Alexander's own professed beliefs in his divine parentage, was in fact ingeniously combined with it to form the version of the story found in the romance tradition. The Libyan god, Ammon, provides the link between the two alternative accounts, for not only had he been appropriated by the Greeks, and identified with their god, Zeus, but he had also been assimilated by the Egyptians into their pantheon, and equated with the ram-headed god, Amun, the creator of the universe, and the divine father of the pharaoh.[10] It was Amun's role as the begetter of the pharaoh – a function that he performed by making love to the

---

one of Daniel's prophetic visions: 'Then I lifted up mine eyes, and saw, and, behold, there stood before the river a ram which had two horns; and the two horns were high; but one was higher than the other, and the higher came up last. I saw the ram pushing westward, and northward, and southward; so that no beasts might stand before him, neither was there any that could deliver out of his hand, but he did according to his will, and became great' (Daniel 8: 3–4).

[7] The Egyptian background to the romance tale of Alexander's birth is explored by Betty Hill in her article: 'Alexander Romance: The Egyptian Connection', *Leeds Studies in English* 12 (1981), 185–94.

[8] For the fate of Nectanebo, see Lane Fox, *Alexander the Great*, p. 197. In the introduction to his translation of *Pseudo-Callisthenes*, Richard Stoneman explores the Egyptian milieu from which the nationalist legends of Nectanebo and Alexander emerged. See *The Greek Alexander Romance*, pp. 11–12.

[9] The author of *The Greek Alexander Romance* refers to this Egyptian legend at the very beginning of his work: 'Many say that he [Alexander] was the son of King Philip, but they are deceivers. This is untrue; he was not Philip's son, but the wisest of the Egyptians say that he was the son of Nectanebo, after the latter had fallen from his royal state.' See *The Greek Alexander Romance*, Book I, p. 35.

[10] The absorption of Ammon into the system of Egyptian religious belief is discussed by Parke, *The Oracles of Zeus*, pp. 194–7, and Lane Fox, *Alexander the Great*, p. 202.

consort of the reigning monarch in the guise of her husband – that
enabled these two seemingly incompatible legends to be reconciled.[11] For,
once Alexander, who had assumed the title of pharaoh by right of
conquest in the autumn of 332 BC, went on to identify himself as the son
of Ammon at Siwah in 331 BC, it was possible for the Egyptian people to
interpret these claims in the light of their own religious beliefs, and so
assert that in accordance with the customary Egyptian practice, *their* god
Amun had adopted the form of the pharaoh, Nectanebo, in order to
conceive their future king, Alexander.

Thus, the account of Alexander's conception that finally found its way
into the romances was composed of elements drawn from two seemingly
incompatible sources. In this composite story, Alexander could be
identified as the son of both Ammon and Nectanebo, although this
somewhat complex resolution inevitably presented those medieval writers (such as the author of *Kyng Alisaunder*), who were faced with the
task of making sense of the material, and who presumably possessed little
knowledge of either ancient history or comparative religion, with
considerable scope for confusion and misunderstanding.[12]

In *Kyng Alisaunder*, the historical Nectanebo is transformed into the
mysterious figure of the Egyptian king, Neptenabus, a monarch wise in
the arts of astrology and magic, who learns through the exercise of those
arts that his land is soon to be conquered by an army led by Philip of
Macedon. In order to avoid this impending defeat, Neptenabus flees his
kingdom, and – determined to gain his revenge on Philip – he journeys to
Macedoyne, Philip's capital, where Queen Olympias is reigning in her
husband's absence. Overwhelmed by the queen's personal beauty,
Neptenabus manages to obtain a private audience by claiming to be a
revered Egyptian astrologer. During their meeting he prophesies that she
will soon be abandoned by Philip for a new wife, yet he is able to console
her with the news that she will give birth to a son begotten by the god,
Ammon, and that her child will grow up to avenge Philip and conquer
the world.

That night while Olympias is sleeping, Neptenabus casts magic spells
over a waxen image of the queen, causing her to have an extraordinary
dream in which a dragon comes to her chamber, enters her bed, and
impregnates her. The following morning, believing the dream to be a

[11] See Betty Hill, 'Alexander Romance', pp. 185–6.
[12] The story of Alexander's miraculous conception is found in four Middle English
works: *Kyng Alisaunder* (71–456); *The Wars of Alexander* (23–405); John Gower's
Confessio Amantis (6: 1789–2366), in G. C. Macaulay, ed. *The Complete Works of
John Gower: English Works*, Vol. 2, EETS ES 81 (London, 1901); and a fragmentary account of Alexander's life consisting of 1242 lines of alliterative verse, which
is thought to have been composed in the third quarter of the fourteenth century,
and which is known as *Alexander A*. See *Alexander A* (453–790), in *The Romance
of William of Palerne*, ed. W. W. Skeat, EETS ES 1 (London, 1867).

confirmation of Neptenabus's prophecy, and now entirely confident in the truthfulness of his testimony, Olympias invites him to become a member of her household, and entrusts him with all of her private affairs. That night, Neptenabus secretly disguises himself as Ammon by covering his body with dragon skin and concealing his face behind a mask of a ram's head, and in this guise he comes to Olympias's bed, where she conceives Alexander, her son.

Paradoxically, then, Neptenabus is revealed to be both a charlatan and a true prophet. Motivated by a mixture of lust and vengeance, he manages to trick his way into Olympias's bed by fabricating a fictitious story about the god, Ammon, and yet as a result of their adulterous union the queen does indeed give birth to a remarkable son, just as Neptenabus prophesied. The magical dream that Neptenabus induces in the queen is absolutely central to the deception that he practises on her, and – reflecting the ambiguous character of its author – the dream itself turns out to be both a misleading travesty, and a truthful prophecy, of future events:

> þe leuedy in her bed lay,
>
> Aboute myd-niȝth, ar þe day,
> Whiles he made his coniuryng,
>
> She seiȝ ferly in her metyng.
>
> Hire þouȝth a dragoun adounc liȝth
>
> To hire chaumbre and made a fliȝth.
> Jn he com to hire boure
> And crepe vnder her couertoure.
> Many siþe he hire kyste
> And fast in his armes þriste,
> And went away so dragon wylde;
> Ac gret he lete hir wiþ childe.   (343–54)

A 'dragon wylde' (353) is in fact a suitably alien and awe-inspiring form for a divine being to adopt, for not only does it aptly suggest the otherness of a god's nature, but its appearance, like that of a god, is liable to instil in any human observer a profound sense of fear. Terror is certainly the overriding emotion experienced by Olympias on waking up – 'Olympias of slepe awook. / She was a-grised for þe nones, / þat alle quakeden hire bones.' (356–8) – and in the dream itself it would seem that her extremely submissive response to the approach of the domineering dragon is motivated by her fear of him. Whatever its pleasures and compensations, then, sex with a god – at least as depicted in Olympias's dream – would seem to be a profoundly shocking and frightening experience, and any child born of such an unnatural union, it is reasonable to assume, would inevitably inherit some of the superhuman powers of its divine father.

On the following night, Neptenabus attempts to reproduce Olympias's dream experience in reality by first changing his appearance to resemble that of a dragon, and then making love to the queen in that guise:

Jn bed wook dame Olympyas,
And aspyed on vche manere

ʒif she miʒth ouʒth yhere
Hou Amon þe god shulde come.
Neptenabus his charme haþ nome,
And takeþ hym hames of dragoun,
From his shuldre to hele adoun;
His heued and his shuldres fram

He diʒtteþ in fourme of a ram.
Ouere hire bed twyes he lepeþ,
þe þrid tyme and jn he crepeþ.
Offe he cast his dragons hame
And wiþ þe lefdy playeþ his game.
She was þolemood and lay stille;
þe fals god dude al his wille.
Also ofte so he wolde,
þat game she refuse nolde.   (380–96)

It has been suggested that the poet's treatment of this incident, with the emphasis on Neptenabus's deception and sexual exploitation of Olympias, owes more to the genre of fabliau than romance.[13] The passage certainly has a low-comic tone, and it is immediately apparent that 'þe fals god' (394), Neptenabus, bears very little resemblance to the awesome figure of Olympias's dream. Indeed, far from transforming himself into a dragon, the exiled king merely assumes a vaguely dragon-like appearance by covering his body with dragon skin, and then leaping twice over the queen's bed (presumably in imitation of a dragon's flight), before creeping into bed with her. Thus, Neptenabus is presented not as a powerful god, but as a lecherous trickster who is able to take advantage of the queen's credulity in order to satisfy his lust.[14]

The contrast between Olympias's fabulous dream and the rather squalid reality that she actually experiences should have implications for the character of Alexander, since romance convention dictates that a

[13] See Betty Hill, 'Alexander Romance', p. 189.
[14] Of course, as well as covering himself with dragon skin – which he removes once he gets into bed with the queen – Neptenabus also wears a mask of a ram's head, no doubt as a gesture towards the ram-headed Ammon. However, by combining both dragon and ram elements in his disguise, Neptenabus ends up resembling neither the dragon of Olympias's dream, nor the ram-headed god of Libyan tradition. In a sense, Neptenabus invests himself with too much significance, and his attempt to forge onto his one body two quite separate symbolic identities merely has the effect of exposing him still further as a fraud.

child's heroic stature is determined by both the identity of his father, and the circumstances of his conception. The miraculous nature of Olympias's dream calls to mind those marvellous tales from classical mythology (such as the stories of Leda and the swan and Europa and the bull), in which immortal gods – having assumed animal form – father children on mortal women.[15] As we have just seen, however, according to *Kyng Alisaunder* and the romance tradition to which it belongs, Alexander is descended not from a god, but from 'þe fals god', Neptenabus, a fact that would seem to compromise his claim to heroic status, and deny him the power and privileges conventionally accorded to the son of a divine being. Indeed, rather than being a source of pride, Alexander's origins in an adulterous union might be regarded as dishonourable and belittling, yet strangely the Macedonian king is depicted in the romances as no less of a hero for being a bastard, and no less god-like for failing to have a divine father.[16]

There is therefore something slightly puzzling, indeed paradoxical, about the story of Alexander's conception, since the portrait of Neptenabus as a fraud and an impostor is difficult to reconcile with the fact that Alexander himself is presented as a figure possessing all of the heroic attributes conventionally enjoyed by the son of a divine being. The ambiguous nature of Neptenabus's character is perhaps due to the Egyptian origins of the story, and results from a sense of confusion – first manifested by the author of the original Greek romance, and subsequently shared by the work's countless translators and adaptors – about the precise nature of the relationship between the Egyptian god, Amun, and the pharaoh, Nectanebo (Neptenabus). As Betty Hill has noted, whereas in Egyptian belief the god Amun assumes the form of the reigning pharaoh in order to father the future king, this chain of events is reversed in the tradition of the Alexander romances, with Nectanebo impersonating the god Ammon as a way of seducing Olympias, an act that only incidentally results in the conception of the future pharaoh, Alexander.[17] It could be argued, then, that during the process of cultural

---

[15] Zeus is said to have transformed himself into a swan before making love to Leda, who laid an egg from which was hatched Helen of Troy. See Euripides, *Helen*, 212 ff., in Euripides, *The Bacchae and Other Plays*, trans. Philip Vellacott (Harmondsworth, 1954), p. 132. On another occasion Zeus took on the attributes of a bull, in which guise he carried off Europa, on whom he fathered Minos, the king of Crete. See Ovid, *Metamorphoses* II (836–75), trans. Mary M. Innes (Harmondsworth, 1955), pp. 72–3.

[16] A similar sense of confusion over the identity of the hero's father is to be found in the story of the conception of King Arthur. Through the magical powers of Merlin, Uther Pendragon (Arthur's father), has his appearance altered to resemble his enemy, the Duke of Cornwall. In this guise, Uther visits the Duke's wife, Elaine. Believing Uther to be her husband, Elaine has sex with him, and so conceives their son, Arthur. See Sir Thomas Malory, 'The Tale of King Arthur', in Malory, *Works*, ed. Eugene Vinaver 2nd edn (Oxford, 1971), pp. 4–5.

[17] See Betty Hill, 'Alexander Romance: The Egyptian Connection', p. 190.

transmission, the esoteric details of Egyptian religious practice were jumbled and misunderstood by the author of the Greek romance, as a consequence of which Nectanebo came to be assigned a very different role in the Alexander romances from the one that he had originally performed in the nationalist Egyptian legend.

This sense of confusion about both the extent of Neptenabus's powers and the motives underlying his actions, is also evident in two further scenes from *Kyng Alisaunder* in which the exiled Egyptian king is depicted in animal form. Because Olympias fears that she will be abandoned by her husband when he hears of her pregnancy, Neptenabus directs magic spells towards the pavilion where Philip – who is still campaigning with the army – is sleeping, causing him to have a dream in which he is both forewarned of Olympias's pregnancy, and led to believe that it is caused by divine intervention. In the dream, a goshawk settles on Philip's sleeping-quarters, where it opens its mouth, and stretches out its wings. This is witnessed by a dragon that flies from his lair, approaches the queen, and then blows a breath of fire into her mouth. Soon afterwards, a lion springs from the queen's navel and darts forth into the east, conquering all before him:

> þat ilk niȝth Neptenabus
> Made so stronge sorcery,
> And adressed it by þe sky,
> þat it com to þe pauyloun
> þere þat lijþ kyng Philippoun,
> Also he lijþ in slepe by niȝth,
>
> Hym þinkeþ a goshauk in grete fliȝth
> Settleþ on his herbergeynge,
>
> And ȝyneþ, and sprat abrode his wenge.
>
> A dragoun of his denne gan fleiȝe,
>
> Whan he þat goshauk yseiȝe,
> And settleþ sone after þas
> On stede þere þe quene was.
> Sone so he þe quene fonde,
> Jn hire mouþe he blew a bronde.
>
> þere-after nouȝth swiþe lang
> A lyoun at hire nauel out sprang.
> þe lyoun smoot in to þe est;
> Ne durst hym wiþstonde beest,
> þe goshauk of hym was a-gast   (478–98)

Unsure as to the meaning of the dream, Philip asks his various scholars and counsellors to explain its significance. Eventually, Abyron, the 'Wisest clerk of euerychon' (504), is able to interpret the vision for him (505–16), explaining that Philip himself is represented by the goshawk, while the dragon symbolises some god or 'sterne man' (509), who – having slept with the queen – has begotten on her a son (represented by the lion), who is destined to reign over the whole world.

Because it alludes both to the strange circumstances of Alexander's birth, as well as to his subsequent career of conquest and world domination, Philip's dream can be seen as presenting a highly condensed version of the romance itself, cast in the form of a beast allegory. The nobility of the hawk and the royalty of the lion (which, as we have seen, are the traditional symbolic attributes of the two animals), make them fitting emblems of Philip and Alexander respectively, while Neptenabus's supernatural power and god-like status is suggested not only by his dragon form, but also by the highly symbolic way in which he impregnates the queen, an act which – as G. V. Smithers has pointed out – recalls the moment in the second creation story of the Book of Genesis, when God animated Adam by filling his nostrils with the breath of life (Genesis 2: 7).[18]

But, in addition to appearing in Philip's dream in the guise of a dragon-god, Neptenabus actually transforms himself into a real fire-breathing dragon in order to defend Olympias from the anger of her husband. According to the author of *Kyng Alisaunder*, having learnt of the queen's pregnancy, Philip is determined to denounce her as an adulteress at a public banquet. However, before he has the opportunity of making his accusation, a dragon flies into the hall, breathing fire from his nostrils and scattering the assembled company with his long tail:

> For a dragon þere com jn fleen,
> Swithe griselich on to seen.
> His tayl was fyue fadem lang;
> þe fyre out at his nose-þerles sprang.
> By þre, by foure, myd þe tayle
> To þe grounde he smoot saunz fayle.
> Wiþ þe mouthe he made a beere
> So al þe halle shulde ben a-fere.
> þe kyng had wele grete hawe;
> Alle his barouns to chaumbre drawe.
>
> þe lefdy ȝede vnto þe drake.
> He lete his rage for hire sake,
> And laide his heued in hire barme
> Wiþouten doyng of any harme.   (545–58)

Unlike the previous occasions on which dragons of one form or another make an appearance, the huge creature that flies into Philip's hall – whose tail alone is said to be five fathoms long – has far too palpable a

---

[18] See Smithers, ed. *Kyng Alisaunder*, Vol. 2, p. 74. Smithers has also noted that this detail is not to be found in any of *Kyng Alisaunder*'s sources.

physical presence to be mistaken either for a dream symbol, or for a man disguised in a dragon costume (Neptenabus's two previous dragon incarnations). Furthermore, because the ability to transform oneself into a ferocious fire-breathing monster would seem to be a task beyond the reach of even the most knowledgeable magician, the performance of such a feat by Neptenabus once again raises questions about the nature of his identity, and in particular the balance in its composition between the natural and the supernatural, and the human and the divine. Although he is roundly exposed by the poet earlier in the narrative as a base impersonator of the god, Ammon, Neptenabus's dramatic defence of Olympias is the kind of undertaking that only a god would have the power to accomplish.

The sense of confusion surrounding the figure of Neptenabus – a confusion that ultimately has its origins in a Greek misunderstanding of the religious practices of the ancient Egyptians – is reflected in the dragon symbol that is variously used in *Kyng Alisaunder* to depict the exiled Egyptian king. Combining potency with an inhuman otherness, the dragon is powerfully suggestive of divinity, and it is no doubt for this reason that in the two dreams that he magically induces – the first in Olympias, the second in Philip – Neptenabus chooses the figure of the dragon to represent the god, Ammon. Of course, in the romance tradition, Neptenabus is not a god himself, but merely an imitator of one, a fact that is highlighted in the comic scene in which he disguises himself as a dragon in order to seduce Olympias. Paradoxically however, although he is presented as both a trickster and a fraud, Neptenabus is also depicted as a figure who possesses the attributes of a god, as he spectacularly reveals in Philip's hall with his awesome display of power and majesty.

As we have seen, this sense of ambivalence surrounding Alexander's claims to divinity is central to many aspects of his life and legacy. In his lifetime, even his own troops received with some incredulity his demand to be considered the natural son of Zeus Ammon. By the medieval period, this ambivalence was compounded by the confusion of the inherited sources, and Christian scepticism about pagan spirituality. And yet, an aura of the supernatural persistently surrounds Alexander. His refusal to accept the conventional limitations of human ambition has prompted many commentators to ascribe to him superhuman powers, whether metaphorical or literal: he is a figure who stands at the nexus of the human, the natural, and the supernatural worlds. According to the romance tradition, he inherited something of Neptenabus's supernatural power, and the young prince's divine (or semi-divine) nature is revealed at the very moment of his birth, which is marked by the whole of the natural world with a series of wonders; the earth trembles, the sky turns black, the sea becomes green, thunder and lightening strike, and everyone is said to be afraid (638–44).

132

According to the romances, Alexander ability to dominate the world of nature – to make it his subject rather than to be subject to it – remained with him throughout his life. It is a theme that becomes particularly important in the accounts of his travels through India and the East, where he is repeatedly confronted by strange natural phenomena, such as monstrous beasts of prodigious size and power. I shall examine Alexander's response to the exotic yet perilous flora and fauna that he encounters in the East, in the following chapter.

11

The Wonders of the East

THE Middle English romance *Kyng Alisaunder* is divided into two approximately equal sections, with the first half (1–4738) describing Alexander's miraculous conception and birth, his childhood and adolescence, and his various campaigns against the Greeks and the Persians, while the second half (4739–8021) is principally concerned with his travels through India and the East, and tells of his war against Porus, the Indian king, and his encounters with the many exotic peoples and animals of that land. Although this account of Alexander's career is entirely lacking in reliable historical and geographical detail, its basic structure does roughly follow the trajectory of the Macedonian emperor's life and travels, and it is also worth noting that despite its extensive use of legendary material, most of *Kyng Alisaunder*'s cast of characters – such as his human parents Philip and Olympias, his principal adversaries Darius and Porus, and his two generals Ptolemy and Perdiccas – are genuine historical figures. Moreover, in both romance and historical narratives, the pivotal moment in Alexander's life – the incident that brings to an end the first phase of his military career, and inaugurates the second – is the final, decisive victory that he gained over the Persian emperor, Darius III.

Alexander inflicted a crushing blow on the forces of Darius at the battle of Gaugamela in 331 BC, and although Darius himself fled from the battlefield unharmed, he was never able to recover from the huge losses that he suffered, and was killed soon afterwards by two of his own satraps – Bessus and Nabarzanes – before Alexander had the chance to overtake and capture him.[1] However, in spite of the fact that Alexander's victory at Gaugamela eliminated the only serious threat to his sovereignty in Central Asia, a number of the tribes that inhabited the eastern provinces of the former Persian Empire – in particular the Bactrians, Sogdians, and Scythians – continued to oppose his rule, and as a consequence Alexander had to postpone his planned invasion of India for a number of years while he forced them into submission. According to Quintus Curtius Rufus's account of this period, on one occasion Alexander was

---

[1] For a modern account of Alexander's victory at Gaugamela, and the assassination of Darius, see Bosworth, *Conquest and Empire*, pp. 74–85, and pp. 94–100.

visited by a Scythian ambassador, who addressed him in the following defiant manner:

> Had the gods willed that your stature should match your greed the world could not hold you. You would touch the east with one hand and the west with the other, and reaching the west you would want to know where the mighty god's light lay hidden. Even as it is, you covet things beyond your reach. From Europe you head for Asia; from Asia you cross to Europe. Then, if you defeat the whole human race, you will be ready to make war on woods, on snow, on rivers, on wild animals.[2]

Taking its cue from the comments of the ambassador, the romance tradition actually describes how Alexander – having completed his conquest of Darius's empire – marches on into India where he proceeds to wage war not just on the country's human population, but on its wild animals as well.

The extraordinarily bellicose nature of India's indigenous animals is first indicated early on in Alexander's Indian campaign, when a number of Macedonian troops who happen to be swimming across a river are set upon and eaten by terrifying hippopotami – animals that are said to be larger than elephants.[3] Soon afterwards, Alexander's army is attacked by a bewildering succession of ferocious beasts, including boars, bears, lions, elephants, tigers, dragons, unicorns, leopards, scorpions, snakes of incredible size dripping poison from their eyes, crabs whose shells are harder than the skin of crocodiles, white lions larger than bulls, a horse-like animal both larger and fiercer than an elephant (known as an 'Anddontrucion'), mice as big as foxes, and bats as large as doves. The Macedonian troops are initially dismayed by the size and savagery of the creatures that attack them, but taking their lead from their heroic king, they eventually manage to fight off the army of animals, although not without first suffering considerable casualties.[4]

The world of nature, then, at least as it manifests itself in India, is presented in the Alexander romances as a hostile, threatening force that exists in direct opposition to humanity. But it is a force that Alexander – with his customary display of invincibility – is able to subdue in much the same way that he overcomes all of his previous foes. And yet it is interesting to note that the Indian animals that assail the Macedonian army are said to be both larger and more ferocious than creatures from other countries (for instance, India's white lions are the size of bulls, while its mice are as large as foxes). John Block Friedman has argued

---

[2] Curtius Rufus, *The History of Alexander*, Book VII, 8, 12–13, p. 168.

[3] This incident is recorded in *Kyng Alisaunder* (5157–62). It can also be found in *The Wars of Alexander* (3969–75), and *The Prose Life of Alexander*, p. 69.

[4] For a description of the attack on Alexander's army, see *Kyng Alisaunder* (5215–446), *The Wars of Alexander* (3977–4075), and *The Prose Life of Alexander*, pp. 69–72.

that such representations belong to a tradition in Western literature that can be traced back as least as far as Ctesias, a Greek travel writer of the early fifth century BC, who depicted India as a land inhabited by terrifying animals and monstrous peoples, in which the normal laws of nature did not apply.[5]

But, in addition to waging war on the creatures of the East, Alexander is also said to have been driven by a spirit of scientific curiosity into observing their many peculiar anatomical and behavioural character-istics, characteristics that he is believed to have recorded – along with a number of observations on India's geography, natural history, and monstrous peoples – in a letter to his teacher, Aristotle, known as the *Epistola Alexandri Magni ad Aristotelem Magistrum Suum de Situ et Mirabilibus Indiae* (*The Letter of Alexander the Great to His Teacher Aristotle about the Geography and Wonders of India*).[6] Although *The Letter of Alexander to Aristotle* clearly belongs to the romance tradition, containing as it does fabulous descriptions of India's miraculous flora and fauna, it nonetheless came to be regarded in the Middle Ages as a work of serious scholarship, which was thought to have provided the philosopher Aristotle with much of the material from which he compiled his work on natural history, *De Animalibus*.[7] Alexander certainly received much praise during the later Middle Ages for his supposed contribution to the study of the natural sciences. For instance, the fourteenth-century English Benedictine monk, Ranulf Higden, whose encyclopaedic work

---

[5] See John Block Friedman, *The Monstrous Races in Medieval Art and Thought* (Cambridge Massachusetts, 1981), p. 5.

[6] Based on a Greek original (which was possibly written as early as the third century AD), the *Epistola Alexandri ad Aristotelem* survives in three Latin versions. The first frequently accompanies the *Zacher Epitome* of Julius Valerius's *Res Gestae Alexandri Magni*, the second is a unique copy preserved in the famous Bamberg Manuscript containing Leo of Naples's Latin translation of *Pseudo-Callisthenes* (Bamberg, Staatliche Bibliothek, MS E.iii.14), while the third (which is consider-ably longer than either of the other two), dates from the ninth century, and was by far the most popular of the three. For a discussion of the textual history of the *Epistola*, and a modern English translation of the text, see Lloyd Gunderson, *Alexander's Letter to Aristotle about India* (Meisenheim am Glan, 1980). The *Epistola* was translated into Old English perhaps at the beginning of the tenth century (the first Alexander text to have been translated into any medieval language), and is preserved in the Nowell codex, which contains the unique copy of *Beowulf*. See *Three Old English Prose Texts: Letter of Alexander the Great, Wonders of the East, Life of St Christopher*, ed. Stanley Rypins, EETS OS 161 (Oxford, 1924). The *Epistola* was also translated into Middle English in the third quarter of the fifteenth century, and is found in a single manuscript: Worcester Cathedral F.172. See Vincent DiMarco and Leslie Perelman, ed. *The Middle English Letter of Alexander to Aristotle*, in *Essays on English and American Language and Literature* n. s. 13 (1978).

[7] For a discussion of the medieval reception of the *Epistola*, see Friedman, *The Monstrous Races in Medieval Art and Thought*, pp. 6–7, and Cary, *The Medieval Alexander*, pp. 105–10.

the *Polychronicon* related the whole of human history from Creation to his own day, claimed in his chapter on the life of Aristotle that Alexander – inflamed by a burning desire for knowledge, and eager to gain an understanding of all creatures – had sent his teacher many animals from Asia (along with thousands of men to look after them), in order to assist him in his researches. According to John Trevisa's late-fourteenth-century Middle English translation of Higden's original Latin:

> þe grete Alisaundre brende in covetise of knowleche of þe kynde of bestes, and sente to Aristotel meny þowsandes of men of Grees, of Asia, and of Tracia, þat fedde bestes and foules wilde and tame, and al þat beeþ i-take wiþ haukynge, oþer wiþ hontynge, and hadde alle maner bestes in kepyng in hyves, in layes, in fisshe weres and pondes, for he wolde knowe al þing þat is broȝt forþ in kynde. Aristotel examyned hem al besiliche, and made aboute an fifty volyms of þe kynde of bestes.[8]

Alexander was thus regarded as a man with a great longing not just for new conquests, but for knowledge as well, and these two aspects of his reputation converge in the romance accounts of his journey through India to produce a figure who was seen as the embodiment of philosophy in action. Nowhere is this combination of worldly ambition and intellectual curiosity better illustrated than in the two legendary stories – both of which were recorded in the *Historia de Preliis* and its derivatives – that tell of Alexander's aerial flight and his journey to the depths of the ocean.[9] Consumed with a desire to explore the heavens, Alexander orders the construction of a flying machine consisting of a chariot surrounded by an iron grating, so that he can sit safely inside the device while in flight. Securing four griffins to the chariot with metal chains, and attaching a bait of meat to a spear that he suspends above the chariot just beyond the creatures' reach, the Macedonian king is lifted high into the heavens by the four animals. After making his celestial journey, Alexander is then overtaken by a similar desire to examine the creatures inhabiting the depths of the ocean. To achieve this end he orders his men to build a transparent glass barrel that is to be fastened with iron chains. Entering the barrel, he commands his strongest soldiers to lower it over the side of a ship into the sea, thus enabling him to view the many fish and monsters that

---

[8] Ranulf Higden, *Polychronicon Ranulphi Higden Monachi Cestrensis: Together with an English Translation of John Trevisa and an Unknown Writer of the Fifteenth Century*, ed. C. Babington and Joseph Rawson Lumby, Vol. 3 (London, 1871, rpt. 1964), Book III, Chapter 24, p. 367.

[9] These two episodes can be found in *The Wars of Alexander* (5633–80) and *The Prose Life of Alexander*, pp. 105–6. For a discussion of the artistic treatments of the story of Alexander's flight, see Victor M. Schmidt, *A Legend and Its Image: The Aerial Flight of Alexander the Great in Medieval Art* (Groningen, 1995).

live beneath the surface of the waves, and that were previously unknown to humanity.

Of course, Alexander's insatiable curiosity means that he is forever dissatisfied with his condition, constantly thirsting for yet more conquests, and a better understanding of the world. Richard Stoneman has observed that Alexander's refusal to accept the normal limits of human ambition – his desire both physically and intellectually to go 'where no man has gone before'[10] – tended, as we have seen, to provoke an ambivalent response even within the romance tradition itself. On the one hand, his restless ambition and all-consuming appetites were regarded as moral failings, which stood in stark contrast to the self-denying contentment experienced by philosophers and sages. And yet, as Stoneman has also noted, it was precisely this moral flaw in the king's character that has made him such an enduring hero, a figure who more than any other came to be seen as the embodiment of the restless, questioning, questing spirit of humanity.[11]

The confused and ambivalent response to Alexander's god-like aspirations is perhaps best encapsulated in the *Collatio Alexandri cum Dindimo*, a legendary text that describes how the Macedonian king – having travelled to the very edge of the known world – enters into a correspondence with Dindimus, the philosopher king of the Brahmans, in which they debate both the meaning of human existence, and the nature of nature itself.[12] The Brahmans of the *Collatio* are said to be a nation of Indian sages who inhabit the land lying to the east of the river Ganges, where they lead a life of extreme self-denial. The text consists of five letters, with Alexander opening and closing the correspondence, in which the two protagonists vehemently contest the merits of their respective customs and religious beliefs. Essentially, then, the *Collatio* is a dialogue in epistolary form, that debates the questions: what does it mean to be a human being, and what is the nature of humanity's relationship with the natural world.

[10] See Richard Stoneman, 'Romantic Ethnography: Central Asia and India in the Alexander Romance', *The Ancient World* 25 (1994), 93–107, pp. 95–6.

[11] See Stoneman, 'Romantic Ethnography', p. 102.

[12] The origins of the *Collatio* are obscure. It is thought that the text was originally written in either the fifth or sixth century AD, although it achieved great popularity from the eleventh century onwards after it was incorporated into the J[1] interpolated recension of the *Historia de Preliis*, from where it found its way into numerous Alexander romances. In Middle English, the correspondence is preserved in *The Wars of Alexander* (4316–841), and the *Prose Life of Alexander*, pp. 77–89. It can also be found – along with a description of Alexander's encounter with another tribe of Indian philosophers, the Gymnosophists – in a fragmentary work of alliterative verse dating from the fifteenth century, known as *Alexander B* or *Alexander and Dindimus*. See *The Alliterative Romance of Alexander and Dindimus*, ed. W. W. Skeat, EETS ES 31 (Oxford, 1878). For an account of the textual history and reception of the *Collatio*, see George Cary, 'A Note on the Medieval History of the *Collatio Alexandri cum Dindimo*', *Classica et Mediaevalia* 15 (1954), 124–9.

Alexander's fictional encounter with Dindimus would seem to have been inspired by a number of genuine meetings that he had with philosophers and wise men during his army's occupation of the Indian city of Taxila, in 326 BC. For instance, the historian Arrian tells of a conversation between Alexander and an Indian ascetic called Dandamis, who was strongly critical of the Macedonian emperor's arrogance and insatiable ambition:

> Dandamis . . . refused either to join Alexander himself or to permit any of his pupils to do so. 'If you my Lord' he is said to have replied, 'are the son of God, why – so am I. I want nothing from you, for what I have suffices. I perceive, moreover, that the men you lead get no good from their world-wide wandering over land and sea, and that of their many journeyings there is no end. I desire nothing that you can give me; I fear no exclusion from any blessing which may perhaps be yours. India, with the fruits of her soil in due season, is enough for me while I live; and when I die I shall be rid of my poor body – my unseemly housemate.[13]

This brief encounter between the world-conquering hero, whose appetite for power and glory was unquenchable, and the ascetic sage, entirely satisfied with his lot, contains the essential features of, and rehearses the same arguments as, the fictional correspondence between Alexander and Dindimus, to which I shall now turn.[14]

---

[13] See Arrian, *The Campaigns of Alexander*, Book VII, p. 350.

[14] The meeting also recalls the encounter that took place almost a decade earlier in the Greek city of Corinth between Alexander and Diogenes of Sinope, the founder of the Cynic school of philosophy. According to Plutarch's account of the incident (Plutarch, *Life of Alexander*, 14, p. 266), Alexander sought out Diogenes, whom he found lying in the sun: 'The king greeted him and inquired whether he could do anything for him. "Yes," replied the philosopher, "you can stand a little to one side of my sun." Alexander is said to have been greatly impressed by this answer and full of admiration for the hauteur and independence of mind of a man who should look down on him with such condescension. So much so that he remarked to his followers, who were laughing and mocking the philosopher as they went away, "You may say what you like, but if I were not Alexander, I would be Diogenes."' The similarity between the disdainful attitude of Diogenes, and that of the Indian sages whom Alexander encountered in Taxila, has caused some modern commentators to suggest that figures such as Dandamis (or Dindimus) were used by the historians of Alexander's reign simply as mouthpieces through which to express Cynic, and later Stoic and Christian ideas. For instance, see Beverly Berg, 'Dandamis: An Early Christian Portrait of Indian Asceticism', *Classica et Mediaevalia* 31 (1970), 269–305. However, this view is disputed by Richard Stoneman, who has argued that both historical and romance accounts of Alexander's dealings with Eastern philosophers preserve some authentic Indian details. See Richard Stoneman, 'Who are the Brahmans? Indian Lore and Cynic Doctrine in Palladius' *De Bragmanibus* and its Models', *Classical Quarterly* 44 (1994), 500–10, and 'Naked Philosophers: The Brahmans in the Alexander Historians and the Alexander Romances', *JHS* 115 (1995), 99–114.

According to the romance accounts of the correspondence, Alexander's confrontation with Dindimus occurs at the very end of his military career, after he has successfully defeated all of his adversaries.[15] With his numerous victories behind him, he continues to advance through India until he finally comes to the River Ganges, which proves impassable because of the many hippopotami, crocodiles, and scorpions that are swimming in its waters. Seeing a number of men standing on the opposite bank, Alexander calls out to them in the Indian language, and asks who they are. On hearing that they are Brahmans, he is filled with the desire to communicate with Dindimus, their king, and so, ordering the construction of a small boat built of reeds, he sends one of his knights to the opposite shore with a letter for Dindimus, in which – after referring to himself as the king of kings and the son of the god Ammon – he asks the Brahman king to explain the customs and beliefs of his people.

Dindimus responds to this letter with a letter of his own in which he claims that it would be difficult for Alexander to embrace the Brahman way of life since the manners and customs of their two peoples are very different. According to Dindimus, the Brahmans lead a simple and pure existence. They do not commit any sins and they deny themselves everything that is not absolutely necessary for the maintenance of life. The Brahmans do not practice agriculture, as they refuse to plough the soil, plant food, hunt, or fish. Instead, they eat only what nature – their bountiful mother – provides for them. The Brahmans go around naked and are able to endure physical hardship with patience and equanimity, and because they have conquered all of their internal enemies, they are not afraid of their external foes, and so lead a life entirely free from fear. The Brahmans have no need for law courts since there are no criminals for them to prosecute, and they live in a society in which everyone is equal, and everything is shared. They reject the art of rhetoric and the schools of the philosophers, choosing instead to speak and live simply, and while they do not enjoy playing games, they are able to experience wonder and delight in observing natural phenomena, taking particular pleasure in the sight of leaping dolphins, the smell of flowers, and the sound of bird song.

After expounding the ascetic philosophy of the Brahmans, Dindimus then goes on to offer a vigorous critique of Alexander's worldly way of life. He accuses Alexander of tyranny, claiming that he interferes with the course of justice, and deprives free men of their liberty. Dindimus also condemns Alexander's insatiable lust for power, arguing that although he had conquered a vast empire, the boundaries of the earth are not large enough to contain his limitless ambition. In a striking analogy, Dindimus compares Alexander to Cerberus, the canine guardian of the Underworld,

---

[15] I shall be basing my discussion of Alexander's encounter with Dindimus on the version of the correspondence found in the *Prose Life of Alexander*.

claiming that like the three headed monster of myth, the Macedonian emperor is completely incapable of satisfying his voracious appetite, however much he might consume.

Having condemned Alexander for his boundless ambition, Dindimus then launches a fierce attack upon the Greek gods, whose sinful deeds both encourage and justify immoral behaviour in humanity. Dindimus argues that Alexander is completely in thrall to these wicked gods, and that he is driven by their example to commit ever more lewd and depraved acts. In contrast to the idolatry of Alexander, Dindimus claims that the Brahmans have rejected the Greek gods in favour of the one true God who reigns in heaven. Finally, after completing his denunciation of Alexander's religious beliefs, Dindimus concludes his letter by declaring that in the life to come, the Macedonian emperor is destined to suffer grievous torments as a punishment for his sins.

George Cary has shown that Dindimus – with his strict ascetic practices, emphatic rejection of the Greek gods, and unstinting espousal of monotheism – came to be viewed by the medieval readers of the *Collatio* as a figure who offered a recognisably Christian alternative to the worldly, pagan values that were embodied by Alexander.[16] This specifically Christian interpretation of Dindimus and the Brahmans can also be found in *The Book of Sir John Mandeville*, an extremely popular (although entirely fictitious) mid-fourteenth-century account of an imaginary English knight's journey through the Holy Land and the East.[17] The Brahmans are praised by the author of *Mandeville's Travels* for worshipping the one true God, observing the ten commandments, and abstaining from every kind of sin,[18] and having enunciated their proto-Christian credentials, the author goes on to claim that as a reward for their moral purity and religious observance, God has made their land more blessed than the territory of any other people:

[16] See Cary, 'A Note on the Medieval History of the *Collatio Alexandri cum Dindimo*', pp. 126–9. For instance, Cary cites Peter Abelard's *Introductio ad Theologiam* (*PL* 178: 1033–4), in which Dindimus is said to have been one of the four pre-Christian kings (along with David, Solomon, and Nebuchadnezzar), who foresaw the coming of Christ.

[17] Almost the only thing that can be said with any certainty about the author of *The Book of Sir John Mandeville* is that he was not called Sir John Mandeville. The text was originally written in French in 1357, although translations into Latin and the vernacular languages of Western Europe (including several Middle English versions) soon followed. For a discussion of the relationship between the different Middle English versions, see M. C. Seymour, *English Writers of the Late Middle Ages: Sir John Mandeville* (Aldershot, 1993). All references will be to Seymour's edition of the so-called Cotton version (London, British Library, MS Cotton Titus C. xvi), which was written at the beginning of the fifteenth century. See *Mandeville's Travels*, ed. M. C. Seymour (Oxford, 1967).

[18] See *Mandeville's Travels*, Chapter 32, pp. 211–12.

And because thei ben so trewe and so rightfulle and so fulle of alle gode condicouns, thei weren neuere greued with tempestes ne with thonder ne with leyt ne with hayl ne with pestylence ne with werre ne with hunger ne with non other tribulacioun as wee ben many tymes amonges vs for our synnes. Wherefore it semeth wel that God loueth hem and is plesed with hire creance for hire gode dedes.[19]

The description of the land of the Brahmans in both the *Collatio* and *Mandeville's Travels* would appear to owe something to the tradition of the Earthly Paradise, for in both texts Dindimus and his people are shown leading a life of innocence and holiness similar to that enjoyed by Adam and Eve in the Garden of Eden, before nature and humanity had suffered the corruption of the Fall. Like Eden, the world of the Brahmans is one entirely without conflict or struggle, in which all creatures live in harmony with one another, and have their needs supplied by the bounty of the earth. It is perhaps for this reason that – from the point of view of the fallen world – Dindimus's account of Brahman society seems to be both utopian and unobtainable, and why Dindimus himself appears to possess a very different nature from, and inhabit an alternative world to, Alexander and the Greeks.[20]

It is Dindimus's wholly benign conception of the natural world, and his somewhat naive understanding of humanity's place within it, that Alexander criticises most forcefully in his response to the Brahman king. According to Alexander, if what Dindimus says is true, then only the

---

[19] *Mandeville's Travels*, Chapter 32, p. 212. The rather more diffuse treatment of this theme can be found in *The Prose Life of Alexander*, pp. 78–83.

[20] This identification of the land of the Brahmans with the Earthly Paradise is further suggested by its geographical location on the eastern bank of the River Ganges, which was traditionally believed to have been one of the four rivers that flowed from the Garden of Eden. For instance, St Jerome – in a letter to a certain young monk called Rusticus – identified the Ganges with the River Phison, which according to Scriptures (Genesis 2: 11) had its source in Paradise. See St Jerome, 'Letter CXXV: "To Rusticus"', in *Select Letters of St Jerome*, ed. and trans. F. A. Wright (London, 1933), pp. 402–3. Drawing on the traditional Western view of India as a place of wonder, Jerome (p. 403) went on to describe the territory surrounding the Ganges in a way that echoes the marvellous depictions of India found in the Alexander romances: 'This land is the home of the carbuncle and the emerald, and those gleaming pearls which our great ladies so ardently desire. There are also in it mountains of gold which men cannot approach because of the dragons and griffins and other huge monsters set there to show us what sort of guardians avarice employs.' A Jewish legend of Alexander that bears no direct relation to the romances, but which was nonetheless translated into Latin some time during the twelfth century under the title *Alexandri Magni Iter ad Paradisum* (*The Journey to Paradise of Alexander the Great*), describes how the Macedonian king actually discovered the site of the Earthly Paradise on an island in the River Ganges, but was prevented from entering the sacred land by the high wall that surrounded it. See *Alexander the Great's Journey to Paradise*, in Richard Stoneman, ed. and trans. *Legends of Alexander the Great* (London, 1994), pp. 67–75.

Brahmans are good men, and every activity undertaken by the Greeks is sinful. Indeed, Alexander declares that it is impossible for the Brahmans to follow human nature, since their beliefs and practices force them to condemn all those activities that are habitually carried out by human beings. However, Alexander claims that in reality it is poverty and not choice that determine the simple and austere life of the Brahmans. As proof of this contention he points out that they are such a primitive and impoverished people that they have not yet acquired a knowledge of agriculture. Alexander therefore regards their simplicity as contemptible, and he compares their dependence upon plants to the predicament of hungry cattle. He argues that unlike the Brahmans – who idealise poverty and self-denial – it is admirable to practise moderation and self-control amid one's wealth

Furthermore, Alexander considers that the unwillingness of the Brahmans to study philosophy provides yet more proof of their inhuman lack of ambition, and their kinship with the beasts. He claims that for rational men with free will, life offers many pleasures, yet because the world is forever changing, unhappiness is an unavoidable condition of human existence, and that sadness inevitably follows joy. Alexander believes that there are many harmless, sensual activities that can lead to human happiness such as singing, dancing, and eating. In addition, all the abundant produce of the earth is available for human consumption. Therefore, a figure like Dindimus who abstains from worldly pleasures is either too proud to accept such abundant gifts, or envious that they have been more generously bestowed elsewhere. Thus, Alexander concludes his letter by arguing that Dindimus's life of self-denial owes more to folly than to wisdom.

Perhaps what is most striking about this letter is that Alexander reveals himself to be not the debauched and decadent figure portrayed by Dindimus, but a rather reasonable spokesman for 'decent' and 'moderate' worldly values. Unlike Dindimus, Alexander sees nothing sinful in satisfying the desires of the body. On the contrary, he rejects the Brahman way of life precisely because he believes that the renunciation of sensual pleasure constitutes a denial of one's humanity. For Alexander, then, the Brahmans are reduced by their life of abstinence to the level and condition of the beasts.

In his final letter, Dindimus rejects the worldliness of Alexander by arguing that humans are not the masters of the world, with rights of ownership and permanent residence, but merely pilgrims passing through life on a journey to their lasting place of abode. However, Dindimus claims that the Greeks are so bloated with wealth and pride that they have forgotten that they are mortal, and actually believe themselves to be gods. After roundly condemning Alexander for his pride, Dindimus then accuses the Macedonian emperor of avarice. He argues that gold and silver are utterly worthless since they can neither sustain the body nor save the soul. Moreover, unlike food that satisfies hunger, and water that quenches the thirst, gold is especially pernicious because the more of it one possesses, the more covetous one becomes.

Alexander is equally combative and uncompromising in his final letter. He tells Dindimus that as a consequence of their refusal or inability to travel, the Brahmans have failed to mix with people from other nations, and so have remained confined within their own land as though incarcerated in prison. He therefore argues that the Brahmans suffer the same torments that the Greeks impose on their prisoners, and he concludes by claiming to mourn for the wretched and miserable lives that they are forced to endure. After completing this last letter of the correspondence, Alexander raises a large pillar of marble which marks the furthest limit of his empire, on which he inscribes a brief account of his many achievements.

This final act of Alexander is full of symbolic meaning. In a sense, the pillar is an emblem that both triumphantly proclaims the full extent of his worldly achievements, while at the same time establishing a boundary beyond which he does not, or cannot, pass. Thus, in the same way that the opinions of Alexander and Dindimus are fundamentally irreconcilable, so their worlds do not meet. This complete failure of Alexander and Dindimus to resolve their differences is one of the most interesting features of the correspondence. The *Collatio* is not a dialogue between an evidently correct and incorrect point of view, and the text refuses to condemn the values of either participant, but treats both protagonists as exponents of equally legitimate and coherent philosophies.

This refusal of the text to proclaim either protagonist a winner – despite the fact that Dindimus clearly represents a proto-Christian point of view – unsettled many of the medieval writers who referred to the encounter, and it prompted some authors to rewrite the dialogue in a more didactic, less open-ended way. For instance, Ranulf Higden devoted four chapters of the *Polychronicon* to the life of Alexander (Book III, Chapters 27–30), one of which (Chapter 29) is concerned with the Macedonian emperor's encounter with Dindimus.[21] In Higden's account, Dindimus both initiates and concludes the correspondence, and it is his opinions that are clearly intended to be seen as correct. Indeed, Higden's Dindimus is invested with such natural authority that Alexander emerges from the debate a completely broken man; he is forced by the unwavering moral integrity of the Brahman king to concede defeat, and admit to leading a miserable and fearful life. After making this confession, Alexander offers Dindimus an array of expensive

[21] See *Polychronicon Ranulphi Higden Monachi Cestrensis*, Vol. 3, Book III, Chapter 24, pp. 454–79. Higden's treatment of this episode is also discussed by Gerrit Bunt in his useful survey of Middle English Alexander literature. See Gerrit H. V. Bunt, *Alexander the Great in the Literature of Medieval Britain*, pp. 37–8.

presents as a sign of his esteem, but the only gift that Dindimus is prepared to accept is oil, which he immediately throws onto the fire. Of course, the radical changes that are introduced by Higden, changes that greatly alter both the tone and meaning of the correspondence, actually demonstrate just how genuine a balance is maintained between the two protagonists in the *Collatio*, a fact that is all the more remarkable considering the profound importance to a medieval audience of the issues under debate.

Although the *Collatio* is a text in which theological concerns feature very prominently – with the idealised figures of Alexander and Dindimus representing an active, worldly paganism on the one hand, and a contemplative, ascetic Christianity on the other – the correspondence is not exclusively concerned with narrowly religious issues, for it can also be seen as a debate between two fundamentally different ways of thinking about the natural world, and humanity's place within it. Thus, the attitude of Alexander and the Greeks, who see nature not only as an arena of struggle and conflict between humans and animals, but also as a vast reservoir of resources to be used by human beings for their own benefit, is placed in direct opposition to the reverential, self-denying view of the Brahmans, who abstain on principle from any interference with, or exploitation of, what Dindimus refers to as, 'þe erthe oure allere moder'.[22] Dindimus's conception of the underlying harmony of all living things is reflected in his account of Brahman society, which is entirely lacking in any form of violence or human conflict, while for Alexander on the other hand, the inherent harshness of the natural world has a salutary effect on human nature, forcing individuals to use their intelligence and ingenuity to better their natural condition, thus enabling them to rise above the level of the beasts. Moreover, by cultivating human intelligence through the study of philosophy – something that the Brahmans conspicuously fail to do – Alexander claims that the Greeks have not only acquired the necessary skills with which to overcome the challenges of life, but that they have also gained the intellectual capacity to make moral and aesthetic judgements, a capacity that – according to Alexander – the Brahmans (along with animals) do not possess:

> 3e hafe na liste to studie aboute lerynge, ne 3e seke na mercy ne does nane till oþer. And all this 3e hafe in comon wit beste3. For ri3te as beste3 hase nowþer reson ne discrecion, ne hase na felynge of gode, ri3te so þay hafe na delite in gode.[23]

In the *Collatio*, then, the familiar aspects of Alexander's reputation – his insatiable ambition, his love of learning, and his determination to gain

[22] *The Prose Life of Alexander*, p. 79.
[23] *The Prose Life of Alexander*, p. 86.

145

ascendancy over both humans and animals – are once again in evidence. Significantly however, for the first time in his career the Macedonian emperor is confronted by an adversary whom he is not able to defeat. Dindimus's respect for the sanctity of the natural world is profoundly at odds with Alexander's wish to dominate and exploit it, and their ensuing debate – in which both parties powerfully advance their positions, and from which neither emerges victorious – provided the extensive medieval audience of the Alexander romances with both the opportunity, and the conceptual framework within which, to reflect upon humanity's relationship with the natural world.

Conclusion:
Representing Nature in Medieval Literature

TO the modern scholar, particularly one investigating medieval attitudes towards the natural world, one of the most interesting and revealing features of the *Collatio Alexandri cum Dindimo* is the actual dialogic form in which the narrative is cast. For, in bringing together two conflicting and mutually exclusive accounts of humanity's relationship with the natural world, and exploring each in sufficient detail to establish their philosophical coherence and legitimacy, the text demonstrates that the culture of the late Middle Ages was capable of speaking with more than one voice when it came to debating humanity's place within the wider world of nature. While the opinions of Alexander the Great – who claims that human beings are the undisputed masters of creation, and as such are entitled to exploit its abundant resources for their own ends – reflects the anthropocentric world view that characterises so many late-medieval texts, the same cannot be said for Dindimus, whose reverence for the natural world makes him see any human interference in its processes as a violation of its sanctity. Of course, as Richard Stoneman has suggested, the great respect that Dindimus accords to all forms of life may reflect the fact that the *Collatio* preserves some of the authentic opinions of the various Eastern philosophers – whether Buddhist, Hindu, or Jain – whom Alexander actually encountered on his Indian campaign.[1] However, whatever Dindimus's origins, it is significant that medieval writers such as Peter Abelard and Ranulf Higden seem to have held him in high esteem, and interpreted his harmonious relationship with the natural world in the light of Christian tradition, seeing it as evidence of his pre-lapsarian innocence and holiness.

The opposition between the self-assertive, secular attitude of Alexander, and the self-denying, proto-Christian view of Dindimus, draws attention to perhaps the central feature of this study; the crucial role that was played by the two narrative genres of hagiography and romance in determining how animals and the natural world were portrayed in the imaginative literature of the period. As we have seen, one of the key ideas that underpinned the treatment of the animal kingdom in the early Lives

---

[1] See Richard Stoneman's two articles on the historical and romance accounts of Alexander's meeting with the Brahmans: 'Who are the Brahmans? Indian Lore and Cynic Doctrine in Palladius' *De Bragmanibus* and Its Models', *Classical Quarterly* 44 (1994), 500–10, and 'Naked Philosophers: The Brahmans in the Alexander Historians and the Alexander Romances', *JHS* 115 (1995), 99–114.

of Francis of Assisi was the belief that the saint's remarkable purity and innocence enabled him to re-establish the state of peace and harmony that had originally been enjoyed by Adam, Eve, and the animals in the Garden of Eden before the Fall. Francis's extraordinary affinity with the animal kingdom was therefore presented by his biographers as a sign of the very high favour in which he was held by God.

Because hagiography enjoyed such high cultural prestige during the later Middle Ages, saintly virtues (such as penitence and humility) proved to be just as important to many of the heroes of romance as the more conventionally heroic attributes of nobility and courage. For instance, as we saw in Part 2, Sir Gowther's sanctity is integral to his role as a knightly hero, and one of the ways in which he manifests his holiness is through his relationship with dogs. Thus, the hagiographical motif of the return to Paradise was used extensively in the canon of Middle English romance to suggest that the secular qualities of the aristocratic hero were closely related to, and merged imperceptibly with, the religious characteristics of the saint. However, as well as using the animal kingdom to indicate that holiness was an essential component of a knight's identity, a very different set of ideas about animals – and their relationship to humanity – was invoked by the authors of the same Middle English romances. Reflecting the class divisions within feudal society, the animal kingdom is presented in *Sir Isumbras*, *Sir Gowther*, *Octavian*, and *Sir Orfeo* as profoundly hierarchical in structure. Those beasts especially favoured by the aristocracy – such as lions, falcons, greyhounds, and horses – are identified as inherently noble in nature, and thus are seen to share not only a natural sense of empathy with their counterparts in the human world, but also a common feeling of superiority to all creatures – whether human or animal – of low degree.

These two fundamentally different ways in which animals are represented and understood in the hagiographical and romance literature of the period – the one ostensibly spiritual, the other social – present us with some rather unexpected conclusions. As we have seen, St Francis's modern reputation as a lover of animals and nature is to a very great extent based on an anachronistic misreading of the early sources. Francis and his medieval biographers tended to value creatures not for their own sake, but as objects that reflected, partook of, and pointed towards the goodness of God, their Creator. However, this failure of Francis to engage with the animalness of the various animals he encountered stands in contrast to the experience of at least some of the protagonists of the romances that I have examined. For instance, Florent, one of the two young heroes of *Octavian*, displays a genuine sense of affection for the falcon that he purchases with his adoptive father's money. Of course, Florent's fondness for the 'aristocratic' bird is used by the poet as a device to draw attention to the prince's own innately noble nature, a nature which – in spite of the humble circumstances in which he finds himself – cannot be suppressed. However, what members of the medieval aristocracy (even fictional ones like Florent) prized in falcons, and what led to the bird's identification as a noble creature, was its power, speed, and sleekness: the very qualities that made it such an efficient hunter of prey. This sense of an authentic engagement with the falcon *qua* falcon is also evident in the scene in *Sir Orfeo*, where the eponymous hero chances upon the hawking party in the wilderness, and laughs for sheer joy at witnessing the skill and proficiency with which the avian predators dispatch their game. Thus, it is the potency and ruthlessness of the falcon – rather than any symbolic qualities that it might possess – that is admired by Florent and Orfeo; a fact that tells us much about the values and self-image of the medieval aristocracy.

Finally, perhaps what this study has demonstrated most definitively is the sheer multiplicity of representations of, and attitudes towards, animals and nature that are to be found in medieval literature. In the different narratives I have examined, animals perform a range of symbolic, allegorical, and mimetic functions, although the divisions between these categories are sometimes difficult to draw. Thus, St Francis treated real animals such as pigs, goats, and sheep as though they were religious symbols enacting a spiritual drama within the book of nature, while the story of Alexander's miraculous conception and birth – involving as it does a dragon that is at one and the same time a figment of a dream, a man dressed in a dragon costume, and a genuine fire-breathing monster – resists all attempts at classification. The abundance and complexity of such images would seem to indicate that both the producers and consumers of medieval literature were capable of engaging with the natural world in a rich and varied way. While this study has in no way exhausted the range and diversity of representations of animals in medieval culture, it has demonstrated that the commonplace view of the Middle Ages as unified and simplistic in its outlook is misconceived.

Bibliography

Primary Sources

Abbo of Fleury. *Life of St Edmund*, in Michael Winterbottom, ed. *Three Lives of English Saints* (Toronto, 1972), pp. 65–87.

Actus Beati Francisci et Sociorum Eius, ed. Paul Sabatier (Paris, 1902).

Alexander A, in *The Romance of William of Palerne*, ed. W. W. Skeat, EETS ES 1 (London, 1867).

Alexander's Letter to Aristotle about India, trans. Lloyd Gunderson (Meisenheim am Glan, 1980).

Alexander the Great's Journey to Paradise, in *Legends of Alexander the Great*, ed. and trans. Richard Stoneman (London, 1994), pp. 67–75.

The Alliterative Romance of Alexander and Dindimus, ed. W. W. Skeat, EETS ES 31 (London, 1878).

Ancrene Wisse: The English Text of the Ancrene Riwle, ed. J. R. R. Tolkien, EETS OS 249 (London, 1962).

Arrian. *The Campaigns of Alexander*, trans. Aubrey de Sélincourt (Harmondsworth, 1971).

St Athanasius. *The Life of St Anthony*, trans. Sister Mary Emily Keenan, in Roy J. Deferrari, ed. *Early Christian Biographies*, The Fathers of the Church, Vol. 15 (Washington, 1952), pp. 125–216.

St Augustine. *Concerning the City of God against the Pagans*, trans. Henry Bettenson (Harmondsworth, 1984).

Aulus Gellius. *The Attic Nights of Aulus Gellius*, 3 Vols, ed. and trans. John C. Rolfe (London, 1927).

Bede. *Life of Cuthbert*, trans. J. F. Webb, in J. F. Webb, ed. *Lives of the Saints* (Harmondsworth, 1965).

Benson, Larry D. ed. *King Arthur's Death: The Middle English Stanzaic Morte Arthure and Alliterative Morte Arthure* (Indianapolis, 1974).

Boethius. *The Consolation of Philosophy*, ed. and trans. H. P. Stewart and E. K. Rand (London, 1918).

St Bonaventure. *The Major Life of St Francis*, The Classics of Western Spirituality, trans. Ewert Cousins (New York, 1978).

——*Major and Minor Life of St Francis with Excerpts from Other Works*, trans. Benen Fahy, in Marion A. Habig, ed. *St Francis of Assisi, Writings and Early Biographies: English Omnibus of the Sources for the Life of St Francis of Assisi*, 4th edn (Chicago, 1991), pp. 789–831.

Caesarius of Heisterbach. *The Dialogue on Miracles*, 2 Vols, trans. H. von E. Scott and C. C. Swinton Bland (London, 1929).

Caxton, William. *The Book of the Ordre of Chyualry*, ed. A. T. P. Byles, EETS OS 168 (London, 1926).

——*Caxton's Aesop*, ed. R. T. Lenaghan (Cambridge Massachusetts, 1967).

Chaucer, Geoffrey. *The Riverside Chaucer*, ed. Larry D. Benson *et al.* (Oxford, 1987).

Cheuelere Assigne, ed. Henry H. Gibbs, EETS ES (London, 1868, rpt. 1932).

Chronica XXIV Generalium, in *Analecta Franciscana* 3 (Quaracchi, 1897), 1–575.

Curtius Rufus, Quintus. *The History of Alexander*, trans. John Yardley (Harmondsworth, 1984).

Brother Elias. 'The Letter of Brother Elias', trans. Marion A. Habig, in Marion A. Habig, ed *St Francis of Assisi, Writings and Early Biographies: English Omnibus of the Sources for the Life of St Francis of Assisi*, 4th edn (Chicago, 1991), pp. 1955–60.

Euripides. *The Bacchae and Other Plays: Ion, The Women of Troy, Helen, The Bacchae*, trans. Philip Vellacott (Harmondsworth, 1954).

St Francis. *The Writings of St Francis*, trans. Benen Fahy, in Marion A. Habig, ed. *St Francis of Assisi, Writings and Early Biographies: English Omnibus of the Sources for the Life of St Francis of Assisi*, 4th edn (Chicago, 1991), pp. 1–175.

Geoffroi de Charny. *The Book of Chivalry of Geoffroi de Charny: Text, Context, and Translation*, ed. and trans. Richard W. Kaeuper and Elspeth Kennedy (Philadelphia, 1996).

Gower, John. *The Complete Works of John Gower: English Works*, ed. G. C. Macaulay, EETS ES 81, 82 (London, 1901).

The Greek Alexander Romance, ed. and trans. Richard Stoneman (Harmondsworth, 1991).

St Gregory the Great. *Dialogues*, trans. Odo John Zimmerman, The Fathers of the Church, Vol. 39 (New York, 1959).

Guy of Warwick, ed. J. Zupizza, EETS ES 42, 49, 59 (London 1883–91).

Henry, Archdeacon of Huntingdon. *Historia Anglorum*, ed. and trans. Diana Greenway (Oxford, 1996).

Hieronymus noster, in *PL* 22: 175–84.

Higden, Ranulf. *Polychronicon Ranulphi Higden Monachi Cestrensis: Together with the English Translations of John Trevisa and of an Unknown Author of the Fifteenth Century*, ed. C. Babington and J. Lumby, 9 Vols (London, 1865–6, rpt. 1964).

Horrall, Sarah M. ed. *The Southern Version of Cursor Mundi* Vol. I (Ottawa, 1978).

Jacobus of Voragine. *The Golden Legend of Jacobus de Voragine*, trans. Granger Ryan and Helmut Ripperger (London, 1941).

Jacques de Longuyon. *Les Voeux de Paon*, ed. R. L. G. Ritchie, in *The Buik of Alexander*, STS 12, 17, 21, 25 (Edinburgh, 1921–9).

St Jerome. *Select Letters of St Jerome*, ed. and trans. F. A. Wright (London, 1933).

—— *The Life of St Paul the First Hermit*, trans. Sister Marie Liguori Ewald, in Roy J. Deferrari, ed. *Early Christian Biographies*, The Fathers of the Church, Vol. 15 (Washington, 1952), pp. 217–38.

—— *The Life of St Hilarion*, trans. Sister Marie Liguori Ewald, in Roy J. Deferrari, ed. *Early Christian Biographies*, The Fathers of the Church, Vol. 15 (Washington, 1952), pp. 239–80.

—— *The Life of Malchus*, trans. Sister Marie Liguori Ewald, in Roy J.

Deferrari, ed. *Early Christian Biographies*, The Fathers of the Church, Vol 15. (Washington, 1952), pp. 281–97.

Jordan of Giano. *The Chronicle of Brother Jordan of Giano*, trans. E. Gurney Salter, in E. Gurney Salter, ed. *The Coming of the Friars Minor to England and Germany* (London, 1926), pp. 127–90.

Kyng Alisaunder, ed. G. V. Smithers, EETS OS 227, 237 (London, 1952–7).

Langland, William. *The Vision of Piers Plowman: A Complete Edition of the B Text*, ed. A. V. C. Schmidt (London, 1987).

The Legend of Perugia, trans. Paul Oligny, in Marion A. Habig, ed. *St Francis of Assisi, Writings and Early Biographies: English Omnibus of the Sources for the Life of St Francis of Assisi*, 4th edn (Chicago, 1991), pp. 957–1101.

The Legend of the Three Companions, trans. Nesta de Robeck, in Marion A. Habig, ed. *St Francis of Assisi, Writings and Early Biographies: English Omnibus of the Sources for the Life of St Francis of Assisi*, 4th edn (Chicago, 1991), pp. 853–956.

Leo of Naples. *Historia de Preliis Alexandri Magni*, trans. Dennis M. Kratz, in Dennis M. Kratz, ed. *The Romances of Alexander* (New York, 1991).

Life of Friar Juniper, in T. Okey, trans. *The Little Flowers of St Francis* (London, 1910), pp. 134–47.

Lindsay, Sir David. *Sir David Lindsay's Works: The Minor Poems*, ed. J. A. H. Murray, EETS OS 47 (London, 1871).

The Little Flowers of St Francis, trans. Raphael Brown, in Marion A. Habig, ed. *St Francis of Assisi, Writings and Early Biographies: English Omnibus of the Sources for the Life of St Francis of Assisi*, 4th edn (Chicago, 1991), pp. 1267–530.

Livy. *The Early History of Rome: Books I–V of The History of Rome From Its Foundations*, trans. Aubrey de Sélincourt (Harmondsworth, 1960).

Lybeaus Desconus, ed. M. Mills, EETS OS 261 (London, 1969).

Malory, Thomas. *Works*, 2nd edn, ed. Eugene Vinaver (Oxford, 1971).

Mandeville's Travels, ed. M. C. Seymour (Oxford, 1967).

Marie de France. *Lais*, ed. Alfred Ewert (Oxford, 1960).

—— *The Lais of Marie de France*, trans. Glyn S. Burgess and Keith Busby (Harmondsworth, 1986).

—— *Fables*, ed. and trans. Harriet Spiegel (Toronto, 1987).

The Middle English Dictionary, ed. Hans Kurath *et al.* (Ann Arbor, Michigan, 1956–).

The Middle English Letter of Alexander to Aristotle, ed. Vincent DiMarco and Leslie Perelman, in *Essays on English and American Language and Literature* n.s. 13 (1978).

The Mirror of Perfection, trans. Leo Shirley Porter, in Marion A. Habig, ed. *St Francis of Assisi, Writings and Early Biographies: English Omnibus of the Sources for the Life of St Francis of Assisi*, 4th edn (Chicago, 1991), pp. 1103–265.

Moschus, Joannes. *Vita Abbatis Gerasimi*, in *Pratum Spirituale*, in *PL* 74: 172–4.

Octovian, ed. Frances McSparran, EETS OS 289 (London, 1986).

Octovian Imperator, ed. Frances McSparran, Middle English Texts 11 (Heidelberg, 1979).

Orosius, Paulus. *The Seven Books of History against the Pagans*, trans. Roy J. Deferrari (Washington, 1964).

Ovid. *Metamorphoses*, trans. Mary M. Innes (Harmondsworth, 1955).

The Oxford English Dictionary, 2nd edn, prepared by J. A. Simpson and E. S. C. Weiner, 20 Vols (Oxford, 1989).

The Parlement of the Thre Ages, ed. M. Y. Offord, EETS OS 246 (Oxford, 1959).

Perry, Ben Edwin, ed. and trans. *Babrius and Phaedrus*, Loeb Classical Library (Cambridge Massachusetts, 1965).

Plato. *The Republic of Plato*, trans. Francis MacDonald Cornford (Oxford, 1941).

Plerosque nimirum, in *PL* 22: 201–14.

Plutarch. *The Life of Alexander*, trans. Ian Scott-Kilvert, in Plutarch. *The Age of Alexander* (Harmondsworth, 1973), pp. 252–334.

The Poems of the Pearl Manuscript: Pearl, Cleanness, Patience, Sir Gawain and the Green Knight, ed. Malcolm Andrew and Ronald Waldron (London, 1978).

Polo, Marco. *The Book of Ser Marco Polo the Venetian Concerning the Kingdoms and Marvels of the East*, 2 Vols, ed. and trans. Henry Yule, 3rd edn (London, 1903).

The Prose Life of Alexander from the Thornton Manuscript, ed. J. S. Westlake, EETS OS 143 (London, 1913).

Rilke, Rainer Maria. *Orpheus, Eurydike, Hermes*, in J. B. Lieshman, ed. and trans. *Rainer Maria Rilke, New Poems* (London, 1964), pp. 142–7.

——*Sonnets to Orpheus*, in A. Poulin Jr, ed. and trans. *Diuno Elegies and Sonnets to Orpheus* (Boston, 1977).

Robert of Sicily, in Walter Hoyt French and Charles Brockway Hale, ed. *Middle English Metrical Romances*, Vol. 2 (New York, 1964), pp. 931–46.

Scripta Leonis, Rufini et Angeli Sociorum S. Francisci, ed. and trans. Rosalind B. Brooke (Oxford, 1970).

Seutonius, *The Twelve Caesars*, trans. Robert Graves (Harmondsworth, rev edn, 1979).

Shakespeare, William. *The Merchant of Venice*, ed. M. M. Mahood (Cambridge, 1987).

——*Henry IV Part 1*, ed. David Bevington (Oxford, 1987).

——*Macbeth*, ed. Kenneth Muir (London, 1962).

Sir Beues of Hamtoun, ed. Eugen Kölbing, EETS ES 46, 48, 65 (London, 1885–94).

Sir Cleges, in Walter Hoyt French and Charles Brockway Hale, ed. *Middle English Metrical Romances*, Vol. 2 (New York, 1964), pp. 875–930.

Sir Degaré, in Anne Laskaya and Eve Salisbury, ed. *The Middle English Breton Lays* (Kalamazoo, 1995), pp. 89–144.

Sir Gowther (MS Advocates), in Anne Laskaya and Eve Salisbury, ed. *The Middle English Breton Lays* (Kalamazoo, 1995), pp. 263–307.

Sir Gowther (Royal MS), in Thomas C. Rumble, ed. *The Breton Lays in Middle English* (Detroit, 1965).

Sir Isumbras, in Madwyn Mills, ed. *Six Middle English Romances* (London, 1973).

Sir Isumbras, in Harriet Hudson, ed. *Four Middle English Romances: Sir Isumbras, Octavian, Sir Eglamour of Artois, Sir Tryamour* (Kalamazoo, 1996).

Sir Orfeo, ed. A. J. Bliss. 2nd edn (Oxford, 1966).

Sir Orfeo, in Anne Laskaya and Eve Salisbury, ed. *The Middle English Breton Lays* (Kalamazoo, 1995), pp. 15–59.

Sir Perceval of Galles, in Mary Flowers Braswell, ed. *Sir Perceval of Galles and Ywain and Gawain* (Kalamazoo, 1995), pp. 1–76.

Sir Tristrem, ed. G. P. McNeill, STS 8 (Edinburgh, 1886).

St: for saints, see under given name.

Thomas of Celano. *The First Life of St Francis*, trans. Placid Hermann, in Marion A. Habig, ed. S*t. Francis of Assisi, Writings and Early Biographies: English Omnibus of the Sources for the Life of St Francis of Assisi*, 4th edn (Chicago, 1991), pp. 225–355.

—— *Legenda ad Usum Chori*, in *Analecta Franciscana* 10 (1941).

—— *The Second Life of St Francis*, trans. Placid Hermann, in Marion A. Habig, ed. *St Francis of Assisi, Writings and Early Biographies: English Omnibus of the Sources for the Life of St Francis of Assisi*, 4th edn (Chicago, 1991), pp. 357–543.

—— *Treatise on the Miracles of Blessed Francis*, trans. Placid Hermann, in Marion A. Habig, ed. *St Francis of Assisi, Writings and Early Biographies: English Omnibus of the Sources for the Life of St Francis of Assisi*, 4th edn (Chicago, 1991), pp. 545–611.

Thomas of Eccleston. *On the Coming of the Friars Minor to England*, trans. E. Gurney Salter, in E. Gurney Salter, ed. *The Coming of the Friars Minor to England and Germany* (London, 1926), pp. 1–126.

Thomas of Kent. *The Anglo-Norman 'Alexander' (Le Roman de Toute Chevalerie)*, ed. B. Foster, ANTS 29, 31 (London, 1976).

Three Old English Prose Texts: Letter of Alexander the Great, Wonders of the East, Life of St Christopher, ed. Stanley Rypins, EETS OS 161 (Oxford, 1924).

Vincent of Beauvais. *De Vita et Actibus Sancti Hieronymi Presbyteri et Gestis Eiusdem*, in *Speculum Historiale Vincentii* (Venice, 1494), Book XVI, Chaps. 18–88, and 92–93, Fols. 198–207.

Virgil. *Georgics*, trans. L. P. Wilkinson (Harmondsworth, 1982).

Vita Fratris Juniperi, in *Analecta Franciscana* 3 (Quaracchi, 1897), pp. 54–64.

Von Strassburg, Gottfried. *Tristan*, trans. A. T. Hatto (Harmondsworth, 1967).

Waddell, Helen, trans. *Beasts and Saints* (London, 1934).

The Wars of Alexander, ed. Hoyt N. Duggan and Thorlac Turville-Petre, EETS SS 10 (Oxford, 1989).

William of England, in *The Complete Romances of Chrétien de Troyes*, trans. David Staines (Bloomington and Indianapolis, 1990).

Ywain and Gawain, ed. A. B. Friedman and N. T. Harrington, EETS OS 254 (London, 1964).

Secondary Sources.

Aerts, W. J., E. R. Smits, and J. B. Voorbij, ed. *Vincent of Beauvais and Alexander the Great: Studies in the Speculum Maius and its Translations into Medieval Vernaculars* (Groningen, 1988).

Allen, Dorena. 'Orpheus and Orfeo: the Dead and the Taken', *Medium Aevum* 33 (1964), 102–11.

Anderson, Andrew Runni. 'Bucephalas and his Legend', *American Journal of Philology* 51 (1930), 1–21.

Anderson, W. S. 'The Orpheus of Virgil and Ovid: *flebile nescio quid*', in Warden, John, ed. *Orpheus: The Metamorphoses of a Myth* (Toronto, 1982), pp. 25–50.

Armstrong, Edward A. *Saint Francis, Nature Mystic: The Derivation and Significance of the Nature Stories in the Franciscan Legend* (Berkeley, 1973).

Arnold, David. *The Problem of Nature: Environment, Culture and European Expansion* (Oxford, 1996).

Baldwin, Dean R. 'Fairy Lore and the Meaning of *Sir Orfeo*', *Southern Folklore Quarterly* 41 (1977), 129–42.

Barron, W. R. J. *English Medieval Romance* (London, 1987).

Baxeandall, Michael. *Painting and Experience in Fifteenth-Century Italy: A Primer in the Social History of Pictorial Style* (Oxford, 1988).

Berg, Beverly. 'Dandamis: An Early Christian Portrait of Indian Asceticism', *Classica et Mediaevalia* 31 (1970), 269–305.

Bergner, H. '*Sir Orfeo* and the Sacred Bonds of Matrimony', *Review of English Studies* n.s. 30 (1979), 432–4.

Beston, John B. 'How Much Was Known of the Breton Lai in Fourteenth-Century Engaland?', in Benson, Larry D., ed. *The Learned and the Lewed: Studies in Chaucer and Medieval Literature* (Cambridge Massachusetts, 1974), pp. 319–36.

Bishop, Morris. *Saint Francis of Assisi* (Boston, 1974).

Bloomfield, Morton W. 'Episodic Motivation and Marvels in Epic and Romance', in *Essays and Explorations: Studies in Ideas, Language, and Literature* (Cambridge Massachusetts, 1970).

Bordman, Gerald. *Motif Index of the English Metrical Romances* (Helsinki, 1963).

Bosworth, A. B. *Conquest and Empire: The Reign of Alexander the Great* (Cambridge, 1988).

Bradstock, E. M. 'The Penitential Pattern of *Sir Gowther*', *Parergon* 20 (1974), 3–10.

——'*Sir Gowther*: Secular Hagiography or Hagiographical Romance or Neither?', *AUMLA* 59 (1983), 26–47.

Braswell, L. '*Sir Isumbras* and the Legend of Saint Eustace', *Medieval Studies* 27 (1965), 128–51.

Brodeur, Arthur Gilchrist. 'The Grateful Lion', *PMLA* 39 (1924), 485–524.

Brooke, Rosalind. *Early Franciscan Government: Elias to Bonaventure* (Cambridge, 1959).

—— 'The *Lives* of St Francis', in Dorey, T. A., ed. *Latin Biography* (London, 1967).

—— 'Recent Work on St Francis of Assisi', *Analecta Bollandiana* (1982), 653–76.

Brown, Peter. *The Body and Society: Men, Women and Sexual Renunciation in Early Christianity* (London, 1989).

Bunt, Gerrit H. V. *Alexander the Great in the Literature of Medieval Britain* (Groningen, 1994).

Camille, Michael. *The Gothic Idol: Ideology and Image-making in Medieval Art* (Cambridge, 1989).

—— *Image on the Edge: The Margins of Medieval Art* (London, 1992).

Carson, Gerald. 'Bugs and Beasts Before the Law', *Natural History* (2000), 4, 6–19.

Cary, George. 'A Note on the Medieval History of the *Collatio Alexandri cum Dindimo*, in *Classica et Mediaevalia* 15 (1954), 124–9.

—— *The Medieval Alexander*, ed. D. J. A. Ross (Cambridge, 1956).

Cassese, Giovanna. 'Niccolò Colantonio', in Jane Turner, ed. *The Dictionary of Art*, Vol. 7 (London, 1996), pp. 542–4.

Chesterton, G. K. *St Francis of Assisi* (London, 1996).

Chiarelli, Renzo and J. C. Pollard. 'Pisanello', in Jane Turner, ed. *The Dictionary of Art*, Vol. 24 (London, 1996), pp. 860–5.

Childress, Diana T. 'Between Romance and Legend: "Secular Hagiography" in Middle English Literature', *Philological Quarterly* 57 (1978), 311–22.

Cohen, Jeffrey Jerome. *Of Giants: Sex, Monsters, and the Middle Ages* (Minnesota and London, 1999).

Cohen, Jeremy. *'Be Fertile and Increase, Fill the Earth and Master It': The Ancient and Medieval Career of a Biblical Text* (Ithaca, 1989).

Constable, Giles. *Three Studies in Medieval Religious and Social Thought: The Interpretation of Mary and Martha, The Ideal of the Imitation of Christ, The Orders of Society* (Cambridge, 1995).

Crane, Susan. *Insular Romance* (Berkeley, 1986).

Crane Dannenbaum, Susan. 'Guy of Warwick and the Question of Exemplary Romance', *Genre* 17 (1984), 351–74.

Cummins, John. *The Hound and the Hawk: The Art of Medieval Hunting* (London, 1988).

Davies, Constance. 'Classical Threads in *Sir Orfeo*', *Modern Language Review* 56 (1961), 155–9.

Delehaye, Hippolyte. *The Legends of the Saints*, trans. Donald Attwater (London, 1962).

Doob, Penelope B. R. *Nebuchadnezzar's Children: Conventions of Madness in Middle English Literature* (New Haven, 1974).

Douie, Decima L. *The Nature and the Effect of the Heresy of the Fraticelli* (Manchester, 1932).

Dunkerton, Jill, Susan Foister, Dillian Gordon, and Nicholas Penny. *Giotto to Durer: Early Renaissance Painting in the National Gallery* (New Haven, 1992).

Elliott, Alison Goddard. *Roads to Paradise: Reading the Lives of the Early Saints* (Hanover and London, 1987).

Emerson, O. F. 'Legends of Cain, Especially in Old and Middle English', *PMLA* 21 (1906), 831–929.

Emmerson, Richard K. and Ronald B. Herzman. *The Apocalyptic Imagination in Medieval Literature* (Philadelphia, 1992).

Evans, E. P. *The Criminal Prosecution and Capital Punishment of Animals* (London, 1906).

Farmer, David Hugh. *The Oxford Dictionary of Saints* (Oxford, 1992).

Fellows, Jennifer. 'St George as Romance Hero', *Reading Medieval Studies* 19 (1993), 27–54.

Finlay, Alison. 'The Warrior Christ and the Unarmed Hero', in Kratzmann, Gregory and James Simpson, ed. *Medieval English Religious and Ethical Literature: Essays in Honour of G. H. Russell* (Cambridge, 1986), pp. 19–29.

Fleming, John V. *An Introduction to the Franciscan Literature of the Middle Ages* (Chicago, 1977).

—— 'The Iconographic Unity of the Blessing of Brother Leo', *FS* 63 (1981), 203–20.

—— *From Bonaventure to Bellini: An Essay in Franciscan Exegesis* (Princeton, 1982).

Fox, Robin Lane. *Alexander the Great* (London, 1973).

—— *The Search for Alexander* (London, 1980).

Friedman, John Block. *Orpheus in the Middle Ages* (Cambridge Massachusetts, 1970).

—— *The Monstrous Races in Medieval Art and Thought* (Cambridge Massachusetts, 1981).

Friedmann, Herbert. *A Bestiary for Saint Jerome: Animal Symbolism in European Religious Art* (Washington, D.C., 1980).

Frye, Northrop. *Anatomy of Criticism* (Princeton, 1957).

—— *A Natural Perspective: The Development of Shakespearean Comedy and Romance* (New York, 1965).

—— *The Critical Path: An Essay on the Social Context of Literary Criticism* (Bloomington, 1971).

—— *The Secular Scripture: A Study of the Structure of Romance* (Cambridge Massachusetts, 1976).

Gilson, E. *The Philosophy of Saint Bonaventure*, trans. I. Trethowan (London, 1938).

Glacken, Clarence J. *Traces on the Rhodian Shore: Nature and Culture in Western Thought from Ancient Times to the End of the Eighteenth Century* (Berkeley, Los Angeles, and London, 1967).

Grimaldi, Patrizia. 'Sir Orfeo as Celtic Folk-Hero, Christian Pilgrim, and Medieval King', in *Allegory, Myth, and Symbol*, ed. Morton W. Bloomfield (Cambridge Massachusetts, 1981), pp. 147–61.

Gros Louis, Kenneth R. R. 'The Significance of Sir Orfeo's Self-Exile', *Review of English Studies* n.s. 18 (1967), 245–52.

Guthrie, W. K. C. *Orpheus and Greek Religion: A Study of the Orphic Movement* (London, 1934, rpt. 1952).

Guzman, Gregory G. 'A Growing Tabulation of Vincent of Beauvais' *Speculum Historiale* Manuscripts', *Scriptorium: International Review of Manuscript Studies* 29 (1975), 122–5.

Hassig, Debra. *Medieval Bestiaries: Text, Image, Ideology* (Cambridge, 1995).

Heffernan, Thomas J. 'An Analysis of the Narrative Motifs in the Legend of St Eustace', *Medievalia et Humanistica* n.s. 6 (1975), 63–89.

—— *Sacred Biography: Saints and Their Biographers in the Middle Ages* (Oxford, 1988).

Hill, Betty. 'Alexander Romance: The Egyptian Connection', *Leeds Studies in English* 12 (1981), 185–94.

Hopkins, Andrea. *The Sinful Knight: A Study of Middle English Penitential Romance* (Oxford, 1990).

Hornstein, Lillian Herlands. '*King Robert of Sicily*: A New Manuscript', *PMLA* 78 (1963), 453–8.

—— '*King Robert of Sicily*: Analogues and Origins', *PMLA* 79, (1964), 13–21.

Houwen, L. A. J. R., ed. *Animals and the Symbolic in Medieval Art and Literature* (Groningen, 1997).

Hume, Kathryn. 'Structure and Perspective: Romance and Hagiographic Features in the Amicus and Amelius Story', *JEGP* 69 (1970), 89–107.

Hurley, Margaret. 'Saints' Legends and Romance Again: Secularization of Structure and Motif', *Genre* 8 (1975), 60–73.

Irwin, Elanor. 'The Song of Orpheus and the New Song of Christ', in Warden, John, ed. *Orpheus: The Metamorphoses of a Myth* (Toronto, 1982), pp. 51–62.

Janson, H. W. *Apes and Ape Lore in the Middle Ages and the Renaissance* (London, 1952).

John Paul II, Pope. 'Apostolic Letter *Inter Sanctos*', *AAS* 71 (1979), 1509f.

—— 'The Ecological Crisis: A Common Responsibility. Message of His Holiness Pope John Paul II for the Celebration of the World Day of Peace, January 1, 1990', in Margaret Atkins, *Must Catholics Be Green?* (London, 1995), pp. 21–32.

Jolly, Penny Howell. 'Jan Van Eyck and St Jerome: A Study of Eyckian Influence on Colantonio and Antonello da Messina in Quattrocento Naples' (University of Pennsylvania Ph.D. thesis, 1976).

Kantra, Robert A. 'Jerome and Erasmus in Renaissance Art', *Proceedings of the PMR Conference* Vol. 1 (Villonova P.A., 1976), 105–10.

Keen, Maurice. *Chivalry* (New Haven, 1984).

Kelly, J. N. D. *Jerome: His Life, Writings, and Controversies* (London, 1975).

Klausner, David N. 'Didacticism and Drama' in *Guy of Warwick*, *Medievalia et Humanistica* n.s. 6 (1975), 103–19.

Klingender, Francis. *Animals in Art and Thought to the End of the Middle Ages*, ed. Evelyn Antal and John Harthan (London, 1971).

Knapp, James F. 'The Meaning of *Sir Orfeo*', *Modern Language Quarterly* 29 (1968), 263–73.

Lagorio, Valerie M. 'The *Joseph of Arimathie*: English Hagiography in Transition', *Medievalia et Humanistica* n.s. 6 (1975), 91–102.

Lambert, M. D. *Franciscan Poverty: The Doctrine of the Absolute Poverty of Christ and the Apostles in the Franciscan Order, 1210–1323* (London, 1961).

—— *Medieval Heresy: Popular Movements from Bogomil to Hus* (London, 1977).

Langmuir, Erika, *The National Gallery Companion Guide* (New Haven, 1994).

Lawrence, C. H. *The Friars: The Impact of the Early Mendicant Movement on Western Society* (London, 1994).

Legge, M. Dominica. 'Anglo-Norman Hagiography and the Romances', *Medievalia et Humanistica* n.s. 6 (1975), 41–9.

Lerer, Seth. 'Artifice and Artistry in *Sir Orfeo*', *Speculum* 60 (1985), 92–109.

Loewe, Raphael. 'The Medieval History of the Latin Vulgate', in G. W. H. Lampe, ed. *The Cambridge History of the Bible*, Vol. 2 (Cambridge, 1969), pp. 102–54.

Longsworth, Robert M. '*Sir Orfeo*, The Minstrel and the Minstrel's Art', *Studies in Philology* 79 (1982), 1–11.

Lovejoy, Arthur O. *The Great Chain of Being: A Study of the History of an Idea* (Cambridge Massachusetts, 1957).

Mann, Jill. 'Sir Gawain and the Romance Hero', in Leo Carruthers, ed. *Heroes and Heroines in Medieval English Literature* (Cambridge, 1994).

—— 'Beast Epic and Fable', in *Medieval Latin: An Introduction and Bibliographical Guide*, ed. F. A. C. Mantello and A. G. Rigg (Washington D.C., 1996), pp. 556–61.

Manselli, Raoul. *St Francis of Assisi*, trans. Paul Duggan (Chicago, 1988).

Marchalonis, Shirley. '*Sir Gowther*: The Process of a Romance', *The Chaucer Review* 6 (1971), 14–29.

Marx, C. W. *The Devil's Rights and the Redemption in the Literature of Medieval England* (Woodbridge, 1995).

Matthews, William. *The Tragedy of Arthur: A Study of the Alliterative 'Morte Arthure'* (Berkeley and Los Angeles, 1960).

Matzke, John E. 'The Legend of Saint George: Its Development into a Romance D'Adventure', *PMLA* 19 (1904), 449–78.

Maxwell O'Brien, John. *Alexander the Great: The Invisible Enemy, A Biography* (London, 1994).

McGinn, Bernard. *The Calabrian Abbot: Joachim of Fiore in the History of Western Thought* (London, 1985).

Mehl, Dieter. *The Middle English Romances of the Thirteenth and Fourteenth Centuries* (London, 1968).

Meiss, Millard. 'French and Italian Variations on an Early Fifteenth Century Theme: St Jerome in His Study', *Gazette des Beaux-Arts* 61 (1963), 147–70.

—— *Giovanni Bellini's St Francis in the Frick Collection* (New York, 1964).

—— 'Scholarship and Penitence in the Early Renaissance: The Image of St Jerome', *Pantheon* 32 (1974), 134–40.

Mockler, Anthony. *Francis of Assisi: The Wandering Years* (Oxford, 1976).

Moorman, John R. H. *The Sources for the Life of S. Francis of Assisi* (Manchester, 1940).

—— *A History of the Franciscan Order from its Origins to the Year 1517* (Oxford, 1968).

Morenz, Siegfried. *Egyptian Religion*, trans. Anne Keep (London, 1973).

Nicholas, David. *The Growth of the Medieval City from Late Antiquity to the Early Fourteenth Century* (London, 1997).

Olsen, Alexandre Hennessey. 'The Return of the King: A Reconsideration of *Robert of Sicily*', *Folklore* 93 (1982), 216–19.

Origo, Iris. *The Merchant of Prato: Francesco di Marco Datini* (London, 1957).

Owst, G. R. *Literature and Pulpit in Medieval England* (Oxford, 1961).

Pagels, Elaine. *Adam, Eve, and the Serpent* (Harmondsworth, 1990).

Parke, H. W. *The Oracles of Zeus: Dodona–Olympia–Ammon* (Cambridge Massachusetts, 1967).

Passmore, John. *Man's Responsibility for Nature: Ecological Problems and Western Traditions* (London, 1974).

Pearsall, Derek. 'The Development of Middle English Romance', *Medieval Studies* 27 (1965), 91–116.

Polecritti, Cynthia L., *Preaching Peace in Renaissance Italy: Bernadino of Siena and His Audience* (Washington D.C., 2000).

Ratzinger, Joseph. *The Theology of History in St Bonaventure*, trans. Zachary Hayes (Chicago, 1971).

Reiss, Edmund. 'Romance', in Heffernan, Thomas J. ed. *The Popular Literature of Medieval England* (Knoxville, 1985), pp. 108–30.

Rice, Eugene F. *Saint Jerome in the Renaissance* (Baltimore, 1985).

Riddy, Felicity. 'The Uses of the Past in *Sir Orfeo*', *Yearbook of English Studies* 6 (1976), 5–15.

Rider, Jeff. 'Receiving Orpheus in the Middle Ages: Allegorization, Remythification and *Sir Orfeo*', *Papers on Language and Literature* 24 (1988), 343–66.

Ring, Grete. 'St Jerome Extracting the Thorn from the Lion's Foot', *Art Bulletin* 27 (1945), 188–96.

Robbins, Emmet. 'Famous Orpheus', in Warden, John, ed. *Orpheus: The Metamorphoses of a Myth* (Toronto, 1982), pp. 3–23.

Roberts, Helen. 'St Augustine in "St Jerome's Study": Carpaccio's Painting and its Legendary Source', *Art Bulletin* 41 (1959), 283–309.

Robertson, D. W. Jr. 'Who Were "The People" ?', in Heffernan, Thomas J., ed. *The Popular Literature of Medieval England* (Knoxville, 1985), pp. 3–29.

Robson, Margaret. 'Animal Magic: Moral Regeneration in *Sir Gowther*', *The Yearbook of English Studies* 22 (1992), 140–53.

Ronquest, E. C. 'The Powers of Poetry in *Sir Orfeo*', *Philological Quarterly* 64 (1985), 99–117.

Rooney, Anne. *Hunting in Middle English Literature* (Cambridge, 1993).

Rosenberg, Bruce A. 'Medieval Popular Literature: Folkloric Stories', in Heffernan, Thomas J., ed. *The Popular Literature of Medieval England* (Knoxville, 1985), pp. 61–84.

Ross, D. J. A. *Alexander Historiatus: A Guide to Medieval Illustrated Alexander Literature* (London, 1963).

Rowland, Beryl. *Animals with Human Faces: A Guide to Animal Symbolism* (Knoxville, 1973).

Sabatier, Paul. *Life of St Francis of Assisi*, trans. Louise Seymour Houghton (London, 1894).

Sale, Kirkpatrick. *The Conquest of Paradise: Christopher Columbus and the Columbian Legacy* (London, 1992).

Salisbury, Joyce E. *The Beast Within: Animals in the Middle Ages* (London, 1994).

Sarton, George. *Introduction to the History of Science*, Vol. 2 (Baltimore, 1931).

Scavizzi, Giuseppe. 'The Myth of Orpheus in Italian Renaissance Art, 1400–1600', in Warden, John, ed. *Orpheus: The Metamorphoses of a Myth* (Toronto, 1982), pp. 111–62.

Schlauch, Margaret. *Chaucer's Constance and Accused Queens* (New York, 1927).

Schmidt, Victor M. *A Legend and Its Image: The Aerial Flight of Alexander the Great in Medieval Art* (Groningen, 1995).

Schmitt, Jean-Claude. *The Holy Greyhound: Guinefort, Healer of Children Since the Thirteenth Century*, trans. Martin Thom (Cambridge, 1983).

Segal, Charles. *Orpheus: The Myth of the Poet* (Baltmore, 1989).

Severs, J. Burke. *A Manual of Writing in Middle English, 1050–1500*, Vol. 1: *Romances* (New Haven, 1967).

Seymour, M. C. *English Writers of the Late Middle Ages: Sir John Mandeville* (Aldershot, 1993).

Simmons, I. G. *Environmental History: A Concise Introduction* (Oxford, 1993).

Simpson, James. *Piers Plowman: An Introduction to the B Text* (London, 1990).

Smithers, G. V. 'Story-Patterns in Some Breton Lays', *Medium Aevum* 22 (1953), 61–92.

Sorrell, Roger D. 'Tradition and Innovation in Saint Francis of Assisi's Sermon to the Birds', *Franciscan Studies* 43 (1983), 396–407.

—— *St Francis of Assisi and Nature: Tradition and Innovation in Western Christian Attitudes toward the Environment* (Oxford, 1988).

Southern, R. W. *Saint Anselm and His Biographer: A Study of Monastic Life and Thought 1059–c.1130* (Cambridge, 1963).

Sparks, H. F. D. 'Jerome as Biblical Scholar', in P. R. Ackroyd and C. F. Evans, ed. *The Cambridge History of the Bible*, Vol. 1 (Cambridge, 1970), pp. 510–41.

Spencer, Colin. *The Heretic's Feast: A History of Vegetarianism* (London, 1993).

Stoneman, Richard. 'Who are the Brahmans? Indian Lore and Cynic Doctrine in Palladius' *De Bragmanibus* and its Models', *Classical Quarterly* 44 (1994), 500–10.

—— 'Romantic Ethnogrophy: Central Asia and India in the Alexander Romance', *Ancient World* 25 (1994), 93–107.

—— 'Naked Philosophers: The Brahmans in the Alexander Historians and the Alexander Romances', *JHS* 115 (1995), 99–114.

Sutcliffe, Fr. E. F. 'Jerome', in G. W. H. Lampe, ed. *The Cambridge History of the Bible*, Vol. 2 (Cambridge, 1969), pp. 80–101.

Tarn, W. W. *Alexander the Great*, 2 Vols (Cambridge, 1948).

Taylor, Andrew. 'Fragmentation, Corruption, and Minstrel Narration: The

Question of the Middle English Romances', *The Yearbook of English Studies* 22 (1992), 38–62.

Thomas, Keith. *Man and the Natural World: Changing Attitudes in England 1500–1800* (London, 1983).

Vicari, Patricia. '*Sparagmos*: Orpheus among the Christians', in Warden, John, ed. *Orpheus: The Metamorphoses of a Myth* (Toronto, 1982), pp. 63–83.

Waldron, R. A. 'Langland's Originality: the Christ-knight and the Harrowing of Hell', in Kratzmann, Gregory and James Simpson, ed. *Medieval English Religious and Ethical Literature: Essays in Honour of G. H. Russell* (Cambridge, 1986), pp. 66–81.

Walsh, Martin W. 'The King His Own Fool: *Robert of Cicyle*', in Davidson, Clifford, ed. *Fools and Folly* (Kalamazoo, Michigan, 1996).

Ward, Benedicta. *Miracles and the Medieval Mind: Theory, Record and Event 1000–1215* (Aldershot, 1987).

Wells, John Edwin, *A Manual of the Writing in Middle English, 1050–1400* (New Haven, 1916).

White, Lynn. 'The Historical Roots of Our Ecological Crisis', *Science* 155 (1967), 1203–7.

Woolf, Rosemary. *The English Religious Lyric in the Middle Ages* (Oxford, 1968).

Worster, Donald. 'Doing Environmental History', in Worster, Donald, ed. *The Ends of the Earth: Perspectives on Modern Environmental History* (Cambridge, 1994), pp. 289–307.

Index

Abbo of Fleury, 32
Adam and Eve, 7, 30, 35–7, 142, 148
Aeacas (grandfather of Achilles), 116
Aesop, 1–3
  see also fable
Alexander A, 126 n
Alexander and Dindimus, 138 n
Alexander the Great, 8, 108, 147
  historical tradition, 111–13, 116–19,
    121–2, 123–5, 134–5, 139
  romance tradition, 111, 113–16,
    119–22, 134–46
  superhuman powers, 119–22,
    129–33
  claims to divine parentage, 122,
    123–32, 140
  and 'pagan' spirituality, 8, 132,
    141, 145
  dominion over animals and nature, 8,
    133, 135–6, 145–6
  taming of Bucephalas, 116–22
  travels through India and the East,
    111, 115–16, 122, 134–46, 147
  letter to Aristotle, 136
  ambition for wealth and power,
    134–5, 140–6
  ambition for 'scientific' knowledge,
    136–8
  understanding of the natural world,
    138–46
Alexandri Magni Iter ad Paradisum,
    142 n
Alfonso of Aragon, 14 n
Alliterative Morte Arthur, 112 n
Ammon, 122, 123–32, 140
  see also Alexander the Great
Amun, 125–6
  see also Alexander the Great,
    Ammon
Ancrene Wise, 62 n
anddontrucions, 135
Angelo, Brother, *see* three companions
animals
  anthropocentric view of, 2, 6, 25,
    29–30, 37–8, 44, 48–51, 147
  criminality of, 29–31
  nobility of, 8, 66, 68–70, 84, 85–90,
    91–5, 104–6, 117, 148

'plebeian' animals 8, 92, 106, 148
markers of holiness, 6, 18, 19, 21–2,
    77–80, 88–9, 106, 148
return to prelapsarian state, 30–2,
    36–7, 102–3, 142, 147, 148
human power over, 8, 21–4, 27–9,
    30–2, 33–7, 97–8, 116–22, 135–6
'scientific' investigation of, 136–8
human sympathy for, 7, 14–16, 17,
    50–1, 95, 96, 148
as food, 46–51
narrative function of, 65–6, 68–70,
    80–1, 85–95, 149
see also specific animals, romance
    heroes, saints, hunting
Anthony, St (disciple of Paul of
    Thebes), 18–19
Anthony of Padua, St, 47–8
apes, 83, 90
archetypal criticism, *see* Frye
Aristotle, 20, 111, 115–16, 136–7
  see also Alexander the Great, *Epistla
    Alexandri ad Aristotelem*
Arrian, 113, 123, 139
Artaxerxes III, 125
Arthur (legendary King of Britain), 60,
    112 n, 129 n
Auchinleck manuscript, 98 n, 105, 114 n
Augustine, St, 4–5, 11, 35–7, 112 n
  City of God, 4, 35–7
Augustus, 97
Avianus, 2 n

bats (as large as doves), 135
bears, 56, 135
Benedict of Niola, St, 34 n
Beowulf, 136 n
Bernard of Siena, St, 23 n
Bessus, 134
Bible, 2, 11, 38, 42, 43, 44
  Old Testament, 38, 40, 47 n
    Genesis, 38, 40, 47 n, 131, 142 n
    1 Kings, 80
    Daniel, 40 n, 78–9, 124–5 n
    Tobit, 78
  New Testament, 38
    Gospels, 62
    Matthew, 40 n, 44, 45 n

Bible (*cont.*)
    Mark, 40, 41, 45 n, 102
    Luke, 45 n, 46, 78
    Gospel of Nicodemus, 62
    biblical view of animals, 38, 40–7,
        78–80
    biblical view of nature, 40, 44
birds, 39–41, 44, 48, 51, 67, 68, 93, 97,
    99, 102–4, 137
    pleasure at birdsong, 103–4, 140
    waterfowl, 56, 99, 104
    see also specific birds
Bishop, Morris, 46
Bloomfield, Morton W., 58 n
boars, 135
Boethius, 97
Bonaventure, St, 30, 33, 37, 39, 41, 42,
    45, 60–1
    see also Francis of Assisi
Book of Nature, *see* natural world
Bradstock, E. M., 71
Brahmans, 138–46
Braswell, Laura, 68–9
Breton Lay, 71, 98, 99, 100 n
Bucephalas, 116–22
    see also Alexander the Great, horses
bulls, 119
    Europa and the bull, 129

Cardinalate, 17
    see also galerus ruber
Cary, George, 114 n, 141
Catharism, *see* heresy
Cato (*Dicta Catonis*), 115
cats, 4, 7
Caxton, William,
    Caxton's *Aesop*, 2 n
    Caxton, *Book of the Order of*
        Chivalry, 76, 94
Cerberus, 140
Charlemagne, 112 n
Chaucer, Geoffrey
    Wife of Bath's Prologue and Tale, 1–3
    Knight's Tale, 45 n
    Man of Law's Tale, 85
    Franklin's Tale, 100 n
    Monk's Tale, 111
Cheuelere Assigne, 87
Chrétien de Troyes,
    Guillaume d'Angleterre, 69 n
    Yvain, 90 n
Christ, 19, 22 n, 27, 40, 41, 42, 43, 44,
    45, 46, 47, 49, 51, 65, 141 n
    as feudal lord, 61–2

    as chivalric knight, 62–4
    as stag, 56, 64, 65, 68
civilisation, 16, 19–23, 101, 105
Clare of Assisi, St, 39
Cleanness, 79 n
Colantonio, Niccolò,
    St Jerome and the Lion, 7, 14–18,
        21–3
    St Francis Giving the Rule to the First
        and Second Franciscan Orders,
        14 n, 23
Collatio Alexandri cum Dindimo,
    138–46
    see also Alexander the Great,
        Dindimus, Brahmans
Council of Lyons, 17
crabs, 135
crocodiles, 7, 135, 140
culture, *see* civilisation
Cummins, John, 92 n, 93, 105
Cuthbert, St, 80

Dandamus, *see* Dindimus
Darius III, 111, 134–5
David (King), 112 n, 141 n
deer, 56, 87, 105, 119
desert, 11, 18–23, 34
    desert fathers, 18–23, 102
    see also Jerome, Malchus the Monk,
        Paul of Thebes, wilderness, forest,
        civilisation
Devil, 33, 34, 44, 62–4
    diabolical father of Gowther, 72–3,
        74–5
Diogenes of Sinope, 139 n
Dindimus,
    understanding of the natural world,
        138–46, 147
    as type of Christ, 140–1, 144–5
    see Collatio Alexandri cum Dindimo,
        Brahmans, Alexander the Great
dogs, *see* hounds
dolphins, 140
dragons, 4, 7, 126–32, 135, 142 n, 149
    see also Ammon, Alexander the
        Great

eagles, 80
Edmund, St, 32
elephants, 4, 135
Elijah, 80
Elliott, Alison Goddard, 18–19, 21
Emaré, 100 n
Erle of Tolous, 100 n

Epistola Alexandri ad Aristotelem, 136
Europa, 129
Eurydice, *see* Orpheus and Eurydice
Eustace, St, 8, 55–7, 58, 59, 64–9, 74
   see also Pisanello
Eve, *see* Adam and Eve

fable ('The Lion and the Man'), 1–3, 6
fairies, 98–9, 104
falconry, *see* hunting
falcons, 8, 65, 67–8, 84, 91–3, 95, 99,
   104–6, 148
   nobility of 8, 65, 68, 84, 91–3, 95,
     105–6, 148
Fall, 7, 30–2, 35–7, 102–3, 142, 148
feudalism, 8, 105–6
fish, 47–8, 80, 137
forest, 56–7, 64, 66, 67, 69, 83, 98–9,
   100–6, 120
   see also wilderness, desert, civilisation
Fox, Robin Lane, 117–18
Francis of Assisi, St, 7, 14 n, 23–4,
   25–32, 33–4, 37–8, 39–51, 95, 102,
   148, 149
   and 'Brother Ass', 32, 33–4, 37–8
   and wolf of Gubbio, 25, 27–32
   sermon to the birds, 39–41, 44, 48, 51
   and lambs, 42–6, 149
   and goats, 43–4, 149
   and pigs, 44–6, 49–51, 149
   and larks, 51
   and ecology, 25–7, 29–30
   moral responsibility towards animals,
     7, 25–7, 29, 46–51
   sexuality, 33, 34, 37
   views on the celebration of
     Christmas, 49, 51
   and chivalry, 59–61
Franciscan Order, 14 n, 22–4, 46, 47,
   49 n, 50, 59–60, 76
   Poor Clares, 43
Frederick II, 31
friars, *see* Franciscan Order
Friedman, John Block, 135–6
Frye, Northrop, 106–8, 121

galerus ruber, 14, 17
   see also Cardinalate
Gareth (brother of Gawain), 63
Gentile de Fabriano, 55
Geoffroi de Charny, 76 n
Gerald of Wales, 4
Gerasimus, St, 12
Giovanni d'Andrea, 13–14, 17

goats, 43–4, 149
God, 41, 42, 44, 47, 61, 72, 75, 76, 88,
   148
   as bird, 67, 68
Godfrey of Bouillon, 87, 112 n
goshawks, 129–30
   nobility of, 130
Gower, *Confessio Amantis*, 85, 126 n
Gregory IX, Pope, 31
Gregory the Great, St, 11, 34 n
greyhounds, *see* hounds
griffins, 4, 7, 67, 83, 87, 137, 142 n
Gynosophists, 138 n

Hadrian, 55, 65
hagiography, 6, 7, 33–4, 51, 65–6, 71–2,
   74, 77–81, 90, 101, 106–8, 147, 148
   see also Bonaventure, Jerome,
     Thomas of Celano, the three
     companions, Ugolino di Monte
     Santa Maria, *Little Flowers of St
     Francis*, romance
hares, 56
hawks, *see* falcons, goshawks
Hector, 112 n
Helen of Troy, 129 n
Hercules, 116
heresy, 47–8, 49 n
Higden, Ranulf, 136–7, 147
Hilarion, St, 34
   see also Jerome
Hill, Betty, 129
Historia de Preliis, 114, 137, 138 n
hippopotami, 135, 140
Holy Spirit, 39
Hopkins, Andrea, 71, 74
horses, 7, 8, 56, 67–8, 73, 84, 94–5,
   116–22, 148
   nobility of 8, 68, 84, 94–5, 117, 148
   see also Alexander the Great,
     Bucephalas
hounds, 7, 8, 28, 30, 56–7, 67–8, 73,
   77–81, 148
   nobility of, 8, 68, 80–1, 148
   associated with penitential suffering,
     77–9
   associated with sanctity, 79–81, 148
human body, 33–7
hunting, 56–7, 64, 66, 67, 104, 137
   falconry, 92 n, 93, 104–6, 137, 149
Innocent III, Pope, 39
Innocent IV, Pope, 17
Isabella Chiaromonte, Queen, 14 n
Isidore of Seville, 11

Jacobus of Voragine, 12–13, 55 n
Jacques de Longuyon, *Les Voeux de Paon*, 112 n
Jerome, St, 1, 7, 11–24, 34, 89, 142 n
  encounter with lion, 7, 11–23
  and monasticism, 11, 18–23
  rejection of classical civilisation, 21–2
  Life of Hilarion, 34
  Life of Malchus, 18–22
  Life of Paul, 18–19, 80 n
  see also Colantonio
Jesus, *see* Christ
Joannes Moschus, 12
John, St, 13
John Paul II, Pope, 26
Jolly, Penny Howell, 14 n, 18 n, 23
Joshua, 112 n
Judas Maccabeus, 112 n
Julius Caesar, 112 n
Julius Valerius, *Res Gestae Alexandri Magni*, 114, 136 n
Juniper, Brother, 49–51
Jupiter, *see* Ammon, Zeus

knights, *see* romance heroes
Kyng Alisaunder, 114, 115–16, 126–32, 134–5

lambs, 42–6, 51
Lancelot, 57, 63, 101
Langland, William, *see Piers Plowman*
larks, 51
Lay le Freine, 100 n
Lazarus, 78
Leda, 129
Leo, Brother, *see* three companions
Leo of Naoles, Archpriest, 114, 136 n
  see also Historia de Preliis
leopards, 67–8, 135
Lerer, Seth, 103
Life of St Christopher, 136 n
lions, 1–3, 4, 7, 6, 8, 11–23, 65–6, 67–8, 83–90, 91, 95, 99, 129–30, 135
  nobility of, 8, 85–90, 91, 95, 130
  and sanctity, 88–90
  white lions (large than bulls), 135
Little Flowers of St Francis, 27, 47
Longinus, 63
Lull, Ramón, 76–7, 94
Lybeaus Desconus, 85
Lysimachus, 116 n

Malchus the Monk, 18–22
  see also Jerome

Mandeville, Sir John, 141–2
Marchalonis, Shirley, 75
Marco Polo, 117 n
Marcus Julianus Justinus, 113, 124
Marie de France,
  Fables, 2 n
  Lays, 100 n
  Yonec, 92–2
Mary, Blessed Virgin, 72, 88
meat, *see* animals (as food), Francis of Assisi
Mehl, Dieter, 71, 82, 115
Merlin, 129 n
mice, 4, 14, 22 n
  (as large as foxes), 135
Minos, king of Crete, 129 n
monasticism, 11, 18–23
  see also Francis of Assisi, Jerome

Nabarzanes, 134
natural world, 7, 16, 21–3
  Book of Nature, 39, 43, 149
  human responses to, 7, 21–3, 25–7, 29–31, 40–4, 105–6, 135–46, 147–9
  human power over nature, 121–2, 133, 134–5
  as a force, hostile to humanity, 135–6
  reverence towards, 138–46, 147
  see also animals, Bible, Alexander the Great, Dindimus, Francis of Assisi, Jerome
Nebuchadnezzar, 69, 78–9, 141 n
Nectanebo II, 125–32
Neptanabus, *see* Nectanebo
nine worthies, 112 n
Noah, 47 n

Octavian, 8, 52, 66, 70, 81, 82–95, 105, 106, 148
Olympias (mother of Alexander the Great), 111, 126–32, 134
original sin, 35–7
  see also Adam and Eve, Augustine, Fall
Orpheus and Eurydice, 96–8, 99–100, 101
  see also Sir Orfeo
Ovid, 97–8, 101
oxen, 78–9, 84, 91

Parlement of the Thre Ages, 112 n
Paul, St, 17–18
Paul of Thebes, 18–19, 80
  see also Jerome

Paula (daughter of Eustochium), 20
  see also Jerome
Paulus Orosius, 112 n, 113, 124
peregrine falcon, *see* falcon
Perdiccas, 134
Peter, St, 17–18
Peter Abelard, 141 n, 147
Peter Lombard, 30
Phaedrus, 2 n
Philip II of Macedon, 111, 117–18, 120,
  123, 126, 130–2, 134
Piers Plowman, 59, 61–4
pigs, 44–6, 49–51, 149
Pisanello, *The Vision of St Eustace*, 8,
  54, 55–7, 66
  see also Eustace
Placidus, *see* Eustace
Plato, 22 n
Plutarch, 113, 116, 117–19, 120–1, 123 n
Pompeius Trogus, 113
Porus, king of India, 134
Pseudo-Callisthenes, 113–14
Ptolemy, 134

Quintus Curtius Rufus, 113, 116, 124,
  134

ram,
  ram headed god, Ammon, 123
  ram headed god, Amun, 124
  'ram with two horns' from Book of
    Daniel, 124–5 n
  mask adopted by Nectanebo, 128 n
Raphael, Angel, 78
René d'Anjou, 14 n
Rilke, Rainer Maria, 96 n
Robert of Sicily, 79 n, 90 n
Robert the Devil, 71
romance (genre), 6, 7–8, 51, 71, 86, 87,
  90, 101, 106–8, 147, 148
  relationship to hagiography, 7–8,
    51–2, 57–9, 64, 66–70, 71–2, 74,
    77–81, 89–90, 101, 106–8, 147, 148
  relationship to history, 108, 113–22,
    123–32, 134–5, 139
  relationship to fabliau, 128
romance heroes,
  relationship to saints, 8, 51–2, 57–64,
    66–70, 74, 77–81, 88–90, 101,
    106–8, 148
  relationship to animals, 51–2, 66–70,
    77–81, 85–95, 106–8, 116–22,
    124–32, 148–9
  see also specific romances

Romulus and Remus, 87
Ross, David, 114
Rufino, Brother, *see* three companions

saints, *see* specific saints listed under
    given name
  relationship to animals, 6, 7, 11–24,
    25–32, 33–8, 39–51, 65–6, 68–9,
    88–9, 102–3, 106–8, 147–8
  relationship to romance heroes, 8,
    51–2, 57–64, 66–70, 88–9, 101,
    106–8
Salisbury, Joyce, 4–6
Sallust, 36
Schmitt, Jean-Claude, 80
scorpions, 135
Segal, Charles, 20
Shakespeare, William
  Henry IV Part 1, 86 n
sheep, *see* lambs, rams
Sir Beues of Hamtoun, 86
Sir Degaré, 85, 100 n
Sir Gawain and the Green Knight, 79 n
Sir Gowther, 8, 52, 66, 70, 71–81, 86,
    88, 100 n, 106, 107, 108, 148
Sir Isumbras, 8, 52, 55, 59, 64, 66–9, 72,
    74, 106, 107, 108, 148
Sir Launfal, 100 n
Sir Orfeo, 8, 52, 66, 70, 81, 95, 96,
    98–108, 148, 149
Sir Perceval of Gales, 85
Sir Tristrem, 105
Smithers, G. V., 131
snakes, 135
Solomon, 141 n
Sorrell, Roger, 26 n, 31 n, 41 n, 46
spaniels, *see* hounds
Spencer, Colin, 48
stags, *see* deer, Christ (as stag)
Stoneman, Richard, 138, 147
Suetonius, *Twelve Caesars*, 112 n
Sulpicius Severus, 11
swans,
  Leda and the swan, 129
swine, *see* pigs

Tertullian, 1
Thalestris, queen of Amazons, 116
Thomas, Keith, 3, 37
Thomas of Celano, 21, 33, 41, 42, 45,
    49, 60
  see also Francis of Assisi
Thomas of Kent, *Le Roman de Toute
    Chevalerie*, 114 n

Thornton Prose Life of Alexander,
    114 n, 135 n, 137 n, 138 n, 140–6
three companions of St Francis, 38,
    59–60
    see also Francis of Assisi
Tobias, 78
Tobit, 78
Trajan, 55, 64–5
Trevissa, John, 137
Tristram, 57, 101, 105

Ugolino di Monte Santa Maria, 27, 31,
    32
    see also Little Flowers of St Francis
unicorns, 67–8, 119
Uther Pendragon, 129 n

vegetarianism, *see* animals (as food)

Vincent of Beauvais, 12–13
Virgil, 97, 101

Wars of Alexander, 114 n, 126 n, 135 n,
    137 n, 138 n
White, Lynn, 25–7, 29, 32
wilderness, 18, 69, 83, 90, 98–9, 100–6,
    107
    see also desert, forest, civilisation,
    Francis of Assisi, Jerome
wolves, 25, 27–32, 65–6, 68, 70 n, 87, 99
    wolf of Gubbio, *see* Francis of Assisi
woodland, *see* forest

Zacher Epitome, *see* Julius Valerius
Zeus, 129 n
    Zeus Ammon, *see* Ammon,
    Alexander the Great

Lightning Source UK Ltd.
Milton Keynes UK
UKOW06n2316160815